Conversations With Great Thinkers:

The Classics For People Too Busy To Read Them

by L. James Hammond

Copyright © 2008 L. James Hammond

cover design: Jim De Luzio
                MORRIS | DE LUZIO | DESIGN

Authors depicted on front cover, from left to right:

top row: Thoreau, Kafka, Leonardo
middle row: Joyce, Homer, Nietzsche
bottom row: Ruskin, Dostoyevsky, Proust

Published by: Noontide Press
                58 Jacob St.
                Seekonk, MA 02771
                508-336-5556

                China Film Press (Zhong-guo Dian-ying Chu-ban-she), Beijing, China (in translation)

                China Literature Association Press (Zhong-guo Wen Lian Chu-ban-she), Beijing, China (in translation)

                New Century Publishing, Taipei, Taiwan (in translation)

Third Edition
Copyright © 2008 L. James Hammond
All rights reserved.

Library of Congress Catalog Card Number: 97-69625
ISBN: 1-57502-598-1

Contents

Preface 1
1. Philosophy 5
2. Ethics 28
3. Religion 56
4. Psychology 72
5. Genius 100
6. Sundry Thoughts 113
7. Literature 142
8. Education 198
9. Language 219
10. Modern Times 225
11. Politics 237
12. Physics 249
13. Life- and Death-Instincts 260
14. Decadence and Renaissance 276
Index 292
Feedback 303

A teacher should teach what is new
by resurrecting what is old.
--Confucius

Preface

Most people today never become truly educated—even if they graduate from college. Colleges today emphasize vocational training instead of education in the humanities. Even students who focus on the humanities usually acquire only specialized knowledge, not broad education.

This book brings together the various branches of the humanities—literature, history, philosophy, psychology, religion, etc.—and combines them into a unified whole. It introduces you to the classics of many different fields, and it also introduces you to the people who created those classics. Thus, you'll become acquainted with the classics in an intimate, personal way; you'll feel that you can reach out and shake hands with writers from previous centuries. Reading this book is like traveling to a foreign country—the country of literature and ideas and the classics.

Chapter 1, "Philosophy," describes the Philosophy of Today, a philosophy that relies on intuition rather than reason, feelings rather than logic, and dreams rather than syllogisms. The Philosophy of Today takes a non-rational approach, and also believes that reality itself is non-rational, hence it's receptive to the occult. The Philosophy of Today is influenced not by the rational philosophers of ancient Greece, but by Eastern philosophy, by Jungian psychology, and by sages from all cultures. The Philosophy of Today is spiritual as well as intellectual. While the Philosophy of Today is first discussed in Chapter 1, later chapters explore it further; for example, Chapter 12, "Physics," shows that the Philosophy of Today is consistent with modern physics.

Besides discussing the Philosophy of Today, Chapter 1 discusses the analytic approach to philosophy that is popular in academia, and contrasts this approach with the approach of Montaigne, Thoreau, and others. Chapter 1 describes the origin of philosophy, the aim of philosophy, and the history of philosophy, paying special attention to Schopenhauer, Nietzsche, and Jung.

Chapter 2, "Ethics," discusses meditation, Zen, and the influence of Zen on Japanese culture; it also discusses the Zennish thinking of Thoreau. Chapter 2 sketches the history of moral thinking, from Socrates to Jung, and describes the attempt to set up universal standards of right and wrong. Chapter 2 discusses the impact of culture on people's values and people's lives, it discusses the interplay of culture and ethics.

Chapter 3, "Religion," begins by reviewing atheist arguments, and ends by going "beyond atheism"—looking at new approaches to religion, new definitions of God.

Chapter 4, "Psychology," begins by discussing occult phenomena, and later discusses birth order, social class, national character, the psychology of adolescence, and other subjects. Chapter 4 ends by discussing the importance of psychology in modern thought—the importance of the Psychology Revolution that Freud started, and Jung continued.

Chapter 5, "Genius," enables you to see the classics from the inside, to meet the people behind the books. But it does more than introduce you to writers and artists. Genius is a subset of human nature, just as neurotics are a subset of human nature. Freud focused on neurotics, but his conclusions were relevant to mankind as a whole. Likewise, when we explore the psychology of genius, our conclusions throw light on man in general. Chapter 5 gives you an introduction to psychology, to Freud's work, and to the whole modern movement toward exploring the unconscious. One well-known Chinese scholar, Dong Leshan, said that the chapter on genius is the best piece he has seen on the subject of genius.

Chapter 6, "Sundry Thoughts," discusses a variety of subjects, including Chinese painting, the sadistic side of human nature, and the cult of leadership. Chapter 6 also includes a biographical sketch of Kierkegaard and a new view of Hitler.

Chapter 7, "Literature," attempts to describe the essential features of major writers—Joyce, Proust, Tolstoy, Kafka, etc.

Chapter 7 also discusses the major philosophical questions surrounding literature, such as the purpose of literature, why people enjoy tragedy, and whether literature is subjective or objective. Chapter 7 returns to the subject of the Philosophy of Today, arguing that the Philosophy of Today resembles the so-called Hermetic worldview, and sketching the history of the Hermetic worldview. Chapter 7 also argues that Shakespeare's worldview closely resembles the Philosophy of Today. Chapter 7 looks at Eastern philosophy, discussing Zen thinking in Whitman and Forster.

Chapter 8, "Education," looks at academia, looks at the controversy surrounding the identity of Shakespeare, and looks at how academia handles this controversy. Chapter 8 pays special attention to the views of Twain and Whitman on the Shakespeare controversy. Chapter 8 also discusses the life-enhancing function of culture—that is, how culture can stimulate us, and arouse in us an appetite for living. Chapter 8 argues that academia often overlooks the life-enhancing function of culture, and it discusses two writers who emphasized this life-enhancing function, Bernard Berenson and Kenneth Clark.

Chapter 9, "Language," discusses how the migration of Asian peoples into Europe (the so-called "Aryan migrations") shaped the development of European languages. Chapter 9 also discusses the origin of language, the origin of surnames, and the differences between the Chinese language and European languages.

Chapter 10, "Modern Times," discusses the pros and cons of modern culture, paying special attention to modern art. Chapter 10 also discusses a modern condition that the Spanish philosopher Ortega called "the revolt of the masses."

Chapter 11, "Politics," discusses rationalism in politics and theology. Chapter 11 also discusses Islamic fanaticism, and the spiritual crisis in the Islamic world. Finally, Chapter 11 discusses the causes of the Iraq War, and causality in general.

Chapter 12, "Physics," discusses the connections between modern physics and the Philosophy of Today, and argues that we're now able to create a synthesis of the sciences and the humanities, Western thought and Eastern thought.

Chapter 13, "Life- and Death-Instincts," discusses the biological side of philosophy. It discusses Schopenhauer's idea of a will to life, Nietzsche's idea of a will to power, and Shaw's idea of a life force. It discusses Freud's theory of life- and death-instincts, and argues that this theory resembles Nietzsche's theory of decadence. Chapter 13 introduces the reader to the theory of history that is set forth in Chapter 14, and shows how this theory of history differs from earlier theories of history, such as those of Spengler and Toynbee. Like other chapters, Chapter 13 discusses the history of ideas. Chapter 13 describes how my theory of history was influenced by earlier thinkers, how it synthesizes earlier thinkers.

Chapter 14, "Decadence and Renaissance," sets forth a new theory of history. This theory predicts that there will be a renaissance in our time, the first renaissance in four hundred years. It is our destiny to be alive during a renaissance epoch. This renaissance is beginning now, when people least expect it, when people see only decadence and sterility. Chapter 14 argues that a renaissance is bound to occur when decadence reaches an extreme.

This book makes philosophy as readable as a newspaper article, but it also has the scholarship and the depth of genuine philosophy. It's free from the technical terms that weigh down many philosophical works; it's written in plain English. A reader of this book quickly becomes familiar with the major categories of culture; he becomes familiar with Russian novelists, with German philosophers, with the history of the English language, with the psychology of genius, etc. A reader of this book also becomes familiar with the Philosophy of Today, which is an important new worldview, and a popular approach to religion and spiritual life.

1. Philosophy

1. *Manifesto* The Philosophy of Today is both a religion and a philosophy; it satisfies both spiritual needs and intellectual demands. It has given up on traditional religion, monotheistic religion. It doesn't believe in a Creator God, a Ruling God, a Judging God. But it also is wary of atheism because it believes that the universe is suffused with energy, power, mystery, even a kind of consciousness. Thus, it isn't exactly atheist, and it isn't exactly theist; one might say that it defines god in a different way, or calls god by a different name.

The Philosophy of Today is akin to Eastern worldviews, such as Zen, insofar as those Eastern worldviews are both a philosophy and a religion, and those Eastern worldviews are neither atheist nor theist (in a Western sense). The Philosophy of Today heals the rift that has sundered philosophy and religion since the time of Descartes. Religion has long been based on faith and revelation, while philosophy has been based on reason. But our religion isn't based on faith, and our philosophy isn't based on reason. We've brought religion and philosophy together, and we base both of them on intuition, feeling, and experience, as well as reason.

Instead of separating feeling and reason, we try to make man whole, and we try to develop a worldview that satisfies the whole person. Thus, the Philosophy of Today is akin to the

Renaissance philosophy of Bruno and Pico, which was a religion as well as a philosophy. Just as that Renaissance worldview tried to calm the storms that were raging between Catholics and Protestants by going past religious formalities, so too the Philosophy of Today hopes to bring people together by emphasizing the common essence that is shared by many religions. The Philosophy of Today respects the spiritual core of all religions, as Bruno and Pico did. We don't dismiss religion as madness or superstition, as Nietzsche and Freud did.

We believe that the most fundamental distinction in philosophy is the distinction between rational and non-rational philosophy. Greek philosophers pioneered the rational approach, and were as fond of it as a child is of a new toy. They rejected mythology, and expelled the poet from their ideal republic. We take a different approach. We believe mythology expresses deep spiritual truths, deep psychological truths, truths that rational thinkers overlook. Likewise, we believe that the poet expresses deep truths. We believe that one sees the world best when one's eyes are half closed. We agree with Bruno that Aristotle isn't the prince of philosophers, and we agree with Bruno that philosophy should embrace literature, art, etc.

A non-rational approach to philosophy unites philosophy with other branches of culture, whereas a rational approach leaves philosophy by itself. The rational approach is only popular with academics, but the non-rational approach appeals to both the intellectual and the "man on the street." One of the most popular philosophers of our time is Joseph Campbell, who took a non-rational approach, and explored the wisdom of myths, and the wisdom of the East.

We don't believe in ethical rules, we aren't interested in categorical imperatives. We leave such things to rational philosophers, and to their admirers in academia. We believe in finding one's center, in acting out of one's center. We believe in spontaneity—the spontaneity of the athlete, of the artist. We agree with Nietzsche that morality is a sign of decadence, that only decadent philosophers try to put human nature into the strait-jacket of Reason.

1. PHILOSOPHY

Just as there has long been a rift between philosophy and religion, so too there has long been a rift between philosophy and science. Modern science depicted the universe as mechanical, cold, while philosophy tried to preserve some purpose, some meaning in the human sphere, if nowhere else. We don't think there's friction between philosophy and science; we embrace modern science, especially quantum physics. The discoveries of quantum physics, which baffled the hard-headed scientists who made them, dovetail perfectly with our non-rational worldview. The occult patterns that physicists have found in subatomic particles are strikingly similar to the occult patterns that we see in the world around us. Even before we became acquainted with quantum physics, we were convinced that the world wasn't rational or logical. We're delighted to find that quantum physics confirms our non-rational worldview. Quantum physics didn't form our worldview, it encouraged us in it.

The same is true of Eastern philosophy: it didn't form our worldview, it encouraged us in it. Western philosophy had an Eastern drift even before it became acquainted with Eastern philosophy. Thoreau responded to Eastern wisdom because he was Eastern himself. Some of the most Eastern writers of the nineteenth century, such as Walt Whitman and Walter Pater, didn't study Eastern literature; they reached their Zennish conclusions independently of the East. Eastern philosophy arrived in the West when the West was ready for it. As the old saying goes, "When the student is ready, the master appears."

We believe that the philosophical subject par excellence is the occult, and we're fascinated by all aspects of the occult. Fascination with the occult is characteristic of non-rational thinkers, just as admiration for Aristotle is characteristic of rational thinkers. The thinker who interests us most, Carl Jung, was fascinated by the occult throughout his long life, and had no interest in Aristotle.

We believe that the exploration of the unconscious, which began with Schopenhauer in the early 1800s, is as important for the Philosophy of Today as Eastern philosophy is. We believe that these two movements—the psychology of the unconscious and Eastern philosophy—have left a deep mark on Western philosophy, and have made this moment the most propitious moment in the history of Western philosophy.

We believe that, while Freud is important for philosophy, Jung is even more important. We regard Jung as the leading exponent of the non-rational approach to philosophy. Jung's grasp of the dark side of human nature is unsurpassed, yet he's far from pessimistic. He not only sees the potential for spiritual growth, he argues that human nature has a proclivity for growth, for balance, for finding its center, for becoming whole. Like other non-rational thinkers, Jung and his disciples teach us to respect the wisdom of poetry, of mythology, of fairy tales. They teach us respect that age-old wisdom that is found in all cultures and all religions, that age-old wisdom that is sometimes called the Perennial Philosophy. One might describe the Philosophy of Today as the Perennial Philosophy, or as the Hermetic Philosophy, or as the Non-Rational Philosophy.

The Philosophy of Today isn't nihilistic or pessimistic. We take a positive attitude—as Zen does, as Thoreau does, as Nietzsche does. We respect Nietzsche because he understood atheism and nihilism, and because he foresaw that we would overcome nihilism, and regain a positive attitude. We believe that Nietzsche carried on the humanistic tradition that has its roots on the Acropolis, and we believe that we've enriched that tradition with the help of psychology and Eastern culture. We believe that Nietzsche foresaw the flowering of philosophy in our time, and referred to it as The Great Noontide.

2. *Ruskin's Hammers* John Ruskin was born in 1819, and raised in a pious Protestant household. His mother read the Bible with him, and when they got all the way to the end, they would turn back to page 1, and start again. As Ruskin grew older, his faith dwindled, partly because of advances in science, partly because of Biblical criticism. Geologists undermined Ruskin's faith by showing that the earth was far older than had been thought, far older than the Bible said it was. "If only the geologists would let me alone," Ruskin wrote, "I could do very well, but those dreadful hammers! I hear the chink of them at the end

of every cadence of the Bible verse."[1] It was difficult to reconcile the vast age of the earth with the idea of divine providence, divine planning. If God had made the earth for man, why had man's appearance been delayed for so long? And if God hadn't made the earth for man, then what had He made it for?

The Philosophy of Today has nothing to fear from advances in science, or from a close analysis of Biblical texts. The Philosophy of Today doesn't try to make the world fit into the Procrustean bed of an established religion, or a holy text. The Philosophy of Today accepts the world as it is, and adopts a religious attitude toward the world; one might describe it as a religion of the world.

3. *Pater's New Religion* Walter Pater was born in 1839, twenty years after Ruskin. Pater and Ruskin were colleagues at Oxford. While Ruskin was losing his faith, and sinking into despair, Pater was developing a new faith, a new worldview. Pater broke with traditional religion and morality, and began to think "outside the box."

Instead of focusing on the goal of life, the meaning of life, he focused on life itself, experience itself, the present moment. Though he probably never heard the word "Zen," his worldview has a striking resemblance to Zen. Pater said that his approach to life "might come even to seem a kind of religion... by virtue of its effort to live days 'lovely and pleasant' in themselves, here and now."[2] Zen's two favorite words are "here" and "now," and it urges us to "be here now."

While Thoreau approaches the present moment through nature, such as the crowing of a cock, Pater approaches the present moment through culture, such as a poem that sharpens his awareness of a winter landscape, or a painting that sharpens his awareness of an urban scene. If Thoreau's Zen is a "nature Zen," Pater's is a "culture Zen."

Pater finds Zen currents in Greco-Roman thinkers, especially Epicurean thinkers; one of his chief works is a historical novel

---

[1] Ruskin's letter of May 24, 1851
[2] *Marius the Epicurean*, ch. 9

called *Marius the Epicurean*. Pater doesn't seem to have studied Eastern thought. I suspect that Greco-Roman thinkers were just a prop for Pater's own Zennish tendencies, as Eastern thinkers were just a prop for Thoreau's Zennish tendencies. There is an Eastern drift in Western thought, and this Eastern drift is evident even in writers, like Whitman, who didn't study the ancients or the Orientals. As Alan Watts said, "Zen lies so close to the 'growing edge' of Western thought."[1]

Though Pater was attracted to the Epicureans, he wasn't a hedonist: "Not pleasure, but fullness of life, and 'insight' as conducting to that fullness."[2] Pater's worldview isn't hedonism, Zen isn't hedonism; meditation aims at awareness, not pleasure. But if Zen doesn't seek pleasure, neither does it avoid pleasure; Zen isn't ascetic.

Younger intellectuals grasped the importance of Pater's worldview. Oscar Wilde called Pater's study of the Renaissance his "golden book." Pater influenced the Aesthetic Movement of which Wilde was a leader.

4. *Gibbon* "The various modes of worship," wrote Gibbon in the late 1700s, "which prevailed in the Roman world, were all considered by the people, as equally true; by the philosopher, as equally false; and by the magistrate, as equally useful."[3] Here we have the Enlightenment-Rationalist contempt for religion. The Philosophy of Today, which is non-rationalist, has more respect for religion, and would say, "The various modes of worship were all considered by the philosopher as equally true" (or perhaps I should say "partially true").

5. *Brutal Morality* Jung says that, in Europe, religion and morality had a "brutal, almost malignant character."[4] This is the

---

[1] *The Way of Zen*, preface
[2] *Marius the Epicurean*, ch. 9
[3] *The History of the Decline and Fall of The Roman Empire*, ch. 2, part 1
[4] *Psychology and the East*, "Commentary on the Secret of the Golden Flower," ch. 5, par. 70

sort of religion and morality that aroused the opposition of Nietzsche, and of Enlightenment thinkers like Gibbon and Voltaire. Western religion and morality had this brutal character because Christianity was thrust upon a barbarous people. The barbarous people of Europe, especially Northern Europe, weren't capable of wholeness, weren't capable of integrating Christianity into a whole personality. They were only capable of a repressive spirituality in which the "spiritual man" dominated the "animal man."

It is this violence against the self that Nietzsche opposed. Nietzsche declared that God is dead, and that Christian morality is also dead. Nietzsche's arguments don't apply to Eastern religion and morality. (Nietzsche himself, though, may have taken some jibes at Eastern religion because he didn't understand it.) Eastern religion isn't a traditional monotheism in which God is separate from the world, and Eastern morality isn't a repression of the body by the spirit. The Philosophy of Today doesn't oppose religion and morality, as Nietzsche did, it only opposes traditional monotheism and repressive morality.

6. *Our Critics* The Philosophy of Today will be criticized by hard-headed rationalists and by traditional monotheists, just as the Renaissance philosophy of Pico and Bruno was criticized by rationalists and monotheists. Bruno wanted to replace Christianity with a new, Hermetic religion. Bruno was burned at the stake by the Inquisition.

Bruno's worldview not only collided with the Church, it also collided with the scientific worldview that was developing in the early 1600s. This scientific worldview was concerned with the visible and measurable, and was scornful of mysticism; like the rationalists of today, these early scientists were uncomfortable with the occult and the mysterious.

Because Bruno's Hermetic worldview was opposed by the religious establishment and the scientific establishment, it went underground in the 1600s, and inspired secret societies like the Rosicrucians and Freemasons. Now the Hermetic worldview is becoming widespread once again, as it was in the Renaissance.

We said earlier that Greek philosophers pioneered the rational approach, and were as fond of it as a child is of a new toy. Likewise, the pioneers of the scientific approach placed too much faith in their new methods, and were too contemptuous of the age-old wisdom of mankind, too contemptuous of mystics and alchemists.

7. *Democratic Philosophy* Unlike Nietzsche's philosophy, the Philosophy of Today is democratic, and has broad appeal. We believe that Eastern practices, like meditation and yoga, can be useful for all sorts of people; these practices are effective in prisons, ghettos, etc. While Schopenhauer and Nietzsche developed a Cult of Genius, we're more interested in spiritual growth, which is open to all, and challenging to all. Though we're impressed by the achievements of genius, we're also impressed by the wisdom of the unconscious—a wisdom that everyone possesses—and we're impressed by the anonymous, folk wisdom of fairy-tales and myths—a wisdom that all peoples possess.

8. *Decathlon* Analytic philosophy, which is popular in academia, divorces philosophy from the rest of the humanities, and treats it as a separate subject. On the other hand, the Philosophy of Today joins philosophy to the rest of the humanities. Philosophy is a synthesis of the humanities. Philosophy is to the humanities what the decathlon is to track and field. Philosophy is not a subject, it is all subjects. It is the art of arts, and the science of sciences. It deals with everything under the sun—and a few things over it.

9. *Practical Philosophy* The Philosophy of Today emphasizes the inner life, spiritual growth, and the art of living well. It doesn't treat philosophy as a purely intellectual exercise; rather, it stays close to life itself.

One of the central questions of ancient philosophy was, What is the good life? Ancient philosophers sometimes discussed abstract, metaphysical questions, but usually ancient philosophers stayed close to life, tried to understand the world,

1. PHILOSOPHY

and advised people how to live well. Ancient philosophers advised people how to accept poverty, how to accept illness, and how to accept death. Ancient philosophers tried to live in accordance with their philosophy. Their philosophy was relevant to life, even when it took a pessimistic view of life. (One ancient philosopher, Hegesias, advised people not to live at all, and many of his followers committed suicide. King Ptolemy prohibited Hegesias from lecturing, lest he depopulate the country.)

During the Middle Ages, philosophy no longer advised people how to live. Religion began to play the role that philosophy used to play. Philosophy was reduced to playing the role of "handmaid of theology." Philosophy was no longer relevant to life; it became enmeshed in logic and in the process of thinking, like analytic philosophy today.

During the Renaissance, many people had more respect for Greco-Roman culture than for Christianity. Philosophy was no longer the "handmaid of theology," it resumed the role that it had in ancient times. One Renaissance philosopher, Montaigne, restored the ancient tradition, tried to understand the world, and discussed topics relevant to life.

Emerson and Thoreau worked within the tradition of Montaigne. They stayed close to life, and didn't become enmeshed in purely intellectual questions. Among their most important writings are their journals—a sign that their philosophical efforts weren't divorced from their daily life. One of their contemporaries, Kierkegaard, is also known for his journal, and also tried to connect philosophy to everyday life. According to Kierkegaard, truth should make you a better person: "only the truth that edifies is truth for you."[1] Nietzsche, too, insisted that the life of the mind should be connected to life. Nietzsche thought that philosophy should be practical, not abstract:

> I get profit from a philosopher, just so far as he can be an example to me.... This example must exist in his outward life, not merely in his books; it must follow the way of the Greek philosophers,

---

[1] *Either/Or*, last sentence

whose doctrine was in their dress and bearing and general manner of life rather than in their speech or writing.[1]

The Philosophy of Today is even more practical than Nietzsche, even less interested in logic than Thoreau, even less abstract than Kierkegaard, even closer to life than Montaigne. The Philosophy of Today draws on the tradition of Jung and Freud, a tradition that stays close to life, a tradition that points us toward self-knowledge. We admire the Buddha, who advised his disciples not to be distracted by intellectual questions, but to focus on their inner life. And we admire those Zen sages whose approach is un-intellectual and un-bookish, those Zen sages "whose doctrine was in their dress and bearing and general manner of life rather than in their speech or writing," those Zen sages whose wisdom manifested itself in arts and crafts and sports rather than in syllogisms and definitions.

10. *Lifeless Philosophy* Academic philosophy has become preoccupied with language, with the process of thinking, and with the process of ascertaining truth. These topics have no bearing on life; they neither deepen our understanding of reality nor give us advice about how to live.

If you ask a process philosopher to discuss the goal of life and the goal of the state, he'll say, "First we have to define our terms. What do you mean by 'goal'? By 'life'? By 'state'?" Soon the process philosopher will be enmeshed in a semantic net, and he'll ask you to come back in a week. When you come back, he'll say, "I'm making progress with my definition of 'goal', but I haven't yet begun to define 'life' or 'state'. Come back next week." A week later, he'll say, "I now realize that I don't have a clear idea of what a definition is. Before I go any further, I have to define 'definition'. Come back next week." After hearing this, you'll realize that you asked the wrong person, that a process philosopher can neither deepen your understanding of reality nor give you advice about how to live.

---

[1] *Untimely Essays*, "Schopenhauer As Educator," §3

1. PHILOSOPHY

Since process philosophy doesn't deal with reality, it has no role outside academia. Philosophy should leave the classroom, enter the world, and address the great questions that every human being wants answers to. Philosophy should address questions of substance, not just questions of process. When philosophy concerns itself exclusively with process, it becomes sterile, hollow and empty, and this is what academic philosophy has become.

Process philosophers want to eject philosophers like Thoreau from philosophy, and force them to seek shelter in literature or history. Thoreau discussed values, as a genuine philosopher always does; the process philosopher, on the other hand, doesn't discuss values, doesn't discuss how people should live. Thoreau lived his philosophy, he didn't just discuss it in the classroom and make a living from it; for Thoreau, philosophy was a way of life, not a job. Hence Thoreau will always be read by the layman, he'll always have a place in the world, while the process philosopher will always be ignored by the layman, and will have a place only in academia.

11. *Pressing Done Here* Kierkegaard saw that philosophy is often side-tracked by questions of process, and fails to address the big questions. "What the philosophers say about Reality," Kierkegaard wrote, "is often as disappointing as a sign you see in a shop window, which reads: Pressing Done Here. If you brought your clothes to be pressed, you would be fooled; for the sign is only for sale."[1]

12. *Living Philosophy* Montaigne speaks openly about sexual pleasure, and also about the pleasure of eating and drinking. This is because France, during Montaigne's time, was little influenced by ascetic Protestantism, and little influenced by the Counter-Reformation. Montaigne was a product of the Renaissance, and he shows how close the spirit of the Renaissance was to the spirit of ancient paganism. Christianity had far less influence on Montaigne than ancient culture had.

---

[1] *Either/Or*, Part I, "Diapsalmata"

Emerson was shocked by Montaigne's treatment of sexual matters; Emerson said, "a gross, semi-savage indecency debases [Montaigne's] book." A comparison between Montaigne and Emerson shows how profound the effect of ascetic Protestantism was, even on one who, like Emerson, was removed from it by several generations. A comparison between Shakespeare and Milton also shows the effect of ascetic Protestantism; Shakespeare, a Renaissance spirit, speaks far more openly about sexual matters than Milton, a Puritan spirit.

Montaigne is the most popular of philosophers—everyone likes him. Emerson, for example, though he deplored Montaigne's "indecency," said of Montaigne's essays, "no book before or since was ever so much to me as that." When Flaubert received a letter from a woman who was depressed, he wrote her thus: "You ask me what to read. Read Montaigne.... *He will calm you...* You will love him, you will see." Nietzsche praised Montaigne for his honesty, and then said, "the joy of living on this earth is increased by the existence of such a man." Pascal, who was a devout Christian and was tormented by a scrupulous conscience, wondered at Montaigne's untroubled conscience and his love of life. But Pascal didn't dislike Montaigne. Has anyone ever disliked Montaigne? Montaigne was still popular in the twentieth century; Montaigne was a favorite of the twentieth-century American philosopher, Eric Hoffer.

Why is Montaigne so popular? Montaigne is honest, personal and intimate; he takes the reader into his private thoughts, and into his personal experiences. Montaigne treats literature as a form of friendship; Montaigne said that one of his purposes in writing was to communicate with kindred spirits and form friendships. Montaigne discusses such fundamental topics as education, death, truth, friendship and love, and he illustrates his remarks with quotations from ancient writers. (Montaigne's enthusiasm for learning and his penchant for quotations are typical of the Renaissance.) Montaigne doesn't represent a particular school, party or theory—he writes as a human being, for human beings. Montaigne doesn't concern himself with questions of process, and he has no interest in logic or metaphysics. Montaigne gives us philosophy without sophistry.

However popular Montaigne may be, he's ignored by today's philosophy professors. Today's philosophy professors insist on converting philosophy into an empty abstraction, a sterile mind game. This wouldn't surprise Montaigne, who was familiar with academia's tendency to remove all the sap, all the blood, all the life from philosophy: "It is a great pity," Montaigne wrote, "...that philosophy is now... a vain and chimerical name, a thing of no use or value.... The cause, I think, lies in these quibblings which have blocked the approach to it."[1]

13. *Who's a Philosopher?* When Thoreau was alive, and was publishing articles on wild apples and Mt. Katahdin, who regarded him as a philosopher? When Kierkegaard was becoming known through his writings on Mozart and French drama, who regarded him as a philosopher? The best philosophers are often not regarded as philosophers until long after their death.

Furthermore, the best philosophers often have little interest in The Great Philosophers. Nietzsche, for example, had little interest in Aristotle; he was far more interested in Wagner's operas and Dostoyevsky's novels. Montaigne was more interested in Virgil and Tacitus than in Augustine and Aquinas. Thoreau paid little attention to Kant and Hegel; he preferred to read about an expedition to find the source of the Nile, or about a voyage to the South Pacific. But Nietzsche did read Schopenhauer closely, and Thoreau did read Emerson closely; philosophers like Nietzsche and Thoreau may have little interest in the history of philosophy, but they have a keen interest in One Philosopher, and their work takes this One Philosopher as a starting point.

14. *One Reader* The philosopher writes primarily for one reader, one disciple. This reader resembles himself, is himself at

---

[1] Montaigne, *Essays*, "On the Education of Children." Emerson's remarks on Montaigne can be found in *The Heart of Emerson's Journals*, edited by Bliss Perry, journal entries of 12/25/31 and 3/43; Flaubert's can be found in his *Letters*, 6/57; Nietzsche's can be found in his *Untimely Essays*, "Schopenhauer As Educator," §2

a younger age, himself transplanted into the future. This reader is the only person who fully understands the philosopher's work; he's the philosopher's best critic, and he can surpass the philosopher, and raise philosophy to new heights. Thus, Aristotle was Plato's best critic, and surpassed Plato, while Nietzsche was Schopenhauer's best critic, and surpassed Schopenhauer.

15. *Jung* The most important philosophical thinker of the twentieth century is Jung, but he isn't yet recognized as a philosopher, he isn't given a chapter in the history of philosophy, and he isn't discussed in academic philosophy departments. Much of Jung's work explores that essence of life which Parmenides called Being, which Kant called the thing-in-itself, and which Schopenhauer called the Will.

Schopenhauer had said that the Will is blind and aimless, like a dog chasing its tail; Schopenhauer was pessimistic. But Jung said that the unconscious has a goal. Jung said that the unconscious contains archetypes (images, patterns), and the most important of these archetypes is the archetype of the self, which draws us toward wholeness and balance, as the North Pole draws a compass needle. Jung said that the archetype of the self is identical with God; whether we refer to it as "the archetype of the self" or as "God" is a matter of choice.

Jung wasn't pessimistic, as Schopenhauer was; Jung sees opportunities for spiritual growth. While Schopenhauer and Nietzsche were contemptuous of religion, Jung respected the religious tradition, and Jung points the way to new religious ideas. While Nietzsche said "God is dead," Jung says that God evolves, as the human mind evolves.

Jung didn't draw a sharp distinction between mind and matter. He thought there was a connection between mind and matter, between man and nature, between the inner world and the outer world. An archetype, in Jung's view, was neither purely psychic nor purely physical, it was both, it was "psychoid" (to use Jung's term).

Just as the Romans saw a connection between the flight of birds and the outcome of a battle, just as the Chinese saw a connection between an earthquake and the death of an emperor,

1. PHILOSOPHY

so too Jung saw connections between the human world and the natural world. He referred to these connections as "synchronicity"—that is, meaningful coincidence; he called synchronicity an "acausal connecting principle." Jung was fascinated by occult phenomena of all kinds, and believed that these phenomena deserved further study.

Kant had said that space, time, and causality are merely categories of the human mind, and pertain only to the world of appearance, not to the thing-in-itself. Occult phenomena violate the laws of space, time, and causality. Schopenhauer and Jung, who both studied Kant, tried to explain occult phenomena in terms of the relativity of time and space. For example, when one of Jung's patients shot himself, and Jung felt a pain in the back of his head, he viewed that incident in the light of Kant's theory. You can perceive something that's taking place far away because it isn't really far away—space is relative, not absolute. When Jung had a vision of World War I before the war started, he said that the future can be foreseen because it is prepared in advance—time is relative, not absolute.

Jung's ideas often agree with ancient beliefs, and also with Eastern beliefs. Jung's ideas also agree with those of Western alchemists. Like Jung, the alchemists believed that the psychic and the physical overlap. The alchemists spoke of *unus mundus*, one world, the union of matter and spirit. They also spoke of "subtle bodies" (or "breath bodies"), which are part physical, part psychic. The concept of "subtle bodies" has been used by Jungians to explain psycho-somatic phenomena in the field of medicine.

The power of the mind is boundless; the mind can not only effect changes in the body, it can also effect changes in the external world. As one alchemist put it, the mind can bring about "many things of the utmost profundity outside the body."[1] Mind and matter overlap; there is no "pure spirit", divorced from matter, and there is no "dead matter", lacking all spirit and energy.

---

[1] Michael Sendivogius, quoted in Aniela Jaffé, *From the Life and Work of C. G. Jung*, ch. 2, p. 75

The whole universe is suffused with energy, with a kind of consciousness.

It will be many years before Jung is discussed in academic philosophy departments. Jung deals with the invisible world, the mysterious, while academics prefer to deal with what can be set forth on a blackboard; Jung deals with the non-rational, while academics are dedicated to rational thinking; Jung deals with the occult, while academics avoid the occult, and regard it with a mixture of fear and loathing.

16. *Zen* Like Jung, Zen represents an important part of modern thought, a part that is neglected in philosophy departments. Zen is highly practical, and speaks directly to one's values, and to one's daily life. Zen isn't bookish or abstract, and it can't be put on a blackboard. One can't grasp Zen by reading about it, one must practice it, and feel it. Zen has the positive, affirmative attitude that one finds in Nietzsche, the mistrust of reason that one finds in Jung, and the feeling of kinship with nature that one finds in Thoreau. Like Jung, Zen points the way to spiritual growth, and to new religious ideas.

17. *The Philosopher As Scientist* Although the philosopher deals with the humanities, with man, he has much in common with scientists like Newton and Einstein, who deal with nature, with the physical world. The philosopher and the scientist both aim at truth, at constructing a picture of reality that's more accurate than that constructed by earlier thinkers. The philosopher and the scientist both experience the thrill of discovering truth, and the pleasure of possessing a new view of the world. Those who learn this new view share in this pleasure, and see the world differently than they used to. Many, however, reject this new view and cling to the old view; the philosopher and the scientist both have difficulty persuading people to accept revolutionary theories.

The philosopher deals with different branches of the humanities—psychology, politics, literature, etc. Likewise, the scientist often deals with different branches of science—mechanics, optics, astronomy, etc. The philosopher and the scientist usually arrive at their central ideas when they're young, when they're about twenty. The vague feelings of the child develop into the clear insights of the adolescent, and eventually become the mature work of the adult. The ideas of the philosopher and the scientist seem to have been born with them, like a part of their body. Their ideas are the ideas of their time, and couldn't have been discovered in an earlier century. Their ideas expand on the ideas of earlier thinkers, or combine the ideas of earlier thinkers.

18. *The Idea of the Time* During the time of Christ, one idea of the time was the repression of the unconscious; another idea of the time was the end of the world and the beginning of a Golden Age, which many thought would come soon. During the Renaissance, the idea of the time was that man, by observing and experimenting, could understand the natural world; thus we find a fascination with the natural world in Bacon, Descartes, Leonardo and Montaigne. During the late 1700's and 1800's, one idea of the time was atheism; the French revolutionaries, Schopenhauer, Marx and Nietzsche are examples. Another idea of the time during the 1800's was the evolution of species; Goethe, Wallace and Darwin are examples. During the late 1800's, the idea of the time was the psychology of the unconscious; Schopenhauer, Nietzsche, Charcot, Janet and Freud are examples. During the twentieth century, the idea of the time was the philosophy of history; Spengler, Sorokin, Toynbee and Ortega are examples.

19. *Intuition* There aren't any completely original thinkers. The planting of an idea is done by a thinker's predecessors. Once the idea is fully developed, it becomes the idea of the time, and often more than one thinker takes a hand in the harvest.

A philosopher's most profound ideas are reached by intuition, not by reasoning. A philosopher's most profound ideas usually come to him during his youth. A philosopher is one who, while still young, has an intuitive perception of the idea of his time.

20. *How We Can Surpass Nietzsche* Unless civilization enters a dark age, ideas always progress, knowledge always advances and

consciousness always expands. Thus, the latest philosophy tends to supersede earlier philosophies, and to render them obsolete; as Schopenhauer said, "It has been with philosophy till now as it is in an auction-room, where whoever speaks last annuls all that has been said before."[1]

Schopenhauer enjoyed worldwide fame in the latter half of the 1800s, when it seemed that he had surpassed earlier philosophers. At the end of the 1800s, however, Nietzsche eclipsed Schopenhauer, and Schopenhauer began to sink into obscurity. More than any other philosopher, Nietzsche inspires young people, and Nietzsche is the model that young philosophers strive to attain. But few people understand Nietzsche's chief theories—his theory of decadence, and his theory of morality as decadent. Before a philosopher can be surpassed, he must first be understood.

Our time can surpass Nietzsche with the help of the great psychologists who came after Nietzsche. We can see further than Nietzsche by standing on the shoulders of giants.

21. *What is the origin of philosophy?* According to Aristotle, philosophy originates in awe. Aristotle had in mind the pre-Socratic philosophers who speculated about the stars, the earth, etc. Aristotle supposed that these men had been prompted to philosophize by a feeling of awe and astonishment in the presence of the universe. Philosophers still feel astonishment, but this feeling is now more likely to be prompted by man than by the stars; the modern philosopher is a humanist rather than a scientist, a psychologist rather than a physicist. The modern philosopher is astonished by the powers of the unconscious, by historical events, by artistic works, and by other human phenomena.

But the philosopher isn't motivated by awe alone, he's also motivated by an interest in the problems raised by earlier philosophers. Every philosopher starts where the last philosopher left off. Another driving force behind philosophy is suffering; the philosopher is motivated by the desire to overcome suffering, by

---

[1] Quoted in H. Zimmern, *Schopenhauer: His Life and Philosophy*, ch. 5.

the desire to make life palatable—for himself and for others. And finally, the philosopher is motivated by a life-instinct, a half-conscious, half-unconscious urge to improve the world and to benefit mankind. This urge motivates not only philosophy, but also many kinds of cultural and political behavior.

22. *From Physics to Psychology* The pre-Socratic philosophers looked at the universe, and tried to reduce the multiplicity of the universe to a single physical element—for example, to water, air or fire. Modern philosophers, on the other hand, look at man and try to view human nature in terms of a single psychological element—for example, a will to life, a will to power, or life- and death-instincts. While the pre-Socratics resembled physicists, modern philosophers resemble psychologists. While the pre-Socratics studied the world without, modern philosophers study the world within.

23. *Metaphysics from Parmenides to Schopenhauer* Everyone knows that metaphysics has played an important role in Western philosophy, but few know what it is. What is metaphysics? What is its purpose? How did it originate?

Metaphysics originated with the pre-Socratics, with Parmenides in particular. The history of Western metaphysics is foreshadowed in Parmenides. Parmenides saw that all things changed, that all things came into being and then passed away. Parmenides reminds one of the Persian king, Xerxes, who stood on a hill and watched his huge army pass beneath him, and then wept at the thought that in a hundred years no trace of that army would remain. Parmenides sought something that really existed, something solid, stable and permanent.

Parmenides decided that all particular things emerged from a primary being, and that while particular things were unstable and fluctuating, being itself was static and permanent. According to Parmenides, particular things didn't actually come into being, since being was unchanging, nor did they cease to be; rather, particular things became manifest, then faded from view. Parmenides said that true being was permanent, and could be known only by reason and intelligence. The world of particular things, on the other hand, was illusory and was perceived by the senses. The senses were mortal and perceived what was mortal, while reason and intelligence were immortal and perceived what was immortal. Parmenides' theory is highly abstract; if philosophy is an evolution from the abstract to the concrete, as Hegel said, Parmenides represents an extreme of abstraction, the starting point of philosophy.

Plato, like Parmenides, regarded the world of particular things as illusory. Plato said that true being lay in the world of ideas; the ideas were eternal, akin to God. Most people, according to Plato, lived in the world of the senses, not the world of the ideas. Plato said that those who live in the world of the senses are like people imprisoned in a cave who know nothing of the world except the shadows they see on the walls of the cave. Plato's metaphysics was poetic and metaphorical.

Aristotle considered metaphysics to be "first philosophy," the most important and lofty branch of philosophy. Aristotle said that true being was unchanging and undivided, just as God was; the knowledge of true being was identical with the knowledge of God. Aristotle equated metaphysics with theology. At the center of Aristotle's philosophy was metaphysics, and at the center of Aristotle's metaphysics was God. Hence Aristotle was popular among Christian thinkers, for whom God was all-important. Aristotle's metaphysics exerted enormous influence over medieval philosophers, especially over Aquinas.

After the Middle Ages, Descartes and Spinoza continued the Aristotelian tradition, and sought to define God, and prove God's existence, by metaphysical reasoning, reasoning that aspired to be as clear and indisputable as geometry. Kant argued that man can't prove anything about God, about the world of true being, about the thing-in-itself. Kant said that man can only prove what relates to particular things, to the apparent world, to the phenomenal world. Thus, Kant's metaphysics appeared to be hostile to religion. On closer inspection, however, it became evident that Kant's metaphysics was friendly to religion. While religion couldn't be supported with proofs, according to Kant, there was still room for religious belief. God couldn't be proven, but neither could He be disproven. For Kant, religion was a matter of

1. PHILOSOPHY

belief rather than rational knowledge. Thus, metaphysics was still an ally of religion.

But the long alliance between metaphysics and religion, an alliance that began with Parmenides, finally ended with Schopenhauer. Schopenhauer agreed with earlier metaphysicians that the world of particular things, the world of the senses, was illusory. Where Schopenhauer differed was in his discussion of the world of true being, ultimate reality. Earlier metaphysicians had equated true being with God, but Schopenhauer said that true being was "will." In inanimate matter, this Will was merely mass, gravity. In organic life, this Will was a will to life, a will to live and reproduce. What Schopenhauer called the Will was similar to what later thinkers would call the unconscious.

While Kant had left room for God, Schopenhauer divided the world between Will and idea—that is, between Will and our ideas about particular things. Schopenhauer left no room for God. Thus, metaphysics ceased to be theological, and became psychological. Schopenhauer was the first uncompromising atheist in Western philosophy. But Schopenhauer's atheism wasn't loud and strident, as Nietzsche's was; Schopenhauer simply left God out and put the unconscious in God's place. Earlier thinkers had said that man was essentially conscious and rational; Schopenhauer was the first to say that man was essentially unconscious and irrational, that consciousness was only a skin over the unconscious.

24. *Schopenhauer and Hegel* Schopenhauer is important because he broached the problem of atheism and the problem of the unconscious, and thus set the stage for Nietzsche and Freud. During the early 1800's, when Schopenhauer was young, Hegel was the undisputed king of German philosophy. Hegel thought that he had reached the summit of philosophical wisdom, yet in the very hall where he delivered his lectures, where he discussed how philosophy had reached its final stage, sat a young philosopher, Arthur Schopenhauer, who discovered a continent whose existence Hegel never suspected. While Schopenhauer set the stage for Nietzsche and Freud, Hegel had no influence on Nietzsche or Freud.

Though Hegel was famous for his metaphysics and his logic, Hegel's importance lies in his theory of society as an organism. This theory influenced those who, in the twentieth century, have explored the philosophy of history. While Hegel was preoccupied with history, Schopenhauer paid little attention to it; Schopenhauer overlooked history, just as Hegel overlooked the problem of atheism and the problem of the unconscious. Schopenhauer regarded history as a chain of random events, lacking philosophical meaning. Schopenhauer insisted that Hegel's concern with history was a deviation from true philosophy.

A philosopher generally thinks that he has discovered the whole truth (and his followers agree with him), but a philosopher never discovers more than part of the truth. A philosopher's importance is often misunderstood by his contemporaries, and also by the philosopher himself. A philosopher's importance is most apparent in retrospect, when his influence on later thinkers becomes evident.

25. *Nietzsche* During his early twenties, Nietzsche idolized Schopenhauer. During his early thirties, however, when he wrote *Human, All-Too-Human*, Nietzsche took issue with many of Schopenhauer's views. For example, while Schopenhauer had criticized dueling, Nietzsche praised it, and while Schopenhauer had praised the study of foreign languages, Nietzsche criticized it, and while Schopenhauer had called noise an unpleasant distraction, Nietzsche called noise a pleasant diversion. Nietzsche took issue with Schopenhauer's views in order to emancipate himself from Schopenhauer, to become a philosopher in his own right, and to become Schopenhauer's equal.

After he had emancipated himself from Schopenhauer, Nietzsche no longer felt compelled to take issue with Schopenhauer's views. Nietzsche did, however, accuse Schopenhauer of constructing an elaborate metaphysical argument for the sake of supporting his personal opinions on morality and on the world in general, just as Nietzsche accused Kant of constructing an elaborate metaphysical argument for the sake of supporting his own belief in God and in Christian morality.

Nietzsche thought that elaborate metaphysical arguments were constructed not to ascertain truth, but rather to support a philosopher's personal opinions. And a philosopher's personal opinions, in Nietzsche's view, were the expression of that philosopher's instincts. Nietzsche criticized Kant and Schopenhauer not for constructing faulty arguments, but rather for having decadent opinions and decadent instincts, and for hiding their opinions behind a facade of elaborate reasoning. When Nietzsche chose to write in aphoristic form, he rejected the tradition of German metaphysics, and embraced instead the tradition of the French aphorists.

26. *Lasting Value?* When we surpass Nietzsche, will we render his books worthless? When Nietzsche surpassed Schopenhauer, did he render Schopenhauer's books worthless? What value does a philosopher's work have after it has been surpassed by a later philosopher? Does it have merely historical interest, or does it have lasting value? A philosopher's work usually has lasting value, unlike a scientist's work, which usually has merely historical interest after it has been surpassed.

Some philosophers, like Schopenhauer and Nietzsche, set forth one central idea, and extend the boundaries of human knowledge. But their work doesn't consist only of this central idea, it also contains numerous other ideas. Many of these other ideas have lasting value, even if the central idea is surpassed by later thinkers. Schopenhauer's remarks on style, for example, have lasting value, even if his theory of the unconscious has been surpassed by later thinkers.

Other philosophers, like Emerson and Thoreau, don't set forth one central idea, and don't extend the boundaries of human knowledge. Their work is timeless, and can't be surpassed. They emphasize the spiritual rather than the intellectual. One might compare philosophy to a stool with three legs: Spiritual, Intellectual, and Literary. While Schopenhauer and Nietzsche emphasize the Intellectual and Literary, Emerson and Thoreau emphasize the Spiritual and Literary.

2. Ethics

1. *Four Ideals* The four most attractive ideals in our time are
   1. the Zen ideal: stillness, awareness of the present moment, meditation, yoga;
   2. the Thoreau ideal: love of nature, love of the earth, the attempt to save the earth from pollution and other dangers;
   3. the Jung ideal: communion with the unconscious, listening to one's dreams and feelings, finding a midpoint between consciousness and the unconscious; and
   4. the Nietzsche ideal: the classical Western ideal, which has its roots on the Acropolis; the full development of the individual, inspired by heroic ethics and by culture.

   The Zen and Thoreau ideals are the most practical, they can be applied most readily in our daily life. The Zen and Thoreau ideals overlap: Zen encourages the love of nature, and Thoreau encourages awareness of the present moment. The Jung ideal lies between Zen and Nietzsche, it builds a bridge between East and West. The Nietzsche ideal appeals strongly to young intellectuals, especially young philosophers, because it addresses itself to such individuals, it describes the situation of such individuals.

2. *Jungian Ethics* Here's an example of how listening to our unconscious can shape our actions, our decisions, our daily life:

when Jung was in his eighties, someone suggested that he write a book suitable for a wide audience. Jung thought about it for a while, and finally decided not to. Then he had a dream in which he was speaking to a crowd of people, and they understood what he was saying. As a result of the dream, Jung reversed his decision, and wrote (with the help of some disciples) *Man and His Symbols*.

The case of Macbeth exemplifies the problems that can arise if we ignore our unconscious, ignore our feelings and hunches. Macbeth murders Duncan in defiance of his feelings; Macbeth allows the prophecies of the witches, and the arguments of his wife, to overcome the "still small voice" of his unconscious. "Macbeth's better nature," wrote A. C. Bradley, "incorporates itself in images which alarm and horrify. His imagination is thus the best of him, something usually deeper and higher than his conscious thoughts; and if he had obeyed it he would have been safe."[1]

3. *Beyond Ethics* In sport, as in art, only the beginner follows rules. "The beginner at golf," wrote Wilson Knight, "is usually guilty of 'thinking too precisely on the event'; but not so the expert, whose thought is embedded in, sunk in, dissolved throughout, the living action, mind and body functioning as a unit."[2] The Zen master teaches the archery student to become one with his bow—not to consciously follow rules, not to consciously release the arrow, but to let the arrow release itself, to become unconscious, to become spontaneous, "mind and body functioning as a unit."

Hamlet is like the beginner at golf; Hamlet is too thoughtful, he can't act spontaneously, he can only make a rational calculation of pros and cons. But Shakespeare shows us an image of spontaneity, of "mind and body functioning as a unit"; he describes Lamord's riding skills thus:

> he grew unto his seat;
> And to such wondrous doing brought his horse,

---

[1] *Shakespearean Tragedy*, "Macbeth"
[2] *The Wheel of Fire*, ch. 15, #2

> As had he been incorps'd and demi-natur'd
> With the brave beast: so far he topp'd my thought
> That I, in forgery of shapes and tricks,
> Come short of what he did. (IV, vii)

Lamord is unconscious and spontaneous, beyond description, beyond technique, beyond rule.

What is true in sport and art is also true in life: the beginner follows rules, ethics, but the highest goal is spontaneity. To achieve wholeness, to act out of our center, is to go beyond ethics. If we combine the active and the passive, the masculine and the feminine, the conscious and the unconscious, we go beyond rules, beyond ethics. The New Testament calls this "freedom from the law." It is this freedom that eludes Hamlet; Wilson Knight says that Hamlet is "sunk deep in the knowledge of good and evil and clogged by ethic."

4. *East and West* Generally speaking, Western religion is ethical, it prescribes rules for our behavior toward other people—the Ten Commandments, for example, or "Love thy neighbor as thyself." These rules come from God, and if belief in God erodes, man falls into moral anarchy.

Eastern religion is psychological and metaphysical, rather than ethical. The psychological side of Eastern religion says, "use the following techniques to reduce stress and attain inner peace," while the metaphysical side says, "man is connected to the whole universe, his being/energy is akin to the being/energy in everything else." If the individual achieves inner peace, and is comfortable with his place in the universe, virtuous conduct is likely to result, even without an ethical code.

Reason is more important in Western thought than in Eastern thought, perhaps because reason can be useful in regulating our inter-actions with other people, but it isn't as useful in psychological and metaphysical inquiries.

I began by saying "Generally speaking" because there are counter-currents. While Taoism and Buddhism may be described as psychological and metaphysical, Confucianism has a strong ethical tendency. Western religion sometimes aims at inner peace, as in phrases like "take no thought for the morrow" and "freedom from the law."

5. *Bildung* "Self-culture," said Oscar Wilde, "is the true ideal of man."[1] The ideal of self-culture, self-development, *Bildung* has long been important in Western culture, but it's on the wane in our time. Is it inconsistent with the other ideals mentioned above—the Thoreau ideal, the Zen ideal, and the Jung ideal? No, actually it fuses these three ideals together, since each of these ideals can play a role in self-development; self-development involves listening to the unconscious (the Jung ideal), being aware of the present moment (the Zen ideal), and appreciating nature (the Thoreau ideal).

Why, then, is the old ideal of self-culture fading away? The ideal of self-culture is in collision with the ideal of service to society, which is a popular ideal in our time. The most talented and ambitious college students want to start their own philanthropic organization, or join someone else's. People think that they should feel guilty if they study the humanities, and follow the way of Zen. People think that they should "get involved," help the needy, be politically active, have a social conscience, "give something back to society," etc.

The inner life is neglected, the life of the mind is never mentioned, the search for truth is unfashionable, the love of culture is considered elitist. In 2002, Columbia University inaugurated a new president. At the ceremony, the guests of honor were the Mayor of New York, and the Secretary-General of the U.N. The theme of the new president's speech was "get involved"—get involved with the city, get involved with the world.

The Harvard historian Oscar Handlin said that, in recent decades, "The overall tone of Harvard turned hostile or at best apathetic to scholarly values, now deemed less worthy than the pressing tasks of doing good for the world."[2]

Eric Hoffer perceived that the ideal of service to society was replacing the ideal of self-development; Hoffer said, "How much

---

[1] *The Critic As Artist: A Dialogue*
[2] "A Career at Harvard," *The American Scholar*, winter, 1996

easier is self-sacrifice than self-realization!"[1] Goethe, the greatest champion of *Bildung*, said he feared that "the world will turn into a vast hospital in which everyone will be the devoted nurse of everyone else."[2]

6. *Eastern Wisdom* is becoming increasingly popular in the West. Schopenhauer was one of the first Western philosophers to admire Eastern philosophy; Schopenhauer rejected Christianity, and embraced Indian philosophy. In the nineteenth century, many Western intellectuals were losing faith in monotheistic religions like Judaism, Christianity, and Islam. Schopenhauer was an atheist, hence he was attracted to Eastern belief-systems that lacked a Western-style God—lacked a God who created the universe, ruled the universe, dictated books, etc. Oriental thinkers believed that the world had grown up spontaneously, like a plant; they didn't view the world as a system that was designed and built by an omnipotent being. The Oriental view is consistent with modern science.

Nietzsche wasn't as impressed by Eastern ideas as Schopenhauer was. But some of Nietzsche's aphorisms remind one of Eastern practices, such as meditation; "Lying still and thinking little," Nietzsche wrote, "is the cheapest medicine for all sicknesses of the soul and, if persisted with, grows more pleasant hour by hour."[3] "Thinking little" isn't as easy as it sounds. The mind wanders; it likes to occupy itself with something. India and China have developed a variety of techniques for calming the mind: meditation, yoga, tai chi, etc. These techniques direct the mind onto something simple and relaxing, such as breathing, walking, repeating the same word over and over, or slowly stretching and exercising the body. These techniques are becoming increasingly popular in the West due to their beneficial effect on both body and mind.

---

[1] *Reflections on the Human Condition*, #107
[2] *Goethe: The History of a Man*, by Emil Ludwig, ch. 7
[3] *Assorted Opinions and Maxims*, §361

7. *Meditation* is sitting still—a stillness of the body, a stillness of the mind and a stillness of the will. Meditation is non-doing, and non-doing reduces stress. On the other hand, stress builds up if one does much, thinks much and desires much. Meditation can be defined as sitting still in an erect posture, concentrating on one's breathing.

Nietzsche's prescription—"lying still and thinking little"—could also be considered meditation; indeed, almost anything can be considered meditation if one concentrates on what one is doing. Listening to music, for example, can be considered meditation if one concentrates on the music. Often, however, people listen to music while doing something else—while driving, while eating, while looking at a magazine, etc.

We frequently burden our mind with worries about the future and regrets about the past. Meditation unburdens the mind by concentrating on the present moment. By concentrating and strengthening the mind, meditation helps us cope with pain. Meditation techniques are often taught to pregnant women, in order to help them cope with the pain of childbirth. Meditation techniques are also taught to people who suffer from chronic back pain and other forms of pain.

Meditation can help us cope with temptation as well as pain. Temptation dominates many people's lives, and causes health problems related to eating, drinking, smoking, etc. If one represses temptation, it becomes stronger; repression doesn't solve the problem of temptation. Meditation and other stress-reduction techniques are the best ways of coping with temptation. People often eat, drink and smoke when they have nothing to do, or when they feel stress. By helping people cope with idleness and stress, meditation removes temptations.

Meditation requires no particular personality type, no special intellectual abilities. However, meditation techniques are of no avail if they're done with the wrong attitude; attitude is as important as technique. One should have an attitude of non-striving, of accepting things as they are. Anyone who adopts this attitude, and who makes meditation a priority in their life, can benefit from it.

8. *Non-doing* revolutionizes ethics, just as the invention of zero revolutionized mathematics.

9. *No Thoughts, No Goals* The word "meditation" suggests thinking, and is thus a misnomer. The Chinese have a better word: *da zuo*, meaning "to sit," or "to do a sit."

Descartes said, "I think therefore I am." Zen says, "I don't think, therefore I am."

The best way to understand meditation is to practice it, not to read about it. It should be experienced, not grasped intellectually.

Some people who try it say, "it didn't do anything for me." We shouldn't expect, however, that it will do something for us. The goal of meditation is to do something that has no goal; the goal of meditation is simply to be. "The practice of Zen," wrote Alan Watts, "is not the true practice so long as it has an end in view."[1] In this respect, as in many other respects, Zen resembles The Jungian Way. Jung and his disciples say that we should attend to the unconscious and respect it, not use its power to further our own purposes. The classic fairy-tale hero, Jungians say, goes off into the world with no clear goal in view—like Don Quixote, who said he was going wherever his horse took him.

10. *A Cloud in the Sky* Meditation plays an important role in Zen Buddhism. In fact, if one traces the word "Zen" from Japanese back to Chinese, and from Chinese back to the dialects of India, one finds that "Zen" means meditation. While Zen may have originated in India, it developed in China, where it was influenced by Chinese Taoism, and by the philosophies of Lao Zi and Zhuang Zi. Although Zen left a deep mark on Chinese culture, it achieved its widest application in Japan, where it shaped haiku poetry, archery, the tea ceremony, and many other facets of Japanese life.

Most religions distinguish between the holy and the unholy, but Zen respects and values everything equally. Western religion tends to regard the everyday world as unholy. The Latin word for "world" is *mundus*, which evolved into the English word "mun-

---

[1] *The Way of Zen*, ch. 3

dane," meaning low, unspiritual. But Zen doesn't view the world as unholy or dirty, Zen values the everyday world because Zen isn't preoccupied with The Other World, the Afterlife, Heaven. Zen can appreciate the present moment because it isn't preoccupied with Eternity.

Haiku poetry celebrates the ordinary, everyday world.

> The melons look cool,
> Flecked with mud
> From the morning dew.

This is by Basho, the most famous haiku poet. Here's another haiku by Basho:

> You light the fire
> I'll show you something nice—
> A great ball of snow!

Zen is aware of the present moment, aware of the sights and sounds, the smells and tastes, that one is experiencing right now. People usually eat hurriedly, with their mind on something else; an American meditation teacher begins his class by giving each person one raisin, and asking them to eat it slowly, mindfully.

Zen lives directly, spontaneously, without excessive reflection. One writer on Zen calls Hamlet "the Zen-less man"[1] because Hamlet is reflective. An ancient Buddhist maxim tells us to "awaken the mind without fixing it anywhere."

Zen is devoid of doctrines and theories. A 12th-century Zen master, Tai-E, burned the chief Zen text because he didn't want Zen to become bookish, dusty and intellectual.[2] Zen masters often taught without words—by pointing, gesturing, etc.

> When the Governor of Lang asked Yao-shan, 'What is the Tao?' the master pointed upwards to the sky and downwards to a water jug beside him. Asked for an explanation, he replied: 'A cloud in the sky and water in the jug.'[3]

---

[1] R. H. Blyth, *Zen in English Literature*, ch. 10. Blyth translated the haiku poems quoted above.
[2] Ibid, ch. 4
[3] quoted in *The Way of Zen*, by Alan Watts, II, 2

Just as Zen lacks a Western-style God, so too it lacks a Western-style morality. Zen doesn't preach, it has no moral law, no "categorical imperative." There are many similarities between Zen and Nietzsche. Nietzsche rejected traditional, Western religion and morality; Nietzsche's philosophy is godless, amoral, beyond good and evil. Like Nietzsche, Zen isn't pessimistic or nihilistic, it accepts the world as it is, and celebrates reality. As Nietzsche represents an advanced stage of Western philosophy, so Zen represents an advanced stage of Eastern wisdom. The philosophers of our time will draw upon both Nietzsche and Zen.

11. *Man Becoming God* While there are similarities between Nietzsche and Zen, there are also differences, one of which is that Nietzsche represents ego inflation, while Zen represents ego deflation. In general, Western culture emphasizes the ego far more than Eastern culture. Western painters like Rembrandt were preoccupied with the self-portrait, while Eastern painters concentrated on landscape. What a contrast between Michelangelo's heroic figures and a Japanese rock garden! The West divides the self from the world, while the East merges the self with the world.

While many Western writers have had a high opinion of their own work, ego inflation reached an unprecedented level with Nietzsche. "Since the old God is abolished, I am prepared *to rule the world*," wrote Nietzsche, in a discarded draft of his autobiography, *Ecce Homo*.[1] Nietzsche's ego inflation was a consequence of his atheism. As long as Western man worshipped God, his ego was kept within bounds; Christianity was a school of humility. Loss of faith led to ego inflation. Dostoyevsky perceived that atheism would lead to ego inflation; "If there is no God, then I am God," says one of Dostoyevsky's atheists.[2]

Zen is an antidote to ego inflation; like Christianity, Zen is a school of humility. Meditation is humbling because no one is "good" at meditation, and no one becomes "better" at meditation by doing it.

---

[1] See the appendix to Walter Kaufmann's translation of *Ecce Homo*.
[2] *The Possessed*, III, vi, 2

12. Ten Zen Basics

I. Zen emphasizes the Here and Now, the present moment. Zen teaches us to be aware of the present moment. Awareness and perception are important in Zen—more important than logical, rational thinking. The most eloquent Zen sermon is Buddha's Flower Sermon, in which Buddha said nothing, but simply held up a flower. By de-emphasizing logical, rational, conscious thinking, Zen helps us to connect with our bodies, and with our unconscious. Thus, Zen can make us more whole, more healthy, more happy.

II. Zen loves nothingness, but Zen isn't nihilism. While most people focus on the printed words, Zen loves the margin of life, the blank space. Zen teaches you to enjoy not only pleasant thoughts, but also no thoughts, a blank mind. While most drivers prefer green lights to red lights, Zen likes red lights as much as green lights. Lao Zi said that the most valuable part of a house is not the walls and roof that the builder constructs, but the empty space within. The Zen spirit lives in the Roman saying, *"Liber non est qui non aliquando nihil agit"* (he is not free who doesn't sometimes do nothing).

III. Zen has a long history and a rich literary tradition. It has been tested by Time, and it has passed the test. The genuine Zen spirit is still alive in Japan today (and probably still alive in China and Korea, too), just as the genuine spirit of Hindu mysticism, and of yoga, is still alive in India.

IV. One of the classics of Zen literature is *Zen in the Art of Archery*, which was written by a German philosophy professor, Eugen Herrigel, who lived in Japan in the 1930s. Other Zen classics are *Zen Flesh, Zen Bones*, the works of R. H. Blyth (such as *Zen in English Literature*), the works of D. T. Suzuki (such as *Essays on Zen Buddhism*), and the works of Alan Watts (such as *The Way of Zen*).

V. Zen came to the West around 1900. Zen came to the West from Japan, since Zen sank deeper roots in Japan than anywhere else. Japan was closed to the West until 1854, so

Zen long remained unknown to the West. (Western philosophers like Schopenhauer, Nietzsche, and Thoreau were familiar with Indian philosophy, and perhaps with Confucius, but not with Zen.) The advent of Zen is a recent phenomenon. The advent of Zen is one of the major developments in Western philosophy in the 20th century. Zen currently enjoys broad popularity in the West. Meditation classes are everywhere. Zen is popular with artists and writers, with businessmen, etc.

VI. Like other schools of Eastern thought, Zen sees the Ego, the I, not as an island, but as part of the mainland; Zen sees the Ego not as independent, but as merged with the surrounding world.

VII. By merging the Ego with the surrounding world, Zen puts us in touch with nature, Zen teaches us to appreciate nature. The most Zennish writers (Basho, Thoreau, etc.) are preoccupied with nature. Oriental painters, influenced by Zen and similar worldviews, appreciated nature long before Western painters did.

VIII. Zen is partly a religion, partly a philosophy, and partly a rejection of both religion and philosophy.

IX. Zen is a type of mysticism. It resembles other types of mysticism—Christian, Islamic, Hindu, etc. The Zen spirit can be found in every country and in every religion. The Zen spirit can also be found in literature—in Whitman, in Thoreau, in Wordsworth, etc. Like other types of mysticism, Zen prizes the moment of enlightenment, which it calls "satori." In the moment of enlightenment, you have a keen sense of being alive, a keen appreciation of everyday reality. Zen monks often seek to attain satori with the help of a "koan," that is, a question or problem, posed by their teacher, that is baffling to the rational mind, that forces one to abandon rational thinking.

X. What is the sound of one hand clapping? The sound of silence.

13. *The Moment* "A big bird spreads its wings, and begins to fly"—a famous image in Chinese literature. "A frog jumps into

an old pond... splash!"—a famous image in Japanese literature. Both these images are images of a moment in time, The Moment, The Eternal Now. And both these images are images of action, spontaneous action, unreflecting action. This is how Nature acts. Shouldn't man act this way, too? Shouldn't man act spontaneously, freely? Isn't this "the way of Zen"? Action for the sake of action, doing something for its own sake, life for the sake of living.

14. *Hume and Zen* Zen dissolves the ego, dissolves the boundaries between you and the external world; Zen changes our conception of the word "I". Zen makes it easier to endure suffering and death by teaching us that we aren't separate beings, we're part of the world.

Before Western philosophers became acquainted with Eastern thought, they had begun to question the ego, to dissolve the ego; this was Hume's contribution. But before we discuss Hume, let's look at Hume's ancestors, Locke and Berkeley.

Locke said that objects have primary qualities, such as substance and extension, and secondary qualities, such as color and taste. According to Locke, secondary qualities are subjective; they depend on you and I the perceivers, and don't exist in the object itself. Primary qualities, on the other hand, actually exist.

To illustrate Locke's theory, let's look at a rose. You and I see it as red. A bee, which sees a different spectrum of light than you and I, may see it as yellow. The color of the rose depends on who's perceiving it. In Locke's view, color is one of those secondary qualities that don't actually exist, that are merely subjective. But Locke believed that primary qualities (substance and extension) actually exist, objectively, apart from any perceiver.

Berkeley went further than Locke, and argued that even Locke's "primary qualities" can't be proven to exist apart from a perceiver. According to Berkeley, to be is to be perceived; we can't conceive of being apart from perceiving. Berkeley even rejected Newton's doctrine of absolute space, time, and motion. The view that space and time are relative, subjective—a view that we associate with Kant and Einstein—can be traced to

Berkeley. There was one thing, however, that Berkeley didn't question: the mind, the ego.

Hume went further than Berkeley, and argued that the mind isn't stable and enduring, it's just a series of thoughts and feelings that fly through us intermittently. Because these thoughts come and go rapidly, we perceive them to be continuous, just as we perceive a movie, which is made up of discrete images, to be a continuous image.

Long before Hume, Buddha had reached the same conclusion; Buddhists compared the mind to a torch that is waved rapidly in a circle, and perceived to be a continuous circle of flame. In the West, this idea seemed to be abstract, remote from life, but in the East, this idea sank deep roots, and became "second nature," became a feeling, and affected how people thought about that little word "I", how people dealt with suffering and death. Zen dissolves the walls of the mind, dissolves the ego, and teaches us that we aren't separate beings, we're part of the world.

Indeed, Zen would argue that nothing is a "separate being," everything is part of everything else. Stop reading and look out of the window. You see a tree and you think, "that's a separate thing." Now reflect: the tree grows leaves. Are the leaves part of the tree, or separate from the tree? Part of the tree, no doubt. But if the leaves die and fall to the ground, they appear to be separate from the tree. When they disintegrate, however, and provide nourishment to that same tree, they appear to be part of it, not separate from it. Like leaves, seeds may be seen as part of the tree, or separate from it. If a seed grows into another tree, should we call it separate? Isn't the second tree of the same substance as the first? "Flesh of my flesh, bone of my bone." And if the tree draws its life from sunlight, water and air, can we call it a separate thing? Is it not part of the sunlight, the water, the air? Is it not just another form of sunlight, another form of water and air? Could it be that everything is a form of everything else, everything is One?

And if that tree isn't a separate thing, then you and I aren't either, for the same reasons that the tree isn't. Aren't you and I forms of sunlight, water and air, forms of everything else? And if we have a child, is he not separate and yet the same, external yet internal? If an apple is in our ice box, it appears separate, but if it's in our stomach, then what? If it becomes part of our brain, then what?

The boundaries that demarcate things are not as clear as common sense supposes. The boundaries that demarcate things gradually vanish when we look at them closely. We begin to see the world as one world, one process, one stream of change. We begin to see ourselves differently, and we begin to define that little word "I" differently.

15. *Not Twice* Like Western mystics, and like Nietzsche, Zen has a positive attitude toward life and the universe; Zen is affirmative, it says Yes. Here's a Zen story that illustrates this:

> A nobleman asked Takuan, a Zen teacher, to suggest how he might pass the time. He felt his days very long attending his office and sitting stiffly to receive the homage of others. Takuan wrote eight Chinese characters and gave them to the man:
>
> Not twice this day.
> Inch time foot gem.
> (This day will not come again.
> Each minute is worth a priceless gem.)[1]

16. *What Zen Lacks* Zen is a religion without superstition. It has

1. no holy men
2. no holy places
3. no holy books
4. no heaven and hell
5. no commandments or laws
6. no rites or ceremonies
7. no miracles
8. no prophecies (that is, no predictions of the coming of the holy man)

---

[1] *Zen Flesh, Zen Bones,* "101 Zen Stories," #32

Compared to Zen, the three monotheistic religions—Christianity, Judaism and Islam—are all encrusted with superstition.

17. *Both East and West* Our respect for the East shouldn't prompt us to despise the West. We should regard Eastern philosophy as a stage in the evolution of Western philosophy, not as a rejection of Western philosophy. Jung and Joseph Campbell, who both respected Eastern wisdom, warned against abandoning our Western roots. Campbell said that the Western concept of

> the individual, his self-hood, his rights, and his freedom [are] the truly great "new thing" that we do indeed represent to the world and that constitutes our Occidental revelation of a properly human spiritual ideal, true to the highest potentiality of our species.[1]

18. *Thoreau* is the most Zennish writer in Western literature. Like Zen, Thoreau focuses on the present moment:

> In any weather, at any hour of the day or night, I have been anxious to improve the nick of time, and notch it on my stick too; to stand on the meeting of two eternities, the past and future, which is precisely the present moment; to toe that line.... We cannot afford not to live in the present. He is blessed over all mortals who loses no moment of the passing life in remembering the past.[2]

Thoreau wanted to be aware of the sights and sounds around him, but found that his mind was sometimes distracted:

> I am alarmed when it happens that I have walked a mile into the woods bodily, without getting there in spirit. In my afternoon walk I would fain forget all my morning occupations and my obligations to society. But it sometimes happens that I cannot eas-

---

[1] *Myths To Live By*, ch. 4. Compare Jung: "It is sad indeed when the European departs from his own nature and imitates the East or 'affects' it in any way. The possibilities open to him would be so much greater if he would remain true to himself."(*Psychology and the East*, ch. 1, par. 9)

[2] see *Walden*, ch. 1, and the essay "Walking"

ily shake off the village. The thought of some work will run in my head and I am not where my body is—I am out of my senses. In my walks I would fain return to my senses. What business have I in the woods, if I am thinking of something out of the woods?[1]

Don't be in a hurry, says Thoreau:

> Nature never makes haste.... The bud swells imperceptibly, without hurry or confusion, as though the short spring days were an eternity.... Why, then, should man hasten as if anything less than eternity were allotted for the least deed? Let him consume never so many eons, so that he go about the meanest task well, though it be but the paring of his nails.... The wise man is restful, never restless or impatient. He each moment abides there where he is, as some walkers actually rest the whole body at each step, while others never relax the muscles of the leg till the accumulated fatigue obliges them to stop short.[2]

Thoreau's attitude toward music was also Zennish: "Listen to music religiously, as if it were the last strain you might hear."[3]

Like Zen, Thoreau is positive, affirmative, Yes-saying. Compared to the New Testament, Thoreau said, a cock's crow is

> a newer testament—the Gospel according to this moment.... to celebrate this last instant of time.... The merit of this bird's strain is in its freedom from all plaintiveness. The singer can easily move us to tears or to laughter, but where is he who can excite in us a pure morning joy? When, in doleful dumps... I hear a cockerel crow far or near, I think to myself there is one of us well at any rate, and with a sudden gush return to my senses.[4]

At age 45, when he was sick and near death, Thoreau's positive attitude didn't change at all, and in one of his last letters, he said, "I may add that I am enjoying existence as much as ever, and regret nothing."[5]

19. *Zen Anger* "Don't just do something! Stand there!"

---

[1] "Walking"
[2] journal entry from 1840
[3] journal entry from 1851
[4] "Walking"
[5] *The Days of Henry Thoreau,* by W. Harding, ch. 20, §2

20. *Greetings* When you meet someone you know, you usually say, "how are you doing?" If the person is a disciple of Zen, however, you should perhaps ask, "how are you breathing?" And if the person is a disciple of Jung, you should ask, "how are you dreaming?"

21. *The Work Ethic and National Character* One effect of the Protestant work ethic is, of course, a propensity for work. "Work hard in your calling"—this is the motto of the Protestant work ethic. A second effect of the work ethic is the quickening of the tempo of life; one who lives by this ethic is always in a hurry. According to the work ethic, wasting time is sinful. A third effect of the work ethic is a materialistic attitude; you should work, earn money, and become wealthy, not devote yourself to the life of the spirit.

Devotion to work, a hurried lifestyle, a materialistic attitude—all these effects of the work ethic damage culture. The work ethic has damaged culture primarily in the Anglo-American nations, since they're the nations that have been most influenced by ascetic Protestantism. In Germany, on the other hand, Protestantism took a less ascetic form, and in France, Protestantism had little influence. Because the French are predominantly Catholic, they've escaped the Protestant work ethic's damaging effect on culture. To this fact must be attributed, at least in part, the high quality of French culture.[1]

22. *Culture and the Leisure Class* Throughout history, from the time of Pericles to the time of Tolstoy, healthy cultures have always emerged from aristocratic societies, from societies that had a leisure class. Within such a leisure class, there was contempt for working and earning money, and there was respect for culture. Members of the leisure class had to struggle against

---

[1] The high quality of French culture should also be attributed to the fact that the aristocracy, the leisure class, was more developed in France than in any other European country. On German Protestantism, see Weber, *The Protestant Ethic and the Spirit of Capitalism*, §4A.

boredom; they had to invent ways to pass the time. Culture gave them a way to pass the time, and it gave them something to live for. Members of the leisure class patronized artists and writers; the Roman aristocrat Maecenas, for example, patronized Virgil and Horace, and made it possible for them to devote their lives to literature.

In modern, democratic society, there is no leisure class. Modern society is unprecedented in its homogeneity, its classlessness. Modern man has conquered boredom and has found a way to pass the time, to pass an entire lifetime: he works, he accumulates wealth. He tries to make as much money as he can, instead of trying to make as much as he needs. While pretending that he works because he has to, modern man often works because he wants to, because working is the best way to pass the time. Working removes the feeling of futility and emptiness, and replaces it with the illusion of having accomplished something worthwhile. Furthermore, working enables people to acquire wealth, and thereby to acquire both the respect of others and self-respect.

Nowadays, it's no longer a disgrace to work, it's a disgrace not to work. Modern man respects work more than he respects anything else. Even the children of billionaires prefer a life of work to a life of leisure. One American politician was fond of saying, "If you're breathing, I want you working." The current idea of utopia is "full employment," that is, everyone working full-time. If one dares not to work, one is despised and isolated. If one devotes oneself to culture, one is an outcast from society. In such an atmosphere, culture suffocates. As the Portuguese writer Pessoa said, "The ruin of aristocratic influence created an atmosphere of brutality and indifference to the arts."[1]

23. *Medieval Wisdom*   All haste is of the devil's party (*omnis festinatio ex parte diaboli*).

24. *Productive Leisure*   Modern man divides life into work and vacation. He defines a vacation as a period of time that isn't

---

[1] *The Book of Disquiet*, translated by Alfred Mac Adam, #470

challenging and productive. Modern man doesn't understand leisure, doesn't understand that leisure can be both challenging and productive.

Modern man despises those who live off inherited money, despite the fact that many outstanding writers—including Schopenhauer, Kierkegaard and Proust—lived off inherited money, and never earned any money themselves.

25. *Time* In an aristocratic society, people try to pass the time, to "beguile the time," to make time slip away painlessly, to stave off boredom. In an egalitarian society, such as modern society, in which there's no leisure class, people try to use time, and to save time; they say, "time is money." Zen teaches us neither to pass time nor to save time, but rather to focus on the present moment; Zen teaches us to live outside time.

26. *Patronage* What ever happened to patronage? It seems to have died out completely. Nowadays, billions of dollars are given to colleges, orchestras, and other institutions, but who gives money to individuals—to individual writers and artists? Patronage was important in ancient times, and in Renaissance times; there were even wealthy people in the mid-twentieth century who patronized writers and artists. But where are the patrons today? Have we forgotten that culture is created by individuals, not by institutions?

Government funding of the arts might be regarded as organized patronage. But governments are unlikely to fund those who are truly creative. Can you imagine van Gogh receiving a government grant? Real patronage takes place between individuals and individuals. The best way for politicians to help is to lower taxes, so that at least a few people can become patrons, or self-patrons.

Is patronage always beneficial to those who receive it? Writers and artists are sometimes more productive in the rough-and-tumble of life than when a patron raises them above it. Jakob Boehme, the mystic, wrote best when he was torn between mundane affairs and lofty speculations; once he found a patron, his creativity dried up.[1] Jung once advised a wealthy woman that the recipient of her patronage would be better off on his own, and such proved to be the case.[2]

27. *Spoiled Children* When American businessmen discuss their goals and values, they often say that they're working for their children, they want their children to live well, they want to be able to send their children to a good college. But if parents live for children, what do children live for? Children should see adults pursuing some high goal, some goal other than children. When children are given the impression that life has no meaning or purpose besides their own well-being, they lose respect for adults, and become spoiled. Many children are spoiled nowadays; many children think that they're the most important part of their parents' lives, they're the center of the universe.

28. *Talking, Acting* In *The Sound and the Fury*, Faulkner contrasts the ethics of talking with the ethics of acting. Mrs. Compson talks about ethics, but her actions are far from ethical. Like many Protestants, Mrs. Compson believes that the worst vice is selfishness, and the highest value is unselfishness. Her complaint about her daughter (Caddy) is, "never since she opened her eyes has she given me one unselfish thought." When her son, Quentin, commits suicide, Mrs. Compson says, "I didn't believe that he would have been so selfish as to..."

While Mrs. Compson stays in bed, complains, and turns against life, her black servant, Dilsey, works steadily and patiently; "I does de bes I kin," Dilsey says. As one critic said,

> Dilsey accepts whatever time brings. She alone never suffers that moment of rejection which is equated with death.... Dilsey's attitude, as she lives it, is formed by her instinctive feeling that what-

---

[1] *Lectures on Jung's Typology: The Inferior Function*, by Marie-Louise von Franz, ch. 2, "The Introverted Intuitive Type," p. 45
[2] *C.G. Jung Speaking: Interviews and Encounters*, "1954: The World of James Joyce"

ever happens must be met with courage and dignity in which there is no room for passivity or pessimism.[1]

29. *Fundamental Law of Ethics* Always leave a public bathroom a little cleaner than you found it. This might be called a fundamental law of politics, too, since society benefits from people acting responsibly and civilly in the public domain.

30. *Traveling* Since ancient times, thinkers have criticized traveling; Emerson, for example, called traveling "a fool's paradise." Though traveling is often a futile attempt to escape reality, there is something to be said for traveling. Time flies by, and life grows stale, when we're living according to the daily routine to which we're habituated. On the other hand, time passes slowly when we're traveling; as Schopenhauer said, "when we're traveling, one month seems longer than four months spent at home." Traveling often prompts people to make important decisions, and it often forms a turning-point in people's lives.

The desire to travel that young people often have is prompted by a desire to break the emotional bonds that have hitherto tied them to home and family. Breaking old emotional bonds leads to the formation of new ones; the desire to travel is related to sexual desire. Proust often used sexual images when speaking of traveling; he once said, "I was seized with a mad desire to ravish little sleeping towns," playing on the words *villes* (towns) and *filles* (girls). While the desire to travel is related to sexual desire, an aversion for travel is related to an aversion for sex; Immanuel Kant and Emily Dickinson, who never traveled outside the towns in which they were born, were sexually abstinent.

The youth's desire to travel is related not only to a sexual urge, but also to a nomadic urge. Young people pass through a nomadic stage. Every human being, in his development, recapitulates the development of mankind as a whole, and passes

---

[1] Olga Vickery, *The Novels of William Faulkner: A Critical Interpretation*, excerpted in the Norton Critical Edition of *The Sound and the Fury*, Second Edition, 1994

through the stages that mankind as a whole has passed through, including the nomadic stage.[1]

31. *Four Feelings Disappearing* Ambition, pride, respect and contempt usually go together, and are usually found in the same person. Ambition, pride, respect and contempt have virtually disappeared from the West. Western man has ambition and pride only in miniature. He aims to outstrip his neighbors, and is proud if he has done so, but he doesn't compare himself with historic figures, and he doesn't aspire to be remembered by future generations. As Tocqueville said,

> Every American is eaten up with longing to rise, but hardly any of them seem to entertain very great hopes or to aim very high.... Far from thinking that we should council humility to our contemporaries, I wish men would try to give them a higher idea of themselves and of humanity; humility is far from healthy for them; what they most lack, in my view, is pride.[2]

Respect and contempt go hand in hand; one who respects some people will necessarily have contempt for others. Nietzsche observed the connection between respect and contempt, and said, "I love the great despisers, for they are the great venerators." Nowadays, people neither despise nor venerate. They're no longer capable of looking up, of respecting; they regard everyone as equal to themselves. I once heard someone say, "the only person we have contempt for nowadays is the person who has contempt for others."

Not only has contempt for others disappeared from the modern West, but also contempt for oneself. Veneration for someone else is often accompanied by contempt for oneself. Since modern man no longer looks up, he no longer looks down on himself.

---

[1] See Emerson, "Self Reliance"; Schopenhauer, *Counsels and Maxims*, §5; G. Painter, *Marcel Proust: A Biography*, vol. 1, ch. 16. On the connection between the desire to travel and sexual desire, see Weininger, *Sex and Character*, §11, and Freud, "A Disturbance of Memory on the Acropolis," 1937.
[2] *Democracy in America*, II, iii, 19

"The time of the most contemptible man is coming," said Nietzsche, "the man who can no longer despise himself."[1]

32. *The Classics*   The study of the classics aims not only at knowledge, but at action, the good life, the development of personality. The study of the classics enlarges one's thoughts by introducing one to earlier historical periods and to foreign cultures. The study of the classics gives one something to respect, and it inspires one to pursue high goals.

But the study of the classics has drawbacks as well as benefits. It requires concentration and effort, and it sometimes leads to the repression of the unconscious, and to discord within the psyche. A number of scholars, including Weber and Mill, have suffered mental breakdowns from the strain of intellectual work. If wisdom consists in inner peace as well as extensive knowledge, then the classics should be studied in moderation. Any attempt to define the classics should bear this in mind; the classics should be small in number, and as brief and readable as possible.

33. *Art and Morality*   Should art have any moral significance? Plato and Confucius thought it should; they thought that music should improve morality and mold character. They thought that the government should prohibit music that wasn't morally pure; they thought that licentious music would promote licentious behavior, and would eventually lead to moral anarchy and political turmoil. Plato and Confucius wanted literature, as well as music, to be inspiring and uplifting.

Tragic drama and epic poetry are often inspiring and uplifting—in their language as well as their content. Tragic drama and epic poetry depict heroes, and inspire heroic conduct. "Tragedy warms the soul," said Napoleon, "elevates the heart, can and must create heroes."[2] Some visual art, such as the art of Greek sculptors and of Michelangelo, is similar to tragic drama; it

---

[1] *Thus Spoke Zarathustra*, Prologue
[2] *The Mind of Napoleon: A Selection from His Written and Spoken Words*, edited by J. C. Herold, 184

depicts heroic personalities, it gives one a high conception of man. Music, too, is often inspiring and uplifting; Beethoven's music, for example, often has this quality. It's clear, then, that great art often has moral significance, though it doesn't preach moral behavior. Great art often gives one a conception of human greatness, though it doesn't preach moral goodness.

34. *Moral Anarchy* When morality becomes false and hypocritical, it provokes a reaction. The realistic art of the late nineteenth century was a reaction against excessive morality and sentimentality. Now evil has become as fashionable in art as good was formerly. Twentieth-century art, including film, has become obsessed with the morbid and the immoral. Many modern artists seem to think that profundity consists in concentrating on the evil, irrational, morbid side of human nature. The morbidity of modern art is as one-sided, as exaggerated, as fraudulent, as was the sentimentality of early-nineteenth-century art. The moral anarchy of modern art, especially that of popular music and film, contributes to the moral anarchy of modern society.

35. *Universal Standards* In the time of Socrates, the intellectuals known as Sophists argued that morality is relative, that morality varies from place to place, and from time to time. The Sophists pointed out that public nakedness is tolerated here, but condemned there, that homosexuality is tolerated here, but condemned there, etc.

Socrates rejected the moral relativism of the Sophists, and believed that there was an absolute moral standard, applicable in all times and places. Plato also believed in absolute moral standards. Socrates and Plato were rationalists, worshippers of reason. Like many early Greek thinkers, Plato was fond of math, and this may have increased his respect for pure reason. Socrates and Plato seemed to believe that just as $2 + 2 = 4$ in all times and places, so reason can discover moral principles that are true in all times and places.

The Stoics agreed with Socrates and Plato. The Stoics believed that there was a Natural Law, a law that could be discovered by reason, a law that could provide moral guidance in all times and places. Likewise, the English philosopher John Locke believed in Natural Rights that were universally valid. Locke respected reason, as Socrates and Plato did, and he believed that reason could build a foundation for morality and religion.

Hume, who was famous for his skepticism, doubted whether reason was a reliable guide outside the field of math. Hume rejected the old rationalist notion that reason can tell us what's right and what's wrong; according to Hume, reason can't tell us what we ought to do, morality is a matter of feelings. "'Tis not contrary to reason," said Hume, "to prefer the destruction of the whole world to the scratching of my finger."[1]

As if to prove that Reason can lead anywhere, the French revolutionaries, who worshipped Reason, embarked on a policy of genocide. Stalin and the Russian revolutionaries also followed the road of Reason and ended up in genocide. Reason, Hume argued, can justify anything, and doesn't lead to a universal moral standard.

Kant tried to rescue religion and morality from the skepticism of Hume. Kant believed that Western civilization needed a solid moral-religious foundation. Kant declared a universal moral law, his so-called "categorical imperative": "Act as if the maxim of your action were to become through your will a general natural law." Kant's categorical imperative has been described as a re-statement of the ancient Golden Rule, "Do unto others as you would have others do unto you."

Schopenhauer agreed with Kant that an absolute moral standard was possible. Schopenhauer declared his own Moral Law: harm no one but rather, as far as possible, help others.

Nietzsche rejected the idea of an absolute moral standard. In Nietzsche's time, Europeans were exploring the depths of Africa, Australia, etc., coming into contact with a variety of primitive peoples, and collecting primitive beliefs. Nietzsche was fascinated by this new science of anthropology, and studied the various moralities found in various parts of the world. Nietzsche felt that the findings of the anthropologists confirmed the old argu-

---

[1] *A Treatise of Human Nature*, Book 2, Part 3, Section 3

ment of the Sophists that morality is relative, that there is no universal Natural Law. Nietzsche admired the Sophists: "they divine that all attempts to give reasons for morality are necessarily *sophistical*."[1]

Nietzsche argued that some moralities are created by masters, others by slaves. (This argument may have been derived from Gorgias and the other Sophists who argue with Socrates in Plato's dialogues.) A slave morality, in Nietzsche's view, is a morality that extols meekness and compassion; Nietzsche regarded Christian morality as slave morality.

Kierkegaard agreed with the Sophists that reason can't provide us with clear moral guidance. According to Kierkegaard, our view of what is right and decent isn't based on reason: "decency.... has its seat in feeling and in the impulse and consistency of an inner enthusiasm. 'On principle' one can do anything." The reasoning process, which Kierkegaard terms "reflection," can go on forever: "reflection has the remarkable property of being infinite." According to Kierkegaard, Reason can't lead us to a universal moral standard.

Like Kierkegaard, Zen doesn't think that man should live by reason and logic, doesn't think that man should live by principles, or seek universal moral standards. Zen likes to compare human existence to a ball being carried along by a river—every moment is new, every situation is unique. The only principle in Zen is "the principle of not acting according to principles, but according to the circumstances, with a whole mind."[2]

Like Zen, Jung believed in spontaneity, and in paying heed to current circumstances. After reading a book by a Zen Buddhist, Jung said, "it seemed to me that we were talking about the same thing, and that the only difference between us was that we gave different words to the same reality."[3] Jung didn't believe in living by universal moral laws, didn't believe in living by reason; rather, he believed in listening to feelings, hunches, dreams.

---

[1] *The Will to Power*, #428
[2] R. H. Blyth, *Zen in English Literature*, ch. 16
[3] *C. G. Jung Speaking: Interviews and Encounters*, "Talks with Miguel Serrano: 1961"

Thus, the search for moral absolutes seems to have failed. But the age-old argument isn't over yet, and surely new philosophers will appear who will seek to establish new Moral Laws.

36. *Do I Contradict Myself?* Eventually, it may be possible to bring Eastern and Western ideas into a seamless unity, but at present there's still tension between them. A philosopher who respects both East and West will feel this tension, and will reflect it in his writings, hence a reader of his work may say, "this book has contradictions."

Philosophy has always had tensions and contradictions. The Renaissance was torn between its respect for Greco-Roman ideals and its respect for Christian ideals. Only a lifeless, abstract philosophy can be completely consistent. If the tensions in modern philosophy are ever resolved, that resolution will not be lasting; rather, it will beget further tensions. If someone accuses you of contradicting yourself, remind him of Emerson's remark: "A foolish consistency is the hobgoblin of little minds."[1]

A rational thinker is uncomfortable with contradictions, he's uncomfortable with the idea that truth itself is contradictory, he's uncomfortable with the idea that A equals B, and at the same time A doesn't equal B. Leo Strauss, the godfather of the neoconservatives, was fond of rational Greek philosophy. Strauss noticed that philosophers sometimes contradicted themselves, and he felt that this contradiction must be intentional, it must indicate that the philosopher is concealing his true thoughts. Strauss believed that philosophers are prevented from speaking their mind by political pressure. Because he was fond of reason and logic, Strauss couldn't accept that philosophers contradict themselves even if they don't feel political pressure, he couldn't accept that truth itself is contradictory, reality is contradictory.

Reason wants philosophy to be precise and consistent. Reason likes definitions and proofs; it likes geometry. But philosophy shouldn't try to satisfy Reason, it should try to reflect real-

---

[1] "Self-Reliance"

ity. Philosophy should say to Reason, "Sorry, I can't give you definitions and proofs, all I can give you is contradictions."

Physics, too, offers contradictions, not definitions and proofs. Einstein argued that light was made up of particles, though he knew that some experiments demonstrated that light was made up of waves. "[Einstein] was not able to dispute the complete contradiction between this wave picture and the idea of the light quanta," wrote Heisenberg, "nor did he even attempt to remove the inconsistency of this interpretation. He simply took the contradiction as something which would probably be understood much later."[1]

Psychology is even more contradictory than physics. Jung often contradicted himself, and was aware of the contradictions. But Jung felt that contradiction reflected psychic reality better than consistency and logic. Jung's assistant said, "it was high praise, though of an unusual kind, when Jung informed me one day that I had been gloriously inconsistent."[2]

37. *Virtue* is not the performance of an uninterrupted series of good actions. Virtue is the love of good actions, the constant intention to perform good actions, the desire to be better today than you were yesterday, and the willingness to admit that you have erred. Martin Luther said that virtue was always beginning (*semper incipere*).

---

[1] Gary Zukav, *The Dancing Wu Li Masters*, "Beginner's Mind", p. 134
[2] Aniela Jaffé, *From the Life and Work of C. G. Jung*, "From Jung's Last Years," p. 111

3. Religion

1. *A Dialogue Between a Nietzschean and a Believer*

N: Consider the vast emptiness of the universe, the earth's tiny place in the universe, and the series of chance circumstances that has produced consciousness on earth. If God existed, if there were a Creator of the universe, why would He have made so much inanimate matter and so much unpeopled space? Why would He have left consciousness to evolve so slowly, and by such a circuitous route?

B: The ways of the hidden God are inscrutable to men, and we cannot presume to understand them or to question them. Our job is simply to believe in God and to love God.

N: But why postulate God's existence in the first place if you don't have any grounds to do so? If God is totally hidden, shouldn't we conclude that He doesn't exist?

B: God isn't totally hidden; there are some grounds for believing that God exists. Consider, for example, the universe itself. Where did it come from, if not from God? If God doesn't exist, how can you explain why there is something instead of nothing?

N: Why there is something instead of nothing is a question that is, as the poet would say, beyond the reaches of our souls, or at least beyond the present state of our knowledge. But we can't allege our own ignorance as a proof of God's existence. Furthermore, even if we postulate the existence of God, that doesn't make it any easier to explain how the universe was brought into being—the origin of matter is still a mystery.

B: If God doesn't exist, why have so many men, and so many great men, in every century and in every country, believed that God exists?

N: Man has a natural tendency to believe in God. But this tendency doesn't prove that God exists, just as man's tendency to believe in a golden age doesn't prove that there ever was a golden age, and man's tendency to believe in a primordial flood doesn't prove that there ever was a primordial flood, and man's tendency to believe in virgin births doesn't prove that there ever was a virgin birth. The universality of a belief doesn't prove that belief true; the universality of a belief teaches us something about man, about man's psyche, but it teaches us nothing about the external world.

B: If God doesn't exist, how can you account for our innate sense of good and evil?

N: The sense of good and evil is relative, not absolute. Different societies, and different historical epochs, have different moralities. There's no universal morality, no universal sense of good and evil. Thus, morality doesn't force us to postulate God. Nothing forces us to postulate God except our own wishes and the power of tradition.

2. *Biblical Prophecies* Before the birth of Jesus, Jews had long believed that a Messiah would eventually appear. The Old Testament is filled with prophecies of the Messiah; many of these prophecies appear to have been fulfilled in the life of Jesus. For example, the Book of Micah foretells that the Messiah will come from Bethlehem; Isaiah foretells that the Messiah will be born of a virgin; the Psalms foretell that the Messiah will be betrayed by

a "familiar friend"; Zechariah even foretells that the Messiah will be betrayed for "thirty pieces of silver."

Throughout the history of Christianity, the prophecies have been adduced as proofs of the divinity of Christ. Even philosophers like Pascal, who were skeptical of miracles, were impressed by prophecies; "the most weighty proofs of Jesus," said Pascal, "are the prophecies."[1] But once people began to subject the Bible to close scrutiny, they ceased to regard the prophecies as "weighty proofs." Biblical prophecies are as dubious as Biblical miracles; the prophecies don't prove the divinity of Jesus, just as Jesus' alleged ability to walk on water doesn't prove his divinity.

Both miracles and prophecies are indications that the life of Christ, as set forth in the New Testament, is filled with fictitious episodes, episodes designed to convince people that Jesus was the long-awaited Messiah. In order to win converts to their sect, the authors of the New Testament had to make it appear that the life of Jesus fulfilled Old Testament prophecies; they had to tailor their life of Jesus to fit the prophecies. Accordingly, they were quick to point out how the prophecies had been fulfilled; for example, in Acts 1:16, Peter, referring to the betrayal of Jesus, says that the "Scripture must needs have been fulfilled... concerning Judas." The Scripture must be fulfilled—this was the guiding principle of the authors of the New Testament.

3. *Biblical Criticism* Biblical criticism has uncovered a host of contradictions, frauds and forgeries in the Bible. It has shown, for example, that the first five books of the Old Testament, which Judaism and Catholicism ascribe to Moses, were not actually written by Moses. It has also shown that an early reference to the trinity (in the First Epistle of John, v, 7) was actually inserted at a later date. The churches, far from trying to ascertain the truth, have tried to suppress the truth, and have forbidden any questioning of the sacred texts; the Catholic Church, for example, forbade any questioning of the early reference to the trinity.

---

[1] *Pensées*, §335

Some will argue, however, that Biblical criticism can't touch the heart of Christianity; it can't deny that Christian morality is lofty; it can't deny that the Sermon on the Mount is sublime. But Christian morality isn't original, isn't unique to Christianity. Like all morality, Christian morality is the product of its time and place, the product of a certain level of civilization, not the product of divine inspiration. There were Jewish thinkers at the time of Christ who preached a morality similar to Christian morality. A few centuries before the time of Christ, thinkers like Socrates, Buddha, Lao-Zi and Confucius also preached a morality similar to Christian morality; in these four thinkers, one encounters such Christian ideas as "do unto others as you would have others do unto you," and "resist not evil."[1]

4. *Which Religion Is True?* Most people who are raised in Christian families and Christian societies become Christians themselves. Only a few people question the beliefs of their environment, and try to discover the truth for themselves. Many in the West think that Christianity must be true because so many people believe it, and have believed it for centuries. How can so many people be wrong? But people in non-Western countries use the same reasoning about their religions; they assume that since Hinduism, Buddhism, Islam, etc. have won so many adherents, they must be true. If the popularity and longevity of Christianity were an indication of its truth, then Hinduism, Buddhism and Islam, which also enjoy popularity and longevity, are also true. But how can they all be true when they contradict each other?

Some people argue that all religions are false because they contradict each other. Likewise, some people argue that all philosophies are false because they contradict each other, and because they're all superseded by later philosophies. Hegel, however, argued that all philosophies are true, all philosophies represent a part of the truth. We can say the same thing about religion: all religions are true, all religions represent a part of the

---

[1] On Biblical criticism, see S. Reinach, *Orpheus: A History of Religions*, VIII; on Jewish moral thought in the time of Christ, see *Orpheus*, VII.

truth. Religion springs from man's psyche, meets man's psychological needs, and contains psychological truth. The founders of religions embody the thoughts and feelings of their society. Likewise, those who modify a religion are responding to society's needs.

But religions aren't satisfied with psychological truth, with partial truth, with temporary truth, with truth for a particular time and place, with the same degree of truth that all other religions possess. They want more; they claim to possess revealed truth, complete truth, eternal truth, truth for all times and places, truth such as no other religion possesses. And in defending this claim, they use dishonest means.

5. *Bring Religion Closer* Baptism, confirmation, communion, bar mitzvah—all these religious rituals helped the individual to rise from a child to an adult. Likewise, the rites of passage in a primitive society helped the individual to rise from a child to an adult. Myths and legends served a similar purpose; Joseph Campbell has shown how the typical hero myth closely resembles a primitive initiation ceremony.

Nowadays, religious rituals like confirmation have lost much of their force, they've become a shadow of their former selves, perhaps because these rituals—like the religions of which they're a part—have become frozen, stuck in the past. The hero myth in *Star Wars* has probably played a more constructive role in modern life than the ritual of confirmation.

For too long, the West has treated religion as a thing apart—remote, sacred, untouchable. As a result, many Western intellectuals wanted to smash religion completely, and this smashing created a dangerous and unhealthy situation, a spiritual and psychological vacuum, a vacuum that was filled by communism, nationalism, etc. Instead of treating religion as a remote grandfather, we should treat it as a sibling of philosophy and psychology, mythology and literature.

The unconscious produces images that resemble rites of passage, the unconscious tries to guide us through life's passages. The unconscious may give us better advice than ritual and myth, since its advice is tailored to our situation—like the advice of a wise friend or a trained therapist. Perhaps the therapist doesn't give us advice, but rather helps us to hear the advice of our own unconscious. If the unconscious resembles ritual and myth, that's not surprising. After all, where do ritual and myth originate if not in the unconscious? Instead of seeing religion as sacred and remote, we should see it as close to us—no further than our own unconscious.

6. *Atheism and Suicide* According to Christianity, God created the individual in his own image, endowed him with an immortal soul, and watches over him forever. Therefore, according to Christianity, human life per se has value; every human life has infinite importance. Accordingly, Christianity opposed suicide; those who committed suicide were denied Christian burial. Kierkegaard is an example of a Christian thinker who opposed suicide; Kierkegaard called suicide, "a crime against God."

Unlike Christians, the ancients didn't consider human life per se valuable. Hence, the ancients had no scruples about suicide. Cicero, for example, recommends suicide for the victims of misfortune. Many famous Greeks and Romans committed suicide, including Cato the Younger, Brutus and Petronius.

Modern atheism is similar, in many ways, to ancient paganism. Since modern atheists, like the ancients, don't consider human life per se valuable, they too have no scruples about suicide. Nietzsche, for example, said that in certain circumstances, suicide is not only justifiable but praiseworthy.

The Renaissance was akin to paganism and to modern atheism. Montaigne, a product of the Renaissance, agreed with ancient philosophers and with modern atheists on the subject of suicide; "the most voluntary death," wrote Montaigne, "is the finest."[1]

---

[1] See Kierkegaard, *Sickness Unto Death*, I, 3, Ba, and Montaigne, *Essays*, "A Custom of the Isle of Cea." On Cicero's attitude toward suicide, see *Tusculan Disputations*, II, 40 and 41; on Nietzsche's attitude toward suicide, see *Human, All-Too-Human*, §80, *The Wanderer and His Shadow*, §185, and *Thus Spoke Zarathustra*, "Of Voluntary Death."

The Philosophy of Today is neither Christian nor atheist. It merges man with the universe; it finds the same energy, the same spirit, the same essence in man as in the universe as a whole. It takes a positive attitude toward the universe, and toward human life. Though it doesn't regard suicide as blasphemous (as Christianity did), it discourages suicide, just as it discourages melancholy.

7. *Atheism and Eugenics* When people think that human life per se isn't valuable, they often advocate the development of a certain type of human being, that is, they often advocate eugenics. Hence we find advocates of eugenics among the ancients and among modern atheists. Plato, for example, wrote thus: "The best of either sex should be united with the best as often, and the inferior with the inferior as seldom as possible." Such modern atheists as Schopenhauer, Nietzsche, Shaw and Wells also advocated eugenics.[1]

8. *The Death of God* The chief philosophical problem of modern times is the death of God, and its implications for our view of the world and our view of man. This problem was first perceived in the late 1800's; it was perceived independently by Dostoyevsky and by Nietzsche. The death of God means that the world no longer has a plan, a divine order; it also means that human life no longer has absolute value. And since morality—in the West, at any rate—has long been founded on religion, the disintegration of religion entails the disintegration of morality. Hence Nietzsche called himself an "immoralist," and said that mankind was now "beyond good and evil."

The death of God is an epoch-making event in human history; it divides history in two, as Dostoyevsky and Nietzsche both pointed out. Dostoyevsky depicts an atheist, Kirillov, who "rejects morality itself altogether." Dostoyevsky's atheists talk

---

[1] The Plato quotation is from *The Republic*, Book V. On Schopenhauer, see *The World as Will and Idea*, vol. 2, §43; on Nietzsche, see *Antichrist*, §3 and *The Will to Power,* §898; on Shaw, see *On the Rocks*, preface; on Wells, see *Anticipations*, §9.

constantly of suicide and genocide. Dostoyevsky seemed to anticipate the worst atrocities of Hitler and Stalin: "There will be an upheaval!," he wrote; "there's going to be such an upset as the world has never seen before.... The earth will weep for its old gods."[1] Can anyone doubt that there's a connection between the death of God and Soviet genocide? Between the death of God and Nazi genocide? Between the death of God and Cambodian genocide? The phase of the French Revolution known as "The Terror" was an early form of genocide, just as the atheism of the French Revolutionaries was an early form of nineteenth-century atheism.

Though we may dislike the new universe in which we find ourselves, though we may long for God, though we may want to return to the age of faith, the age of religious and moral certainty, the age of the great cathedrals and Thomas Aquinas, nonetheless we must accept the current situation, and learn to cope with it. The wailing infant may prefer to be back in the womb, but he can't go back. Just as the infant grows accustomed to living outside the womb, so too it's possible to develop new approaches to religion and morality. Schopenhauer thought that mankind would outgrow religion, but now the future of religion looks bright. It now seems possible to develop new conceptions of God, new conceptions of religion, and new conceptions of the value of human life.

9. *Nietzsche and Nazism* If Nietzsche first spoke of the death of God, and the death of God is connected to Nazi genocide, did Nietzsche cause Nazi genocide? Do thinkers cause historical events? No, Nazi genocide wasn't caused by Nietzsche; Nietzsche merely popularized the phrase "death of God," and revealed the full implications of the loss of religious belief. As Dostoyevsky's work shows, the ideas of atheism and of going "beyond good and evil" were in the air during the late 1800's; Nietzsche didn't introduce those ideas, he merely found them and expressed them. To find the ideas of one's time and express them is the task of a thinker.

---

[1] See *The Possessed*, I, 3, iv and II, 8.

10. Beliefs Become Policies During the 1940s, when rumors about the Holocaust began to circulate, it seemed unbelievable. People couldn't believe that a nation as advanced, as cultured as Germany was killing millions of people in death-factories.

One might suppose that Hitler alone conceived the idea of a death-factory, or that this idea was unique to the Nazis, or to the Germans. In fact, the idea of a death-factory, the idea of genocide, was widespread in the late 1800s and early 1900s. Many of England's leading intellectuals endorsed the idea, including George Bernard Shaw, H. G. Wells, and D. H. Lawrence. Wells envisioned genocide on a far greater scale than anything seen in the Third Reich; Wells spoke of eliminating "those swarms of blacks, and brown, and dirty-white, and yellow people." Lawrence wrote, "If I had my way, I would build a lethal chamber as big as the Crystal Palace."[1]

The idea of genocide was doubtless as widespread in Germany as it was in England. Nietzsche speaks of, "the greatest of all tasks, the attempt to raise humanity higher, including the relentless destruction of everything that was degenerating and parasitical."[2] Gorky met many people in Russia who subscribed to these ideas; Gorky said that these ideas are "more persistent and more widespread than they are commonly thought to be."[3]

Is it surprising that the idea of genocide, widespread among Western intellectuals, was eventually put into practice? The beliefs of one generation become the policies of the next; as Heine said, "thought precedes action as lightning precedes thunder."

The idea of genocide emerged when religious faith declined. In the early 1800s, Heine said that Christianity had restrained the Germans, and he predicted that the Germans would perpetrate genocide if "that subduing talisman, the cross, be shattered."[4]

---

[1] *National Review Online*, October 18, 2006, "Let It Grow: Population progression," by Jonah Goldberg
[2] *Ecce Homo*, "The Birth of Tragedy," §4
[3] *My Universities*
[4] *Religion and Philosophy in Germany*

11. *Atheism and the Future* As long as people believed in God, their chief concern was doing God's will. As long as people believed in God, they paid little attention to the future of mankind; they left it to God to take care of mankind. As long as people believed in God, they acted like children who think that if their parents love them, they don't have anything to worry about, their parents will take care of them. It's only recently, it's only since people have lost their belief in God, that people have become preoccupied with the future of mankind, have begun to see themselves as responsible for the future of mankind, and have begun to believe that the future will be as bright or as dark as they make it. One of the greatest benefits that atheism has conferred on mankind is a sense of responsibility, a sense that man is responsible for his own future. Conversely, one of the greatest injuries that religion does to mankind is to make man into an irresponsible child, preoccupied with doing God's will, unconcerned about his own future.

12. *Mill* Writing about 1870, Mill said there was an urgent need for a new religion, a new faith. Mill said that this need was so urgent that any "thinking or writing" that didn't help to develop a new religion was of dubious value.

> When the philosophic minds of the world can no longer believe its religion [Mill wrote], or can only believe it with modifications amounting to an essential change of its character, a transitional period commences, of weak convictions, paralyzed intellects, and growing laxity of principle, which cannot terminate until a renovation has been effected in the basis of their belief leading to the elevation of some faith, whether religious or merely human, which they can really believe.[1]

Mill shows wisdom and modesty by not saying precisely what this new religion should be; he speaks of, "some faith, whether religious or merely human." Mill says that the old worldview is "discredited in the more intellectual minds"; this is true today, as it was in Mill's day. (Nietzsche, who writes in a

---

[1] *Autobiography*, ch. 7

more prophetic, more poetic tone than Mill, expressed the same thought when he said, "God is dead".) Mill says that the old religions, discredited though they may be, are still a "powerful obstacle to the growing up of any better opinions." Mill realized that a void had been created by the decline of the old faiths, and that this void would be filled by political schemes, totalitarian schemes. He anticipated the harmful effects of these schemes, and warned against them.

13. *Jung* believed that certain archetypes or images could be found in the unconscious of all mankind, in the "collective unconscious." The most important of these archetypes, according to Jung, was the archetype of the self. In Jung's vocabulary, the term "self" means the whole person, the unconscious as well as consciousness. Jung felt that God was synonymous with the archetype of the self.

Jung felt that man was prone to identify himself with consciousness, with the ego, with reason, and to neglect and despise the unconscious. In other words, Jung felt that man was prone to lapse into rationalism, and to lose contact with his unconscious, with his soul. In Jung's view, religion helped man to maintain contact with his unconscious, and to avoid rationalism and ego inflation. Since modern societies were apt to reject religion, they were also apt to lapse into rationalism. Jung regarded Communism as a lapse into rationalism. Communists tried to use reason to control all human activities; they despised tradition, and they despised religion.

Christ helped man to avoid rationalism and ego inflation, urging people to "become like little children." The message of Christ resembled the message of Zen, since both Zen and Christ steered man away from rationalism and toward the wholeness of the child.

Jung believed that the archetype of God evolved during the course of history. The violent, amoral, unconscious God of the ancient Hebrews evolved into the loving, moral, conscious God of the time of Christ. The existence and evolution of the God archetype took place independently of man, independently of human reason and human volition. Jung didn't regard God as an invention of man. Jung believed in God, and his arguments are the strongest arguments against atheism.

Jung regarded Jesus not merely as a carpenter's son, a Jewish reformer, a genius, but rather as the son of God, as a carrier or embodiment of the son-of-God archetype. Jesus felt himself to embody this archetype, felt himself to be the son of God. Jesus knew that it was his destiny to live this archetype—to die young, etc.

Jung believed that archetypes and myths were embodied in history, they didn't exist only in the mind. Through contact with archetypes, and contact with the unconscious, it's possible for certain people, including Jesus, to anticipate the future. Just before the outbreak of World War I, Jung himself had a prophetic dream of Europe awash in a sea of blood.

14. *Merlin* Some symbols of the self, such as the yin-yang symbol, are a blend of darkness and light, a union of opposites. Christ, however, is a self symbol who emphasizes the light and excludes the darkness; Christ isn't a union of opposites. Hence, it was necessary to offset Christ with a figure of darkness, of evil, such as the devil, or the Antichrist, or Satanaël (the elder son of God).

In an attempt to heal the split between light and dark, Christ and Antichrist, the figure of Merlin grew up in the Western imagination; Merlin united the opposites in one being. Likewise, the alchemical figure Mercurius was a union of opposites; "Mercurius [is] cunning and duplex (double); one text says of him that 'he runs around the earth and enjoys equally the company of the good and the wicked.'"[1] One purpose of alchemy, and of The Grail Legend, was to unite the opposites, to heal the rift between light and dark. The philosopher's stone (*lapis philosophorum*), which was sought by the alchemists, was a blend of light and dark.

15. *The Jungian God* Jung equates God with our own unconscious; that is, he finds God within, instead of projecting God

---

[1] *The Grail Legend*, ch. 22

outside. He says that the unconscious is greater than the ego, beyond the ego, just as God is beyond man. Thus, finding God within ourselves doesn't mean the apotheosis of man, or the abasement of God. Jung respects both God and the unconscious—or should I say, he equates God and the unconscious, respects them, and sees them as beyond our limited ego, our rational mind.

Jung says we shouldn't regard God as outside ourselves, as separate from man, and we shouldn't regard God as all-powerful, all-good, and all-wise. If we do so, we

1. divert our attention from our own souls, our own inner world;
2. ascribe such a high value to God that we end up despising ourselves ("the only thing left behind here is a miserable, inferior, worthless, and sinful little heap of humanity"[1]);
3. create the need for a complement to God—namely, the Devil

But while Jung opposed the traditional, Western view of God, he wanted to continue to use the term "God." He wanted to apply the term "God" to the unconscious—to those forces in the soul that are beyond the rational mind, beyond the ego. Only by using the term "God," Jung argued, could we accurately describe the strength of those forces, and their independence of the conscious mind.

16. *Hiking Philosophers* If Descartes hiked to the top of a mountain in Africa, and sat down on a rock, and looked at the animals in the valley below, and at the vegetation all around him, he might say, "I alone, in this vast scene of teeming life, have a soul." And if Kant hiked to the top of the same mountain, he might say, "I alone am an end in myself." But if Freud hiked to the top of that mountain, he might say, "all these animals and plants have the same basic drives that I have, they all have life- and death-instincts—just like me. Animals and plants are my

---

[1] Jung, *Two Essays on Analytical Psychology*, ¶394

kin. Man is derived from animals, and animals are derived from plants—we're all branches of the same family tree, we're all relatives. Man isn't fundamentally different from animals and plants—as Western thinkers once supposed."

And if Jung hiked to the top of that mountain, he might say, "all those animals have the same Energy, the same Essence, the same Spirit, the same Tao, that is in me. And all these plants have that same Energy, too. And this rock that I'm sitting on, this mountain, this earth—all these have that same Energy, too. I'm akin to the animals, the plants, the rocks—I'm akin to everything in the universe. Man is derived from animals, and animals are derived from plants, and plants are derived from inorganic matter. We're all related! The same universe that produced the rock I'm sitting on also produced *Hamlet*. Man isn't fundamentally different from other forms of life, as Descartes and Kant thought, nor is organic life fundamentally different from inorganic matter, as Freud thought. The same Energy/Essence/Spirit/Tao suffuses everything, produces everything."

Jung's view is similar to that of Eastern philosophers. This view helps to explain why Eastern painters depicted landscapes long before Western painters did. Western painters like Michelangelo were preoccupied with man, perhaps because the West saw man as distinct from the rest of the universe. The East saw the same Tao in everything.

It has been said that the clearest distinction in nature is the distinction between the organic and the inorganic. This distinction is clearer (so the argument goes) than the distinction between one species and another, and clearer than the distinction between plants and animals. But is it really as clear as it appears to be? Isn't it conceivable that some enterprising young scientist will someday connect the organic to the inorganic—just as Darwin connected man to animals? Isn't it conceivable that we'll someday discover intermediate forms—forms that lie between the organic and the inorganic? After all, isn't organic life descended from the inorganic? Darwin speculated on how organic life might have originated:

If (and O, what an if!) we could picture some hot little pool in which all manner of ammoniacal and phosphorous salts, light, heat, electricity and so forth were present, and that a protein compound were to be chemically formed in it, ready to undergo even more complicated changes...[1]

17. *The World Behind* Is the essence of the universe matter or spirit? It is both/and, not either/or, it is a mysterious mix of matter and spirit. It is here, in this mysterious essence, that time and space seem to disappear, it is here that occult phenomena occur. It is this mysterious essence that Kant called the "thing-in-itself," that Kant described as beyond time, space, and causality, and beyond man's power of comprehension. One might call this mysterious essence The World Behind the World.

When physics encounters The World Behind, it's surprised to find matter appearing to act with intention, with consciousness, it's surprised to find mysterious links between distant particles.

When biology encounters The World Behind, it speaks of things that are both material and spiritual—a will to life (Schopenhauer), *élan vital* (Bergson), life- and death-instincts (Freud), etc. Some biologists have argued that evolution couldn't occur without some force or instinct to propel it. These forces and instincts are elusive, mysterious, both material and immaterial.

Chinese thinkers referred to The World Behind as the Tao. The Tao is the mysterious essence of the universe, the thing-in-itself. Lao Zi said,

> There was something vague before heaven and earth arose.... It stands alone, unchanging; it acts everywhere, untiring. It may be considered the mother of everything under heaven. I do not know its name, but call it by the word Tao.[2]

While people in the West often imagine God making the world, the Tao doesn't make the world, it produces the world through spontaneous growth: "The Tao's principle is spontane-

---

[1] *Sophie's World*, "Darwin"
[2] Alan Watts, *The Way of Zen*, ch. 1

ity." The Tao isn't the master of the universe, as God is, and the Tao isn't a conscious being, as God is:

> The great Tao flows everywhere,
> To the left and to the right.
> All things depend upon it to exist,
> and it does not abandon them.
> To its accomplishments it lays no claim.
> It loves and nourishes all things,
> but does not lord it over them.

18. *Animism Encore* One might describe the history of religion as a progression from animism to polytheism to monotheism to atheism. Now, however, we seem to be coming full circle, and developing a new religion that resembles animism. Our new religion sees energy and intelligence suffusing the universe. It doesn't see God as distinct from the universe, or distinct from man. It draws no distinction between spirit and matter, mind and body.

19. *Beyond Atheism* The most promising sources of new approaches to religion are:
1. the unconscious (its wisdom, its power, its tendency to seek psychic harmony);
2. the existence of occult phenomena, which can't be explained by rational-scientific thinking; the possibility of life after death;
3. a feeling of oneness with the universe, and a love of nature;
4. a belief that there is some sort of energy or force permeating the universe.

Mill said that a new faith could be "religious or merely human." It didn't occur to Mill that a new faith could be religious *and* human. Instead of a religion that is centered on a God who created the world and rules the world, why not a religion that sees the world developing through its own forces, and sees man as participating in these forces, not just subject to them? And if someone wants to use the word "God" for the mysterious forces in the universe and in man, why should we object?

4. Psychology

1. *Silent Communication* Communication takes place not only through words, but also through everything that one does, and through everything that one merely thinks or feels. The unconscious of one person can read the unconscious of other people. People often receive letters or phone calls from those who have been occupying their thoughts, as if telepathic communication preceded written or verbal communication. Children and animals are especially sensitive to people's feelings because they're more unconscious than adults; their unconscious isn't impeded by consciousness. Children and animals can often read people's feelings, even when people try to hide their feelings from them.

Goethe noticed that thoughts and feelings are often communicated by non-verbal means.

> One soul [said Goethe] may have a decided influence upon another, merely by means of its silent presence.... It has often happened to me that, when I have been walking with an acquaintance, and have had a living image of something in my mind, he has at once begun to speak of that very thing.... We have all something of electrical and magnetic forces within us.

Feelings can be communicated between people who aren't near each other; the mind can traverse space. This occurs with special frequency between members of the same family. Heinrich Mann heard his sister, Carla, call to him before she committed suicide, though she was in Germany and he was in Italy. "I was strolling," said Mann, "all was still; then I was called; from the house, I thought. So little prepared was I, that in the first moment it did not occur to me: no one here calls me by my given name." Oscar Wilde had a vision of his mother's death, and when his wife told him that his mother had died, he said that he knew it already.

The mind can traverse not only space but time as well. People often have a presentiment of what is about to happen. Mussolini, for example, had a presentiment of danger before an attempt on his life. "On October 31, 1926," said Mussolini, "when I was in Bologna, the spiritual atmosphere seemed to me so oppressive that throughout the day I was anticipating disaster. In the evening there was an attempt on my life."[1]

Psychic powers aren't distributed to everyone in the same measure. Certain people—Swedenborg and Rasputin, for example—have exceptional psychic power. Swedenborg once told a group of people that a fire had just broken out in Stockholm, three hundred miles away, and such turned out to be the case. Swedenborg's abilities were so well verified that even the skeptical Kant was impressed by them. As for Rasputin, he often amazed people by reading their minds. And there's reason to believe, as Jung did, that Nostradamus had prophetic powers. Some have argued that people who are struck by lightning, and survive, end up with exceptional psychic powers.

We should keep an open mind toward the occult, and not dismiss it because it's difficult to explain, and inconsistent with current worldviews. The occult is the largest unexplored continent in the intellectual world. It will probably play a leading role

---

[1] On Goethe, see Eckermann, *Conversations With Goethe*, 10/7/27; on Mann, see Richard Winston, *Thomas Mann: The Making of an Artist, 1875-1911*, ch. 16; on Wilde, see Richard Ellman, *Oscar Wilde*, ch. 19; on Mussolini, see Emil Ludwig, *Talks With Mussolini,* V, 1. Henry IV (King of France) and Hitler also had presentiments of danger before attempts on their lives (see Voltaire, *General History*, ch. 144, footnote, and Toland, *Hitler*, XXVIII, 5 and XXI, 3).

in the intellectual history of the twenty-first century, just as the psychology of the unconscious played a leading role in the twentieth century, and the theory of evolution played a leading role in the nineteenth century.

2. *From God to the Unconscious* As long as Western man was preoccupied with religion and with God, his attention was diverted from himself, diverted from his own psyche, diverted from psychology and from parapsychology. As soon as religious belief declined, Western man began to look within himself. Schopenhauer was the first Western philosopher who rejected religion and turned to psychology instead. Seventy-five years before Freud, Schopenhauer stressed the importance of the unconscious and of sexuality. Schopenhauer also had a keen interest in the occult, and he often told stories about his occult experiences.

Schopenhauer's successor, Nietzsche, also rejected religion and turned to psychology. Schopenhauer and Nietzsche foreshadowed Freud. Freud spoke of "the large extent to which psychoanalysis coincides with the philosophy of Schopenhauer," and Freud said that Nietzsche was "another philosopher whose guesses and intuitions often agree in the most astonishing way with the laborious findings of psychoanalysis."[1]

But while Nietzsche was interested in psychology, he wasn't as interested in the occult as Schopenhauer was, just as Freud wasn't as interested in the occult as Jung was. Jung was receptive to the occult in all its forms; Jung was even receptive to astrology and reincarnation.

3. *Freud and the Occult* Freud was initially hostile to the occult, but he became more receptive as more evidence was presented to him. Eventually he realized that it was an enormous field, and largely unexplored. He said, "If I were at the beginning rather than at the end of a scientific career... I might possibly choose just this field of research, in spite of all difficulties."

---

[1] *An Autobiographical Study*, 5

Freud's disciples were divided on the occult—some were receptive, others skeptical. The skeptics warned Freud that if you give any ground, you'll be overwhelmed. If, for example, you admit that telepathy exists, you'll have to admit all sorts of magical influence. If you study near-death experiences, you'll have to examine the evidence for life-after-death. And how can you stop there? You'll be drawn into the study of ghosts, and that will lead you to the study of vampires.

So the skeptics in Freud's circle, like skeptics today, insisted that the entire subject of the occult must be dismissed. But the evidence won't go away, the subject keeps coming back. We should keep an open mind toward the occult, and keep looking at the evidence, while recognizing that it has always been fertile ground for fraud, superstition, and credulity.

4. *Birth Order* Psychologists have long recognized that birth order has an effect on personality. An only child has a monopoly on parental love. An eldest child also has a monopoly on parental love—until another child is born. Thus, only children and eldest children develop self-confidence and an instinct for dominance. According to Freud, the great man is usually an only child or an eldest child; part of his greatness consists in his self-confidence. "He who has been the undisputed darling of his mother," wrote Freud, "retains throughout life that victorious feeling, that confidence in ultimate success, which not seldom brings actual success with it."

The youngest child is also sometimes "the undisputed darling of his mother," since he's the only child who has not yet grown up. This may be the reason why some youngest children attain eminence. Another reason why some youngest children attain eminence is that their sense of being inferior to their elders fires them with an ambition to become superior. Adler described this type of youngest child thus: "restlessly pushing forward, they surpass everyone by their initiative."[1]

---

[1] On Freud, see "A Childhood Recollection from *Dichtung und Wahrheit*"; on Adler, *see The Practice and Theory of Individual Psychology*, §26.

Since an eldest child is valued by his parents, he sees himself as valuable, takes himself seriously, takes life seriously, and develops self-discipline. A younger child, on the other hand, values himself less, and often lacks self-discipline; this lack of self-discipline shows itself in a variety of ways, including alcohol problems and drug problems. Consider, for example, the Carter brothers, Jimmy and Billy. The elder brother, Jimmy, became President through his self-discipline and determination, while Billy was known for his undisciplined behavior.

The influence of birth order on personality is far-reaching and multi-faceted; once one understands it, one finds examples of it everywhere.

5. *Deformity is Daring*   Just as a youngest child's sense of being inferior sometimes makes him ambitious, so too a handicapped child's sense of being inferior sometimes makes him ambitious. Examples of handicapped people who attained eminence are Demosthenes, Alexander Pope, Lichtenberg, Talleyrand, Byron, Kierkegaard, Toulouse-Lautrec and Goebbels.

As Byron wrote in *The Deformed Transformed*,

> Deformity is daring.
> It is its essence to o'ertake mankind
> By heart and soul, and make itself the equal—
> Ay, the superior of the rest.

6. *The Pendulum*   Human nature tends to maintain a balance between asceticism and self-indulgence, between stoicism and epicureanism. Whenever one reaches an extreme of asceticism or of self-indulgence, one's nature steers one back in the opposite direction. Human nature is self-regulating and avoids extremes. When, for example, one becomes depressed, and loses one's appetite for life, as a result of being hard on oneself and living stoically, one changes direction, becomes indulgent toward oneself, and adopts the epicurean approach to life. The epicurean approach eventually reawakens one's appetite for life. It develops into the stoic approach, and the cycle begins anew.

One could describe this cycle in Freudian terms by saying that when the tyranny of the super-ego has reached an extreme, the id makes a comeback and the ego tastes pleasure. After the ego is restored to harmony and health, it once again listens to the behests of the super-ego, and the cycle begins anew. Anatole France described this cycle by saying, "within every one of us there lives both a Don Quixote and a Sancho Panza to whom we hearken by turns."

Just as human nature compensates for its own extremes, so too human nature compensates for circumstances. The mind overcomes unfavorable circumstances by drawing libidinal energy back into itself and by indulging the id's desires. Tolstoy depicts a prisoner of war who creates his own happiness in the midst of hardships: "the harder his lot became, the more terrible his future, the more independent of his present plight were the glad and soothing thoughts, memories, and images that occurred to him."[1] The super-ego relaxes in times of sickness and misfortune, and becomes more severe in times of good fortune.

7. *Silent Superiority* Lyndon Johnson (the former President) said that sometimes you shouldn't respond to your critics: "Sometimes you have to just stand there and take it, like a jackass in a hailstorm." A leader may be characterized by composure and silence. The Zuni Indians chose their leaders not for their eloquence, but for their silence. Faulkner says that people are "convinced of anything by an assumption of silent superiority"; people have a habit of "attributing wisdom to a still tongue."[2] The best argument is often silence.

Hitler began his speeches with a long silence. This enabled him to establish an unconscious rapport with his audience.

When Ted Kennedy first ran for the Senate, he had a debate with a primary opponent (a fellow Democrat). His older brother, John Kennedy, advised him "he's going to hit you hard, and you're going to have to keep your cool." Ted was indeed attacked, but he assumed a posture of "silent superiority," he

---

[1] See Anatole France, *The Crime of Sylvester Bonnard,* "The Little Saint-George," 4/17, and Tolstoy, *War and Peace,* XIV, 12.
[2] *The Sound and the Fury,* "June Second, 1910"

stood there and took it like a jackass in a hailstorm, and he emerged victorious from the primary.

De Gaulle once put his Free French forces into action without consulting Churchill. Churchill was furious, summoned De Gaulle, and berated him at length. De Gaulle said nothing. After De Gaulle had left, Churchill said to his aide, "That was very fine, wasn't it? I couldn't have done it better myself."

In India, there's a legend about the Buddha's conflict with a horde of demons. The demons attack, armed to the teeth, but the Buddha's lotus throne is empty. The Buddha has entered a plea of *nolo contendere*, he has chosen not to fight. The best response to evil is sometimes no response.

8. *Repose* Wilson Knight said that a great actor understands "the power of the thing left unsaid, the gesture not made."[1] A great actor not only has energy and passion, he also has repose. This repose, Knight says, "will always be partly unconscious and instinctive."

Shakespeare understood acting, and he understood that repose is as important as passion. Hamlet advises the players,

> In the very torrent, tempest, and, as I may say, whirlwind of passion, you must acquire and beget a temperance that may give it smoothness. O, it offends me to the soul, to hear a robustious periwig-pated fellow tear a passion to tatters, to very rags, to split the ears of the groundlings.[2]

Haiku poetry makes use of silence, makes use of "the thing left unsaid." Suzuki said, "When a feeling reaches its highest pitch we remain silent, because no words are adequate. Even seventeen syllables may be too many."[3] Zen has as much respect for repose as Knight does; one might say that Zen is a synonym for repose.

In sports, as in the arts, repose is as important as energy. In baseball, for example, a batter must be able to *not* swing (not

---

[1] *The Wheel of Fire*, ch. 15, #2
[2] III, ii, 4
[3] D. T. Suzuki, "Buddhist, Especially Zen, Contributions to Japanese Culture" (from *Essays in Zen Buddhism*, third series)

swing at a bad pitch). Since the pitch is coming at high speed, the batter only has a split-second to decide whether or not to swing; the batter, like the actor, must be "unconscious and instinctive." In baseball, it's a mistake to swing at everything, but it's also a mistake to swing at nothing; a batter must be active and passive simultaneously, he must attain repose.

Muhammad Ali showed repose in his bout with George Foreman. Ali landed several punches early in the bout, but Foreman was unbowed, landed some punches, and seemed ready to overpower Ali. Instead of attacking, Ali retreated into his legendary "rope-a-dope"—in other words, Ali leaned against the ropes in a defensive posture, and allowed Foreman to punch him.

Foreman took the bait; Foreman had youth, energy, and power, but lacked repose. Foreman was like a batter who is over-eager, and swings at bad pitches. Foreman exhausted himself, and then Ali struck, and knocked him out. I don't believe Ali had ever used the "rope-a-dope" before, or even conceived of it before. It was a stroke of genius, if ever there was a stroke of genius in an athletic competition, and like all strokes of genius, it was spontaneous, intuitive, instinctive. It came from the depths of his soul, and it signified that in those depths, there was repose.

The Roman general Fabius became famous for avoiding battle, for not attacking. Fabius was more successful than other Roman generals in dealing with Hannibal, the Carthaginian general. Fabius was given the nickname *Cunctator*, The Delayer; in English, we describe delaying tactics as "Fabian tactics." One might say that Ali used Fabian tactics against Foreman, or one might say that Fabius used the "rope-a-dope" against Hannibal.

Nothing is more frustrating than being defeated by an opponent who uses Fabian tactics. Foreman was devastated by his defeat, and didn't get over it for months, if not years; Foreman said he should have died in the ring. What makes such a defeat hard to bear is that you know you've been defeated by yourself, by your own eagerness, by your own lack of repose. You're like the raging bull who rushes at the matador, only to be tricked, side-stepped, and run through.

9. *Spite* The death of Socrates is a classic example of people stumbling into a quarrel, and no one being willing to back down. Socrates was accused of impiety, and of corrupting youth. "The penalty proposed was death," J. B. Bury wrote, "but the accusers had no desire to inflict it; they expected that, when the charge was lodged in the archon's office, Socrates would leave Attica, and no one would have hindered him from doing so." But when we try to force someone to do what we want them to do, when we try to put someone in a box, they often resist, and they often find a way to assert themselves, or to strike back at us. The accusers of Socrates should have anticipated that he would be too proud to publicly retreat, too proud to publicly bow down to them. Socrates remained in Athens to face the charge, and he was condemned to death by a narrow majority.

According to Athenian law, a condemned man had the right to propose a lighter punishment than his accusers had proposed, and then the judges would choose one of the two punishments. Here again, Socrates was too proud to bargain for his life, too proud to bargain with his enemies. Instead of proposing a punishment that was significant, but less than death, Socrates proposed a trivial fine (say, 35 cents). By a wide majority, the judges voted to inflict the death penalty.

When a mother asks her son "why did you punch your little brother in the nose?" the response is often "he was asking for it." If one of Socrates' judges was asked, "why did you execute Socrates?" the judge might respond, "he was asking for it."

According to Plato, Socrates died out of obedience to the law, out of loyalty to the legal system that he had lived under. Is Plato's account credible? Isn't it more likely that Socrates wanted to spite his enemies, that Socrates was too proud to publicly bow down to his enemies, that Socrates felt his execution would make his enemies look bad. Is it possible that Plato, when he conversed with Socrates, was too young to understand Socrates' motives? If so, did Plato have a better understanding of Socrates' motives when he grew older?

How does J. B. Bury explain the fact that Socrates didn't try to save his life? "Socrates was full of days—he had reached the age of seventy—and life spent otherwise than in conversing in the streets of Athens would have been worthless to him." Perhaps there is some truth in this, though Sophocles said that no one enjoys life more than an old man, and Socrates' friends would probably have found him a comfortable home outside Athens. Perhaps Socrates stayed in Athens precisely because his enemies wanted him to leave. Bury doesn't consider this possibility.

Nietzsche argued that the death of Socrates was a disguised suicide, that Socrates didn't want to live. But if Socrates wanted to die, why did he choose this particular moment? People who want to die, consciously or unconsciously, can find a way to do so (sickness, accident, suicide, etc.). Assuming Socrates had suicidal impulses, why did he wait until this particular moment to act on those impulses? Like Bury, Nietzsche doesn't consider the possibility that Socrates chose to stay in Athens because his enemies wanted him to leave, because he wanted to spite his enemies. If the death of Socrates is a suicide, it should be compared with the many cases in which someone commits suicide in order to strike a blow at another person—suicide from spite.

10. *Frevel* People often get into trouble through playful teasing, childish daring. In English, we speak of "asking for it," or "looking for trouble."[1] Jungians refer to this as *frevel*, a German word that's related to the English word "frivolous":

> In many stories all over the world there is this kind of infantile daring which is not courage. It looks like it, but it isn't. This pseudo-courage, which is infantile daring out of unawareness or lack of respect, is a common feature through which man steps suddenly into the area of the archetype of evil.[2]

An example of *frevel* can be found in the Beatrix Potter story, "Squirrel Nutkin." Nutkin and some other squirrels go out to Owl Island to gather nuts. When they reach the island, they

---

[1] In Chinese, they say "looking for trouble for yourself" (zi4 zhao3 ma2 fan). Does every language have an equivalent of "looking for trouble"?
[2] *Shadow and Evil in Fairy Tales*, by Marie-Louise von Franz, Part II, ch. 2

pay a call on the owl who lives there. While the other squirrels treat the owl deferentially, and give him various presents, Nutkin is impertinent, and teases the owl. Next day, the other squirrels are again deferential, while Nutkin continues his teasing. Day after day, Nutkin teases the owl. At first, the owl pays no heed to Nutkin, but finally he lashes out, and grabs Nutkin in his talons. Just before Nutkin is devoured, he manages to escape, scarred and mortified. Nutkin was "looking for trouble," "asking for it," being "frevelous."

Like other forms of evil, *frevel* is readily apparent among children, but by no means absent from adults.

Solzhenitsyn was imprisoned in Stalin's Gulag for many years. The cause of his imprisonment was a letter that he wrote to an old friend, a letter that was critical of Stalin. Didn't Solzhenitsyn know that Stalin's secret police opened letters, and that criticizing Stalin could land one in prison? Was Solzhenitsyn tempting fate, was he looking for trouble? Is this a case of *frevel*?

Swann is one of the main characters in Proust's novel, *Swann's Way*. Before Swann falls madly in love with Odette, Proust says that Swann is at a "dangerous age." Swann is idle, he wants to fill up his life, he wants to try something new, he wonders what it is like to "live solely for love," like the people he read about in novels. Swann is playing with fate, playing with life, and he ends up in an emotional Gulag. Is this a case of *frevel*?

Marie-Louise von Franz, a disciple of Jung, wrote

> The one moment when I feel really bad in analysis is when I see in one of my analysands that infantile, daring curiosity about evil. An analysand may say, "Oh I like going to a place where there are murderers!" Or, "I like to experiment with this woman, I know she is an evil woman, but I must have some experience of life and I shall try out sleeping with her, I must explore that!" ....When you act out of a kind of frivolous attitude, or just out of intellectual curiosity, just to find out about it and with a lack of respect

toward the infection and destructiveness of the phenomena, then one feels very uneasy.[1]

11. *Associations* When meeting a person for the first time, one often associates him with a person whom one has known in the past. One thinks, "don't I know him? Haven't I met him before?" Thus, Proust's narrator, when he met new people at the seashore, associated them with people whom he knew at Paris; "in the first few days of our visit to Balbec," wrote Proust, "I had succeeded in finding Legrandin, Swann's hall porter and Mme. Swann herself, transformed into a waiter, a foreign visitor whom I never saw again and a bathing superintendent."[2]

12. *Idealizations* When meeting a person for the first time, one often overrates him. One substitutes for the actual person parts of oneself and parts of one's ideal. One of the characters in *War and Peace*, Prince Andrey, reveres a new acquaintance, Speransky, until he gets to know him, and then he becomes disillusioned with him.

13. *The Hunter* Athletics is a sublimated form of war and hunting, and appeals to those who are aggressive and competitive. Athletes are sometimes said to have a "killer instinct." Tolstoy said, "there are two types of men: hunters and non-hunters,"[3] that is, athletes and non-athletes.

14. *Class* depends neither on money nor on education nor on personality. Class depends only on family background; the grandson of a king is from the highest class in society, though he may be penniless, uneducated and crude. People often marry someone from their own class, neither higher nor lower, just as people often marry someone from their own ethnic group. Likewise, in the business world, certain companies attract people from a certain class. Thus, even in an almost classless society,

---

[1] Ibid
[2] *Within a Budding Grove*, "Place-Names: The Place"
[3] Henri Troyat, *Tolstoy*, §18

even in a thoroughly democratic society, class distinctions are still evident and are still maintained.

Though class distinctions are still evident, they're far less evident than they once were. Class distinctions are a relic of earlier epochs, and they aren't likely to exist for much longer. The upper class will gradually be inter-mixed with other classes, unless the upper class is preserved by strict rules governing marriage—like the rules in ancient Rome that prohibited marriage between a patrician and a plebeian—or unless the upper class is preserved by social customs that forbid marriage between classes.

15. *Amor Fati* The psychiatrist Elisabeth Kübler-Ross worked with terminally-ill patients. She argued that, when people are faced with death, they go through five stages: denial, anger, bargaining, depression, and acceptance. The final stage, acceptance, is characterized by an acceptance of one's fate and one's mortality.

What if someone reached this final stage, and then recovered, and lived on? This is what seems to have happened to Nietzsche; he was gravely ill, he was expected to die, he reached the stage of acceptance of his fate and his mortality, and then he recovered. Nietzsche's later works, beginning with his *Gay Science*, were written from beyond the grave, and often speak of *amor fati*, love of fate. Surely Nietzsche himself was aware of how much he owed to his illness, and how much he owed to the emotional instability that eventually caused him to go mad.

The ancients said, "to philosophize is to learn to die." When one faces death, one learns to die. Nietzsche became a philosopher not only by studying philosophy, but also by facing death.

16. *From Anger to Acceptance* In the final years of life, people often take a more positive attitude toward life than they did in their early years. Shakespeare's final plays have a more positive spirit than his earlier works; one critic said that Shakespeare's final plays, such as *The Tempest*, express a "serene and mystic

joy," while earlier works, such as *Hamlet*, express "spiritual pain and despairing thought."[1]

When Shakespeare was approaching death, he achieved serenity. He was still at the height of his powers; he didn't live long enough to experience senility (he died at 54). He knew he was dying, he didn't die unexpectedly. For purposes of literature, he died at the perfect time. His last three years seem to have been extraordinarily productive—his physical powers ebbing away, but his creative powers at their zenith, and his spiritual progress complete.

17. *Stages of Youth* At the time of puberty, libidinal energy from the id invades the ego, and produces such effects as violence and dishonesty. This libidinal energy also causes affection for both genders; during this period, love and friendship have their origins.

At about age fifteen, the conscious mind, afraid of the libidinal energy that is pouring in from the unconscious, begins to repress and to sublimate this libidinal energy. Repression results in a stoic lifestyle. The young Flaubert exemplifies this stoic lifestyle; Flaubert said that as an adolescent, he considered castrating himself, and "spent two whole years at that time without so much as looking at a woman." The young Gide also lived stoically; he followed a rigid timetable, read the Gospels on the tram and on the playground, slept on boards, and awoke in the middle of the night to pray. H. G. Wells also lived stoically as an adolescent: "Every moment in the day had its task," Wells wrote in his autobiography; "Harris and I would go for one-hour walks and I insisted on a pace of four miles an hour. During this pedestrianism we talked in gasping shouts."[2]

Not only in history, but also in legend, youth represses the unconscious in order to develop a conscious personality. The

---

[1] G. Wilson Knight, *The Crown of Life: Essays in Interpretation of Shakespeare's Final Plays*, ch. 1, v

[2] See Flaubert, *Letters*, 12/27/52 (selected by R. Rumbold, London, 1950); Gide, *If It Die*, I, 8; H. G. Wells, *An Experiment In Autobiography*, IV, 3.

legendary hero Perceval begins his career by killing the Red Knight. According to Jungians, the Red Knight represents Perceval's own shadow:

> This killing of the red shadow-knight corresponds to a violent repression of Perceval's own individual affects and emotions as a first step towards building up a conscious personality. Every young person who grows up in a social milieu and develops into a responsible personality must go through this phase of a merciless subjugation of individual inner primitive emotionality before he can develop further.[1]

During adolescence, libidinal energy is sometimes expressed, sometimes repressed, and sometimes sublimated. While the adolescent's repression of libidinal energy results in a stoic lifestyle, the adolescent's sublimation of libidinal energy results in a ravenous appetite for knowledge. Hume, for example, "suffered a nervous breakdown at eighteen, following a period of intense intellectual discovery and voracious reading." The young Napoleon also had a ravenous appetite for knowledge; "on attaining the age of puberty, [Napoleon's] passion for reading was carried to excess; and he eagerly devoured the contents of every book that fell in his way."[2]

During these years, there is discord in the psyche, the authority of the super-ego is insecure, and the id periodically rebels. As a result, one's moods fluctuate. One is joyful one day and melancholy the next day. One lives like a stoic one day and like an epicurean the next day. These fluctuations of mood are manifested by one's working habits and also by one's eating habits.

If the youth is victorious in his battle with the unconscious, and if his head is filled with fresh knowledge and lofty ideals, he'll be big-headed, proud. Pride is as characteristic of youth as stoicism. If, however, the youth loses his battle with the unconscious, his pride will be shattered; as Jung put it, "The presump-

---

[1] *The Grail Legend*, ch. 3, p. 57
[2] On Hume, see Desmond Morris, *The Book of Ages*, 18; on Napoleon, see Las Cases, *Memorial of St. Helena*, 8/15.

tion of the ego can only be damped down by moral defeat."[1] Just as the youth's moods fluctuate, so too his pride fluctuates.

Repression and moral severity are necessary in order to control the unconscious, and raise the level of consciousness. Repression and moral severity are gradually dispensed with, however, once the unconscious has been controlled and the level of consciousness has been raised. By the age of about eighteen, the moralist has given way to his successor, the theorist. While the moralist is concerned with ethics—with controlling himself and with setting his own house in order—the theorist is concerned with politics and with finding his place in the world and in history.

The theorist, like the moralist, is an unbalanced personality, favoring consciousness at the expense of the unconscious. Since consciousness is individual and the unconscious is collective, favoring consciousness, as adolescence does, results in a hyper-individual, unsocial personality. If mental illness, as Jung says, is either an exaggeration of the individual or an exaggeration of the collective, the mental illness of adolescence consists in an exaggeration of the individual. Adolescence is mild and temporary insanity.

The exaggeration of the individual makes the adolescent a stranger to fellow feeling; he is encased in solitude. In Dostoyevsky's novel, *The Adolescent*, the nineteen-year-old protagonist describes himself thus: "I was in general unaccustomed to the company of people, whoever they were.... I built myself a shell and stayed inside it." The young Descartes was so unsocial that between the ages of eighteen and twenty he hardly ever left his apartment, and he didn't give his address to his family or his friends.[2]

The adolescent often keeps a secret in order to set himself apart from other people, and to strengthen his sense of identity.

---

[1] *Aion* (Collected Works, v. 9, part II), par. 45-47
[2] On Jung, see his Collected Works, vol. 16, §5; on Dostoyevsky, see his *The Adolescent*, I, iii, 3 (Garden City, NY: Doubleday & Company, Inc., 1972, trans. A. MacAndrew); on Descartes, see "The Dreams of Descartes," by L. Feuer, *American Imago*, spring, 1963.

"My 'idea'," says the protagonist of Dostoyevsky's *Adolescent*, "sustained me in my weakness and misery.... Sometimes I felt cold shivers running down my spine when I imagined myself explaining 'the idea' to someone and, having explained it, suddenly realizing that now I had nothing special left."[1] Just as possessing a secret is characteristic of adolescence, so too revealing a secret is characteristic of post-adolescence. The secret is revealed at first to a single friend and later to more and more people. (Not only individuals, but sometimes entire societies, or groups within societies, keep secrets in order to build a sense of identity. Many religious cults in the ancient world emphasized secrecy.)

Why does adolescence keep secrets? Why does it favor consciousness? Why does it exaggerate the individual? Why does it go temporarily insane? These phenomena serve two purposes: they build a sense of identity, and they raise the level of consciousness.

As the adolescent matures, his sense of identity becomes stronger, and the repression of the unconscious abates. Asceticism isn't a goal, it's merely a means. Despite what many philosophers have said, the goal of the individual is not to attain the subjugation of feeling by reason, and the subjugation of the unconscious by consciousness. The goal of the individual is to attain inner harmony and a balanced personality.

18. *Adolescence* One can also describe adolescence in abstract, metaphysical terms. The child, the pre-adolescent, lives in the finite, and is a stranger to the infinite. The adolescent catches a glimpse of the infinite, falls in love with it, and chases after it. While chasing the infinite, the adolescent loses the finite. This is the cause of the adolescent's melancholy. He lives in the clouds, and is a stranger on the earth. He's happy in eternity, but sad in the present moment. The task of the adult is to be equally at home in eternity and in the present moment. While adolescence can be called the discovery of the infinite, adulthood can be called the re-discovery of the finite.

---

[1] See *The Adolescent*, I, v, 4 and I, iii, 4.

19. *Repression Dreams* If youth represses the unconscious, this repression will be evident in dreams—repression dreams, dreams of fighting the animal that symbolizes the unconscious, dreams of fighting the snake, the fish, or the dragon. Philosophers often achieve a high level of consciousness by repressing the unconscious, and this repression is evident in their dreams. Ruskin dreamed that a snake "fastened on my neck like a leech, and nothing would pull it off."[1] Ruskin later went insane. In *Thus Spoke Zarathustra*, Nietzsche describes a snake entering a shepherd's mouth: "the snake had crawled into his throat—and there it had bitten itself fast."[2] Following Zarathustra's advice, the shepherd bites off the snake's head, and spits it out. Then he laughs triumphantly. Nietzsche later went insane.

Repression is natural and healthy as a temporary state, during adolescence, but unhealthy as a permanent state. As Jung said of Nietzsche, "Cases of this kind occur when the unconscious has been resisted for too long on principle, and a wedge violently driven between instinct and the conscious mind."[3]

20. *What Christianity Accomplished* Like the pre-adolescent, the ancient Greeks didn't repress their unconscious; they didn't declare war on their own bodies and their own feelings. Their mind was in harmony with their feelings.

During the time of the Roman Empire, harmony was replaced by excess. The Romans of this period were uninhibited, and indulged their carnal desires without restraint.

This period of moral anarchy was followed by a period of moral tyranny. During this period, Western man had a tendency toward repressing his unconscious. This tendency is evident not only in Christianity, but also in Stoicism, Mithraism and Neoplatonism. Christianity, after triumphing over other religions, introduced conscience and introspection throughout the Western

---

[1] *The Darkening Glass: A Portrait of Ruskin's Genius*, by John Rosenberg, ch. 9
[2] Part III, "Of the Vision and the Riddle," #2
[3] *Symbols of Transformation*, Part II, ch. 7, par. 587

world. Christianity raised Western man's level of consciousness by repressing the unconscious, just as the period of adolescence raises the level of consciousness by repressing the unconscious.

21. *National Character*   People in England and the U.S., who were under the sway of ascetic Protestantism, were more ashamed of bodily pleasures and bodily functions than people on the Continent. In the late 1700s, the English traveler Arthur Young wrote, "In England a man makes water (if I may use such an expression) with a degree of privacy, and a woman never in sight of our sex. In France and Italy there is no such feeling." After seeing a play in Venice, Young wrote:

> There is between the front row of chairs in the pit and the orchestra... a space five or six feet without floor: a well-dressed man, sitting almost under a row of ladies in the side-boxes, stepped into this place, and made water with as much indifference as if he had been in the street; and nobody regarded him with any degree of wonder but myself.

Even today, these attitudes haven't entirely disappeared. Hotels in England have separate bathrooms for men and women, while hotels on the Continent often have one bathroom for both sexes.

People in Russia, Spain, etc. often kiss each other when meeting or separating; this was also customary among the ancient Greeks and Romans. Such a practice would certainly not be found among people influenced by ascetic Protestantism.

When Dostoyevsky traveled in Europe, he noted "the gloomy nature of Englishmen." This gloominess—which has often been remarked—is the result of ascetic Protestantism, which deprived people of spontaneity and joy, and turned life into a task. Stendhal spoke of, "the unhappy look without which one isn't respected in England," and he said that the English had an aversion for "wasting time"; Stendhal spoke of a person who "worked eighteen hours a day, like an Englishman."

When Thoreau was living at Walden Pond, he became friends with a Catholic, a French Canadian.

> He came along early [Thoreau wrote], crossing my bean-field, though without anxiety or haste to get to his work, such as Yan-

kees exhibit. He wasn't a-going to hurt himself. He didn't care if he only earned his board.

Thoreau's friend didn't have the "gloomy nature" of an Englishman: "He interested me," Thoreau wrote, "because he was so quiet and solitary and so happy withal; a well of good humor and contentment which overflowed at his eyes."[1]

22. *Beyond the Family* Jesus said, "Whosoever shall do the will of my Father which is in heaven, the same is my brother, and sister, and mother."[2] As this remark shows, Jesus didn't preach devotion to one's kin, he preached a universal morality. Before the time of Jesus, the individual was wrapped inside the family; Christianity liberated the individual from the family. During the early Middle Ages, Christians were known only by their first names; last names (family names) were added later. But among Greeks, Romans, Chinese, etc., the family name was of primary importance (they would say "Washington George" rather than "George Washington").

In primitive societies, ancestor worship is widespread. Ancestor worship survived until the advent of Christianity, and it still survives in countries where Christian influence is weak. For someone in an ancestor-worshipping society,

> the great interest of human life was to continue the descent, in order to continue the worship. The birth of a daughter did not fulfill the object of the marriage.... The family, like the worship, was continued only by the males.[3]

Even today, a peasant in China or India is eager for a male heir; a woman who is expecting a girl often gets an abortion, and a woman who gives birth to a girl often abandons it. In China, some young men complain that they can't find wives because of the shortage of females.

---

[1] Young, *Travels in France and Italy*, entry for Nov. 4, 1789; Dostoyevsky, *Winter Notes on Summer Impressions*, ch. 5; Stendhal, *Memoirs of an Egoist*, chapters 6 and 7; *Walden*, "Visitors"
[2] Matthew, 12:50
[3] Fustel De Coulanges, *The Ancient City*, II, 3

The ascetic Protestant sects tried to treat everyone like a family member. Hence men were called "Brother John," "Brother Thomas," etc., and women were called "Sister Ann," "Sister Sarah," etc. The Chinese, on the other hand, are known for "unscrupulous competitiveness"[1] toward people outside their family. As Weber said, "the typical distrust of the Chinese for one another is confirmed by all observers. It stands in sharp contrast to the trust and honesty of the faithful brethren in the Puritan sects, a trust shared by outsiders as well."[2] This trust facilitates business transactions. Likewise, extending morality beyond the family facilitates community spirit and community enterprises. Thus, ascetic Protestantism has contributed to the economic and political success of the English-speaking nations. It is doubtful whether democracy can work well in China, where community spirit is lacking, and family spirit is still predominant.

Likewise, it will be difficult to establish democracy in Iraq, where family spirit is far stronger than community spirit. In Iraq, family spirit is strengthened by the custom of marrying one's cousin. Cousin-marriage was once routine in many parts of the world, but "it became taboo in Europe after a long campaign by the Roman Catholic Church."[3] Christian thinkers argued that cousin-marriage fostered family loyalty at the expense of universal love; they wanted morality to go beyond the family.

23. *Romantic Love*   The individual is often a microcosm of society; Shakespeare spoke of, "the state of a man, like to a little kingdom."

In love, indulgence causes satiety, while abstinence causes desire. This is true in the life of society as well as in the life of the individual. The indulgence of the pagans caused satiety, hence the pagans didn't romanticize love or idealize women. But the abstinence of the Christians caused desire, hence the Christians did romanticize love and idealize women. Romantic love

---

[1] Max Weber, *The Religion of China: Confucianism and Taoism*, III
[2] ibid, VIII
[3] *New York Times*, 9/28/03

originates with the medieval troubadours. This love was for an individual, not for preserving a dynasty or strengthening family loyalty.

24. *Transference* is "latching on" to another person—latching on emotionally. Transference is becoming preoccupied with another person, and making that person the focus of positive, often erotic feelings, or negative, hostile feelings. If we think of two people as two separate buildings, transference is an elevated walkway linking the buildings. Since it's often unconscious, it might also be described as a subterranean passage linking the buildings.

To cope with such obsessions, Jungians recommend "active imagination," while Zen recommends meditation. Both active imagination and meditation allow one's emotion to express itself, but detach one from one's emotion, observe it "at arm's length," perhaps even address it. There is a certain kinship between active imagination and meditation, a kinship that is part of the larger kinship between Jungian psychology and Eastern religion.

When Freud began practicing psychotherapy, he noticed that his patients often formed a transference for him, and he sometimes formed a counter-transference for them. He wasn't sure how to handle the situation; he said later that the transference problem delayed the development of his new science for ten years. Eventually, however, he realized that transference was at the core of psychotherapy, and was the best tool in the therapist's toolbox.

Freud tried to purge transference of erotic feelings by bringing these feelings into consciousness, and by showing the patient that he was "proof against every temptation."[1] Once transference was purged of eros, it could bring about a cure. The feelings transferred to the therapist could be drawn back onto the patient

---

[1] "Further Recommendations in the Technique of Psychoanalysis: Observations on Transference-Love" (1915). See also "The Dynamics of the Transference" (1912).

himself, thereby strengthening his ego, his character.[1] If, however, a negative transference developed (feelings of hostility for the therapist), then a cure was impossible. Occasionally transference was simultaneously negative and positive, a situation that therapists called "ambivalence."

Jung, who disagreed with Freud about many things, agreed with Freud that transference was at the heart of psychotherapy. Jung viewed alchemy as a kind of psychotherapy, and he looked for an analogue to transference in the field of alchemy. He found it in the *coniunctio*, which he regarded as the core of alchemy.

Jung noticed that a transference between doctor and patient was often accompanied by telepathy, by occult phenomena. When one of his patients shot himself, Jung felt a pain in the same place where the bullet struck his patient.

25. *Equal Crimes?*   There are three kinds of crime: active, contemplative, and unconscious.

Active	John murders Tim.
Contemplative	John thinks of murdering Tim, and though he doesn't actually do so, he likes the idea, and wishes that it were possible.
Unconscious	John neither murders Tim nor consciously desires to do so, but he has an unconscious will to do so, a will which it is difficult, if not impossible, for him to control. Drawn by this unconscious will, John leads Tim into a fatal accident.

Are these three kinds of crime morally equivalent? Or is active crime more culpable than contemplative, and contemplative more culpable than unconscious? In *The Brothers Karamazov*, Dostoyevsky portrays a man (Svidrigailov) who commits a murder and goes unpunished, and another man (Dmitri) who is punished for that murder though he didn't commit it. There is a

---

[1] The process of transferring feelings and then bringing them back into oneself can be compared to the process of attachment and detachment that we discussed in Chapter 7, #32 ("Proust and Detachment").

kind of justice in this punishment since the man who is punished desired the murder. "It is a matter of indifference who actually committed the crime," writes Freud, in his discussion of *The Brothers Karamazov*, "psychology is only concerned to know who desired it emotionally and who welcomed it when it was done."[1]

But is it really "a matter of indifference who actually committed the crime"? Is lusting after a 5-year-old girl equivalent to raping a 5-year-old girl? One who abstains from active crime, as Dmitri does, may be assumed to have other impulses that outweigh his criminal impulses, and these impulses (let us call them "positive impulses" or "virtuous impulses") may be valuable to society and to the individual himself. As James Hillman said,

> It is not what contents a person carries in his unconscious that reveal his character, for we have our statistical share of the bomber, murderer and pervert, but how one meets these contents.[2]

26. *Abuse and Crime* A criminal's childhood often includes abuse. Stalin and Hitler were both beaten as children. Abuse is sometimes unintentional: the Unabomber (Ted Kaczynski) was a normal, happy child until he was taken from his parents and kept in isolation for an extended period because of a health problem. According to his mother, he was never the same after being isolated.

27. *Broken Home Better?* If one grows up in a warm home, surrounded by parental love, the outside world seems shockingly different. In the outside world, you find yourself dealing with people who don't like you, and whom you don't like, yet somehow you must deal with them, and carry on the battle of life. One might even say that it's an advantage to grow up in a cold home, or a broken home, because then the outside world doesn't seem shockingly different.

---

[1] "Dostoyevsky and Parricide" (1928)
[2] *Lectures on Jung's Typology: The Feeling Function*, ch. 7

28. *Father-less, Precocious*   Three American politicians—Gerald Ford, Bill Clinton, and Barack Obama—came from broken homes, and were raised by single mothers, and later, stepfathers. Throughout history, eminent men have often come from father-less households; such a household seems to breed sturdy independence, precocious maturity, and a gregarious nature.

29. *Freud and Jung*   While Freud was a child of the Western scientific tradition, Jung was inclined toward the mystical, the irrational, and the occult. While Freud respected reason and science, and the critical spirit of the Enlightenment, Jung felt that Western man's worship of science and reason was leading him to spiritual bankruptcy. While Freud wrote essays on Western icons like Shakespeare and Michelangelo, Jung wrote essays on Eastern religion, and on Eastern classics like the *I Ching*. While Freud can't match Jung's depth of thought, Jung can't match Freud's clear, concise style. While Freud deserves credit for pioneering the study of the unconscious, Jung deserves credit for drawing attention to the infinite potential, and deep wisdom, that lies within every human psyche.

Both Freud and Jung had the good fortune to find a career that dovetailed with their intellectual interests, a career that put them into daily contact with the cutting-edge of knowledge. As a youth in Switzerland, Jung was interested in philosophy, and found Nietzsche's *Zarathustra* inspiring. He was also interested in medicine, and decided to go to medical school. Jung says that when he was finishing medical school,

> I was preparing for my final exams, and I also had to know something about psychiatry, so I took up Krafft-Ebing's textbook on psychiatry. I read first the introduction... and then it happened. Then it happened. I thought, this is it, this is the confluence of medicine and philosophy! ....I knew absolutely that this was the thing for me; it came over me with the most tremendous rush. You know, my heart beat so... I could hardly stand it.[1]

---

[1] *C. G. Jung Speaking: Interviews and Encounters*, "1952"

As a young psychiatrist, Jung admired Freud's work, and sent Freud several of his own essays. Freud wrote back to Jung, and in 1906, Jung visited Freud in Vienna. They met at one in the afternoon, and talked for thirteen hours. Later, however, their relationship deteriorated, partly because Jung was fascinated by the occult, and Freud was uncomfortable with it.

While Jung was friendly toward religion in general, he was rather scornful of contemporary Christianity:

> The Christian nations have come to a sorry pass; their Christianity slumbers and has neglected to develop its myth further in the course of the centuries. Those who gave expression to the dark stirrings of growth in mythic ideas were refused a hearing.... A myth is dead if it no longer lives and grows.[1]

The best religion is one that satisfies both head and heart, one that meets both intellectual demands, and spiritual needs. The three major monotheistic religions—Christianity, Judaism, and Islam—no longer meet intellectual demands and spiritual needs, hence there's a need for new approaches to religion.

30. *Queen of the Sciences* "Psychology," Nietzsche wrote, "is now again the path to the fundamental problems.... Psychology shall be recognized again as the queen of the sciences, for whose service and preparation the other sciences exist." Nietzsche spoke of "this immense and almost new domain of dangerous insights."[2] With his gift for anticipating the future, Nietzsche anticipated the Psychology Revolution that Freud started, and Jung continued.

The Psychology Revolution has had a profound impact on our worldview—far more profound than the Darwinian Revolution—and the Psychology Revolution is still in progress. The Psychology Revolution presents today's philosophers with an opportunity and a challenge; never before has philosophy had such a vast field to explore, such a vast crop to harvest, such a vast amount of knowledge to assimilate. In the 20th century,

---

[1] *Memories, Dreams, Reflections*, ch. 12
[2] *Beyond Good and Evil*, §23

many thinkers reacted to the Psychology Revolution by ignoring it: "The unconscious doesn't concern me," they said; "I will have nothing to do with Freud or Jung." Perhaps these thinkers sensed that the Psychology Revolution would shatter their worldview, perhaps they sensed that a lifetime of study was required to grasp Freud and Jung and their disciples. As Nietzsche said of psychology, "There are in fact a hundred good reasons why everyone should keep away from it who—*can*."

Freud is difficult to grasp, but he throws a bright light on human nature, and on the humanities. Jung is even more difficult to grasp, but he throws an even brighter light on human nature, and on the humanities. Jung points the way to wholeness and spiritual growth, hence he's more popular with laymen than Freud.

Jung views marriage as an attempt to reach wholeness; he views something that is apparently sexual (namely, marriage) from a spiritual perspective. Freud does the opposite; he views things that appear to be non-sexual from a sexual perspective. Jung extends the domain of spirituality and religion, while Freud extends the domain of sexuality. Though Jung was critical of Freud's approach, he was wise enough to realize that future thinkers would draw upon both Freud and himself.[1]

A friend once wrote to me,

> The problem with what I've read from Jung and Freud is that their theories seem to exist in a vacuum. They make very powerful reading sometimes, but in the end I am left with the feeling of having briefly shared someone's ungrounded, subjective experience.

Perhaps this is why academia usually ignores Freud and Jung; academia prefers rigorous arguments to profound ideas, academia loves statistics, numbers. But if you have a penchant for introspection, for exploring inner worlds, you'll find that Freud and Jung speak to your own experience, and you'll find that their arguments can be buttressed by your own experience. And if you have a penchant for literature and philosophy, you'll find that

---

[1] *C. G. Jung Speaking: Interviews and Encounters*, "1955"

4. PSYCHOLOGY

Freud and Jung throw light on those subjects, and strengthen their arguments with evidence drawn from those subjects.

Three of the chief issues in psychology are:

1. What is evil? Is evil in every human being? Is it something active and forceful, or merely a lack of good (*privatio boni*)? Is evil relative and subjective, or is it absolute and universal? Can we define evil as turning against life, and allying oneself with death and destruction? Can we define good as accepting life, embracing life?
2. How do we reach wholeness and harmony? How can a professional therapist foster one's spiritual growth? What can an individual do to foster his own growth?
3. How can we explain occult phenomena? Is there any limit to the power of the psyche? Is there any part of us that can survive after death?

"Psychology is now again the path to the fundamental problems." Are we finally ready to explore this "immense and almost new domain"? Are we finally ready to explore ourselves?

5. Genius

1. *What is Genius?* Genius is the sublimation of sexual libido onto cultural and political goals. Libidinal sublimation enables the genius to work toward cultural or political goals with exceptional passion and energy. Genius usually has an innate predisposition toward one of four fields: philosophy, art, science or politics.[1]

2. *Kinds of Genius* Can a person have more than one kind of genius? Samuel Johnson thought that a genius could work in any field; "Had Sir Isaac Newton applied himself to poetry," said Johnson, "he would have made a very fine epic poem.... The man who has vigor, may walk to the east, just as well as to the west."[2] Some have argued that Bacon wrote the plays that are attributed to Shakespeare, and thus that Bacon had both philosophic and artistic genius.

---

[1] Outstanding historians and sociologists—such as Tacitus, Gibbon, Tocqueville and Weber—don't fit into any of these four categories. Likewise, outstanding psychologists, like Freud and Jung, don't fit easily into any of these categories, though they should probably be considered philosophic geniuses. Perhaps a separate category should be set up for psychologists, historians, sociologists, etc.

[2] James Boswell, *Journal of a Tour to the Hebrides*, August 15

There have been a few versatile geniuses, such as Leonardo and Pascal, but it's very unusual for a person to have more than one kind of genius. Most geniuses can work in only one field. It's inconceivable that one person could have written the plays of Shakespeare and the philosophical works of Bacon. If Newton had applied himself to poetry, he wouldn't have written "a very fine epic poem." Since Newton knew his own limitations, he never applied himself to poetry. Most geniuses never attempt to work outside the field for which they were born.

3. *Grades of Genius* Just as there are various kinds of genius, so too there are various grades of genius. The lowest grades of genius resemble the highest grades of talent. Thus, it's difficult to say precisely where the dividing line is between genius and talent; it's difficult to say precisely who has a low grade of genius, and who has a high grade of talent.

4. *Origin of Genius* What is the origin of genius? Schopenhauer, who thought that character came from one's father and intellect came from one's mother, said that genius was the product of an exceptionally strong-willed father and an exceptionally intelligent mother. Karl Abraham, one of Freud's disciples, thought that genius emerged from a family that was declining in vigor and strength, but managed to produce one or two people who combined a neurotic disposition with intellectual gifts. As an example, Abraham cited Ikhnaton, an Egyptian pharaoh whose ancestors were vigorous, practical and warlike, and who combined neurotic traits with genius.

Many geniuses emerged from families that had been successful in practical affairs, and then had declined in vigor and strength. Thomas Mann is an example. Mann's family had a long history of business success and social prominence. His ancestors must have been strong-willed, energetic and intelligent. Mann's generation, however, seems to have been touched by both genius and neurosis—or if not actual neurosis, at least mental instability. While Mann's brother, Heinrich, was a well-known writer— only slightly less famous than Thomas himself—two of Mann's sisters committed suicide.

In Wittgenstein's family, one finds the same combination of business success and mental instability; Wittgenstein's father was a steel magnate, one of the richest men in Europe, but three of Wittgenstein's brothers committed suicide. Mental instability is also found in van Gogh's family; three of van Gogh's siblings had "severe psychological disturbances."[1]

The best solution to the problem of the origin of genius is a solution that combines Schopenhauer's theory with Abraham's theory. Genius is found in a family that is declining in vigor and strength, and in which the father is strong-willed, the mother intelligent.

While genius inherits certain virtues and talents, it usually bequeaths little. Genius doesn't beget genius; genius is an end, not a beginning.

5. *Political Genius* During turbulent times, nations often raise men of genius to positions of leadership. Examples are Caesar, Napoleon, Lenin, Mussolini and Hitler.

6. *Genius and Prophecy* Genius can see into the future. The Roman writer Seneca foresaw the discovery of the Americas. In the thirteenth century, Roger Bacon foresaw the automobile and the airplane. Leonardo foresaw many mechanical inventions, including the steam engine, the airplane, the parachute, the submarine, the tank, and the machine gun. Rousseau, in 1762, foresaw the French Revolution and the demise of the European monarchies. Jefferson, in 1820, foresaw the American Civil War. Tocqueville, in 1835, foresaw that the United States and Russia

---

[1] See J. Gedo, *Portraits of the Artist: Psychoanalysis of Creativity and Its Vicissitudes*, 8, i. Other examples of geniuses whose families had been successful in business are Schopenhauer, Kierkegaard, William and Henry James, Kafka and Faulkner. Schopenhauer's views on the origin of genius can be found in *The World as Will and Representation*, vol. 2, §43; Abraham's views can be found in his "Amenhotep IV" etc., 1912.

5. GENIUS

would one day be the world's most powerful nations.[1] Heine foresaw Nazi militarism and genocide; Heine predicted that the forces found in German philosophy would someday "erupt and fill the world with terror and amazement," and that, "a play will be performed which will make the French Revolution look like an innocent idyll."[2] Kafka predicted that men "will try to grind the synagogue to dust by destroying the Jews themselves." Burckhardt foresaw the misfortunes of Germany; when the Kaiser was crowned at Versailles in 1871, Burckhardt said, "that is the doom of Germany."[3] Nietzsche foresaw the psychology of the unconscious, the world wars and the rise of Russia.

7. *Hitler and Fate* Do individuals control history, or do history and fate control individuals? The prescience of genius is an argument in favor of fate, and an argument against free will; if events can be foreseen long before they occur, they must have been caused neither by individuals nor by circumstances, but by history and fate. It appears that Hitler was the cause of the Holocaust, and that the Depression was the cause of Hitler's rise to power. But if the Holocaust was foreseen a century before it occurred, then it can't be ascribed to particular individuals, or to particular circumstances. While Hitler was the proximate cause of the Holocaust, and while the Depression was the proximate cause of Hitler's rise to power, the root causes of these events lie

---

[1] On Seneca, see his play, *Medea* (chorus' second speech); on Rousseau, see *Emile*, Book 3; on Jefferson, see his letter to John Holmes, April 22, 1820; on Tocqueville, see *Democracy in America*, vol. 1, conclusion.
[2] Heinrich Heine, *Religion and Philosophy in Germany*, "The Meaning of German Philosophy." Heine wasn't the only person who foresaw the Holocaust long before it occurred; a number of passages in Nietzsche's works suggest that he, too, foresaw the Holocaust. See *Human, All-Too-Human*, §475, *The Dawn*, §205, *Beyond Good and Evil*, §§241 and 251, and *Ecce Homo*, "Why I Am A Destiny," §1.
[3] On Kafka, see G. Janouch, *Conversations With Kafka* (New Directions Books, 1971, p. 139); on Burckhardt, see Jung, *Memories, Dreams, and Reflections*, ch. 8.

far deeper than any particular individuals or particular circumstances.

Throughout his life, Hitler acted like one who was the agent of fate. When he wrote *Mein Kampf* in the 1920's, Hitler sketched the history of the 1930's and 1940's. He anticipated a great war, and he anticipated that Germany might be destroyed by the war. Hitler felt that his life and his actions were the result not of accident or of choice, but of fate. With fate supporting him, he felt that he possessed great power, that he was invincible, hence he had complete confidence in himself. His confidence enabled him to speak with passion, energy, and conviction, and it enabled him to captivate a nation.

Hitler relied on his unconscious to reveal what was fated to occur; he relied on hunches and intuitions. "I go the way Providence dictates," said Hitler, "with the assurance of a sleepwalker."[1] Hitler's dependence on fate and on his unconscious was so complete that he lost touch with reality, and wasn't wholly sane.

Napoleon, whose career resembled Hitler's in many ways, felt, like Hitler, that he was the agent of fate, that he could foresee the future, and that he didn't control events but rather was controlled by them. "I always had an inner sense," said Napoleon, "of what awaited me.... Nothing ever happened to me which I did not foresee."[2] Napoleon thought that any attempt to assassinate him, before his fate had run its course, was certain to fail—and in fact, many such attempts did fail.

8. *Mad Genius* How is genius able to see into the future? Partly because genius has a high level of consciousness, and partly because genius is in close contact with the unconscious. The prescience of genius is the result of unconscious feeling, as well as conscious thought. The genius draws from his unconscious ideas, images and intuitions.

Because the genius is in close contact with his unconscious, he runs the risk of becoming insane. Many geniuses have gone

---

[1] *Adolf Hitler*, by John Toland, 14, i
[2] *Napoleon the Man*, by Dmitri Merezhkovsky, ch. 9

5. GENIUS

insane; examples are Tasso, Newton, Swift, Comte, Gogol, Ruskin, Hölderlin, Schumann, Nietzsche, Strindberg and van Gogh.

9. Semi-Mad Genius Many geniuses were partially insane, if not wholly insane; many geniuses lived on the borderline between sanity and insanity. Schopenhauer is an example of a genius who was partially insane. Schopenhauer had many irrational fears and anxieties; fearing that people would misinterpret a trance as death and bury him alive, Schopenhauer "stipulated that his remains be left unburied beyond the usual time." Cézanne is another example of a genius who was partially insane. Cézanne experienced "chronic paranoia"; when his friends threw a party to celebrate his birthday, he left abruptly, thinking they were making fun of him. Gödel was so afraid of being poisoned that he stopped eating, and starved to death.

It is an indication of the genius' partial insanity that he goes to extremes and is one-sided. The genius lacks moderation. Dostoyevsky, for example, said, "I go to the ultimate limit everywhere and in everything; all my life long I have always approached the limit!"[1]

A second indication of the genius' partial insanity is that he's moody, more so than most people are. Genius often oscillates between elation and depression. Kierkegaard is an example of a moody genius. Kierkegaard's mental state was described as "depression, alternating with, but more commonly blended with, a condition of exaltation." Strindberg was also moody; "throughout [Strindberg's] life," wrote one of his biographers, "his moods varied from elation to the blackest depression." The moodiness of genius tends to take the form of depression rather than elation;

---

[1] On Schopenhauer, see E. Hitschmann, *Great Men: Psychoanalytic Studies*, "Schopenhauer"; on Cézanne, see John Gedo, *Portraits of the Artist, etc.*, 9, vi; on Dostoyevsky, see Yermilov's biography of Dostoyevsky, Intro.

genius is melancholy. Kafka is an example of a melancholy genius: "every day," said Kafka, "I wish myself off the earth."[1]

A third indication of the partial insanity of genius is that genius often has a tendency toward illness. Examples of geniuses who were chronically ill are Epicurus, Pascal, Lichtenberg, Schiller, Leopardi, Darwin, Nietzsche and Proust. Illness often has a psychological cause, and chronic illness is often the result of psychological problems. Certain illnesses, such as epilepsy and asthma, almost always have a psychological cause. Several geniuses were epileptics, including Muhammad, Dostoyevsky and Flaubert. Proust's asthma was a symptom of his psychic state, a plea for maternal attention.

While the ideal man, according to the adage, has a healthy mind in a healthy body (*mens sana in corpore sano*), the genius often has an unhealthy mind in an unhealthy body. Is it surprising, then, that so many geniuses die young?

10. *Protean Genius* Genius is multi-faceted and protean; genius has a wide variety of different personalities. Strindberg is an example of a multi-faceted genius; one of his friends addressed Strindberg thus: "O warm, strong, weak, O trusting-suspicious, brave-timid, loving-hating, poetic-prosaic, solicitous-uncaring Strindberg!"[2] Jung also had a variety of different personalities; "Jung left the most contradictory impressions on those who knew him," one scholar wrote, "he was sociable but difficult, amusing at times and taciturn at others, outwardly self-confident yet vulnerable to criticism."[3]

11. *Woman, Child, Genius* Though the genius may be a male, he has some feminine traits, and though the genius may be an adult, he has some childlike traits. Virgil, because of his feminine traits, was nicknamed Parthenias, or The Virgin. Milton was nicknamed The Lady of Christ's (he attended Christ's College).

---

[1] See *Kierkegaard*, by Walter Lowrie, II, 3, and *Strindberg*, by Michael Meyer, ch. 3, and *Franz Kafka*, by Max Brod, 2.
[2] *Strindberg*, by Michael L. Meyer, ch. 9
[3] *Freud: A Life for Our Time*, by Peter Gay, V, i

Chekhov was described as "modest and quiet like a girl. And he walks like a girl."[1] Artistic creation requires an especially high degree of femininity. Philosophical, scientific and political geniuses are less feminine than artistic geniuses, and accordingly they're less inclined toward homosexuality than artistic geniuses are.

12. *Immature Genius* Genius is childlike. Genius approaches the world with naiveté, as if it were new and strange. Leonardo is an example of a childlike genius; "the great Leonardo," wrote Freud, "remained infantile in some ways throughout his whole life....As a grown-up he still continued playing." It was said of Mozart that, "in his art he early became a man, but in all other respects he invariably remained a child."[2]

13. *Cheerful Genius* Though genius is melancholy, it is also, paradoxically, cheerful. Cheerfulness can coexist with melancholy; as the French say, "sad heart, gay spirit (*le coeur triste, l'esprit gai*)." The cheerfulness of genius is an indication of its childlike nature; like the child, the genius can enjoy things that other people have ceased to enjoy. Kant is an example of a cheerful genius; Herder said that Kant, "had the happy sprightliness of a youth." Kafka is another example of a cheerful genius; despite his melancholy, Kafka was said to be "always cheerful."[3]

14. *Playful Genius* The genius, especially the artistic genius, shares with the child a tendency to create imaginary worlds. The genius and the child both turn their backs on the real world, and invent worlds of their own. The artist has often been compared to a child at play.

---

[1] Tolstoy's words, quoted in Gorky, *Reminiscences of Tolstoy*, §2. On the nicknames of Vergil and Milton, see *Paradise Lost and Other Poems*, Mentor Books, 1961, Intro.
[2] See Freud, *Leonardo and a Memory From His Childhood*, §5, and Schopenhauer, *The World as Will and Representation*, vol. 2, §31.
[3] *I Am A Memory Come Alive: Autobiographical Writings of Franz Kafka*, "1923," Schocken Books, New York, 1974

15. *Genius and Narcissism* Why do geniuses have some feminine traits and some childlike traits? What do geniuses have in common with women and children? Women and children have a tendency toward narcissism—toward internalizing their libidinal energy—and genius also has a tendency toward narcissism. Because of their narcissism, geniuses are often solitary and friendless. "I have no friends," said Michelangelo, "need none, and will have none"; Michelangelo was said to be "lonely as a hangman." A woman who knew Kierkegaard and Ibsen said, "I have never seen in any other two persons, male or female, so marked a compulsion to be alone."[1]

As a result of their narcissism, geniuses have difficulty loving another person. The love affairs of geniuses have sometimes been suspected of having a narcissistic nature. It was said of Beethoven that he "loved only love, not women." Ortega said that Stendhal and Chateaubriand, though they were frequently involved in love affairs, never actually loved.

Because it's difficult for them to love another person, geniuses are often bachelors. If they're married and have children, they usually aren't good parents. Rousseau, for example, wasn't a good parent; Rousseau put all his children in an orphanage. Hitschmann said, "If the children of men of genius do not succeed or turn out badly... the narcissism of the fathers should not be forgotten as an explanation."[2] Examples of geniuses whose children turned out badly are Goethe, Melville, Joyce, Hemingway, O'Neill and Einstein.

16. *Genius and Homosexuality* Just as everyone is to some extent insane, so too everyone is to some extent a homosexual.

---

[1] On Michelangelo, see Emil Ludwig, *Three Titans*, "Michelangelo" and W. Niederland, "Clinical Aspects of Creativity" (*American Imago*, spring-summer, 1967); on Ibsen and Kierkegaard, see M. Meyer, *Henrik Ibsen*, ch. 5.

[2] See Emil Ludwig, *Three Titans*, "Beethoven," Ortega, *On Love*, 2, ii, and Edward Hitschmann, *Great Men: Psychoanalytic Studies*, "Goethe," etc.

5. GENIUS

While the average person has some homosexual proclivities, the genius has even more; the genius is closer to homosexuality than the average person is, just as the genius is closer to insanity than the average person is. Many geniuses were homosexuals: Verlaine, Rimbaud, Whitman, Swinburne, Baudelaire, Wilde, Proust, Gide, Forster, Auden, etc.

Why does genius have a proclivity for homosexuality? Geniuses and homosexuals both tend to be effeminate and narcissistic. The narcissism of homosexuals prevents them from loving a body different in gender from their own.

If all geniuses are effeminate and narcissistic, why aren't all geniuses homosexuals? The nature of one's relationships to one's parents is an important factor in determining whether one becomes a homosexual. Freud thought that male homosexuality originated in early childhood, and could usually be traced to one of the following causes:

1. an especially close relationship to the mother
2. a mother with a dominating, masculine personality
3. an absent father
4. a bad relationship with the father

Any one of these causes could hinder the son from identifying with his father, and from acquiring his father's masculine traits. Geniuses who, as a result of one of these causes, couldn't identify with their fathers became homosexuals. Proust, for example, had an especially close relationship to his mother, and his father was often absent; Forster's father died when he was a baby, and Forster was raised by his mother and his aunts; Gide and Wilde had dominating, masculine mothers.[1] While the narcissism of genius makes homosexuality more likely, environmental factors should be taken into account, too.

---

[1] On the relationship between narcissism and homosexuality, see Sandor Ferenczi, "The Nosology of Male Homosexuality," 1911, and Freud, *Three Essays on the Theory of Sexuality*, I, 1, A, footnote. Freud discusses the origins of homosexuality in *Leonardo da Vinci and a Memory of His Childhood*, 3.

17. *Greek Love, Self Love* Homosexuality was open and widespread in ancient Greece; homosexuality is sometimes referred to as "Greek love." Sachs argued that the ancient Greeks were narcissistic, and that their narcissism caused their proclivity for homosexuality, caused them to celebrate the body in their art, caused them to be indifferent to nature, and caused them to avoid technology.

Why were the ancient Greeks narcissistic? Narcissism is characteristic of a primitive society, of a society that hasn't passed through the narcissistic stage of libidinal development and reached the stage of object love, just as narcissism in an individual is characteristic of immaturity, and of not having reached the stage of object love. Thus, primitive peoples have proclivities for narcissism and for homosexuality; according to Freud, "[homosexuality] is remarkably widespread among many savage and primitive races." Though the ancient Greeks weren't in all respects "savage and primitive," they were in some respects immature; the ancient Greeks have often been described as youthful, as adolescents.[1]

18. *Genius and Nature* Just as the narcissism of the ancient Greeks made them indifferent to nature, so too the narcissism of geniuses often makes them indifferent to nature. Flaubert, for example, wrote thus: "I am no Nature addict: her 'marvels' do not move me as much as the miracles of Art." Dostoyevsky was described as "utterly indifferent to natural scenery." "I hate views," said Oscar Wilde; "a gentleman never looks out of the window."[2]

---

[1] On the ancient Greeks, see Hanns Sachs, *The Creative Unconscious*, 4, and Nietzsche, *The Gay Science*, §155. On primitive man, see Freud, *Three Essays on the Theory of Sexuality*, I, 1.
[2] See Flaubert, *Letters*, 7/2/74; A. Yarmolinsky, *Dostoyevsky*, ch. 10; R. Ellman, *Oscar Wilde*, chapters 5 and 8. Anatole France was also indifferent to natural scenery; see *Anatole France Himself*, "The Ladybird in the Engravings."

19. *Genius and Adolescence* Like the genius, the adolescent is narcissistic. The narcissism of the adolescent is manifested by a certain aversion for the opposite sex, especially for the genitals of the opposite sex. Because the ancient Greeks were narcissistic, they too had an aversion for the genitals of the opposite sex. Thus, in Greek mythology, any man who looks at the female genitals, symbolized by the Medusa head, is turned to stone.

In addition to narcissism, many other traits are common to genius and adolescence: melancholy, eccentricity, moodiness, a tendency toward partial insanity, and a tendency to go to extremes. Genius has often been viewed as a kind of adolescence, as protracted or repeated adolescence.

20. *Genius and Infancy* The adolescent and the infant face similar challenges: the adolescent must learn to live outside the family, the infant must learn to live outside the womb. The way in which one copes with adolescence repeats the way in which one coped, at an earlier age, with infancy. Genius often matures slowly and lingers in adolescence, and genius often lingers in infancy, too; Macaulay, Nietzsche and Einstein, for example, were slow in learning to talk.

The infant doesn't distinguish between itself and the external world; the infant hasn't established the boundaries of its own ego. The infant is one with the universe. Genius lingers in infancy, and never completely loses the infant's feeling of oneness with the universe. This feeling of oneness with the universe, this unbounded ego, helps the philosophical genius to understand man and the world, helps the scientific genius to understand nature and the cosmos, helps the political genius to understand his nation, and helps the artistic genius to sympathize with the external world. If genius can be viewed as protracted adolescence, it can also be viewed as protracted infancy.

21. *Genius and Sex* Some geniuses, instead of lingering in adolescence, mature quickly, both sexually and intellectually. Examples are Byron and Rimbaud. According to Freud, "sexual precocity often runs parallel with premature intellectual development."

The combination of sexual and intellectual precocity, though it may be found in artists like Byron and Rimbaud, is never found in philosophers. Philosophers generally arrive at their central ideas while they're young, but they never develop and express those ideas until they've reached at least their late twenties. Philosophy requires a high level of consciousness, which is attained by repression of the unconscious, and repression of the unconscious precludes sexual precocity. Repression of the unconscious sometimes precludes all sexual activity, hence many philosophers have been sexually abstinent. It was said of Plato that he "never touched a woman," and the same is probably true of Pascal, Kant, Kierkegaard, Mill, Carlyle, Thoreau and Nietzsche.

Scientists, like philosophers, often attain a high level of consciousness by the repression of their unconscious. This repression sometimes precludes all sexual activity; according to Eissler, Newton "never had intercourse," and the same is probably true of Mendel.

Art, unlike philosophy and science, doesn't require the repression of the unconscious, but rather the participation of the unconscious. Accordingly, artists are often sexually uninhibited.[1]

---

[1] On precocity, see Freud, *Three Essays on the Theory of Sexuality*, Summary; on Newton and Mendel, see K. R. Eissler, *Talent and Genius: The Fictitious Case of Tausk contra Freud*, ch. 6.

6. Sundry Thoughts

1. *The Life of the Mind: 7 Nevers*
   I. Never separate the life of the mind into different departments (Inter-disciplinary Approach)
   II. Never let intellectual pursuits predominate at the expense of spiritual life; never let the mind predominate at the expense of the whole person (Spiritual Approach)
   III. Never let truth predominate over beauty, never let content predominate over style; respect literary values, even in a non-fiction work (Aesthetic Approach)
   IV. Never become preoccupied with current events, current books, etc.; spend more time with old books than with fresh newspapers (Timeless Approach)
   V. Never let professionals take over, and turn the life of the mind into a job; it should be pleasurable, a leisure-time activity (Pleasure Principle)
   VI. Never insist that the universe make sense; accept the mysterious and the inexplicable (Negative Capability)
   VII. Never focus on the West and ignore the East; on the other hand, don't let respect for the East blind you to the merits of the West; respect both East and West (Global Perspective)

2. *Delicate Balance* Listening to a piece of music for the first time is unenjoyable; as the Greek proverb put it, "unheard melodies are never sweet." Yet it's also unenjoyable to listen to the same piece too many times. In listening to music, there's a delicate balance between novelty and satiety.

3. *Combined Arts* Nietzsche says that the early Greeks had a Dionysian art that combined poetry, music, and dance. But over the course of time, poetry, music, and dance were separated, and became specialized. What we call "classical music" usually doesn't include poetry or dance.

Popular music, however, returns to the old tradition, the tradition in which poetry, music, and dance existed together. Elvis Presley said, "I can't listen to music without moving. I tried, but I can't do it." Michael Jackson danced even in the recording studio. This popular tradition, this Dionysian tradition, has probably existed at all times—below the surface, on the fringe of society, underneath "higher culture."

In China, this popular tradition flourished among minority peoples, while majority Chinese (Han Chinese), were closer to the specialized Western tradition. In the center of China, Han Chinese often listened to music silently, motionlessly, while on the periphery of China, minorities were "moving to the beat."

4. *Farmers and Philosophers* A pumpkin farmer spends only a tiny fraction of his time picking pumpkins. Most of his time is spent in preparatory work—plowing, sowing, weeding, etc. Likewise, a philosopher spends only a tiny fraction of his time writing philosophy. Most of his time is spent in preparatory work—reading, thinking, conversing and, last but not least, living. Every philosopher can understand the pumpkin farmer's irritation when his neighbor says to him, "How can you call yourself a pumpkin farmer? I never see you picking pumpkins! You're not a real pumpkin farmer."

5. *Highest compliment* for a writer: "You didn't make that up yourself. Tell me, who did you copy that from?"

6. *Distant Wisdom* No man is a prophet in his own country. In China, they say "a monk from distant lands can understand the scriptures." Montaigne said, "In my region of Gascony, they think it funny to see me in print. But the further from my own haunts my reputation spreads, the higher I am rated."

7. *Not Entertainment* The highest purpose of literature is spiritual enlightenment, spiritual growth; in other words, the highest purpose of literature is to save the reader's life. Spiritual growth isn't optional; one grows in order to survive. If someone says, "this book isn't a good read, it's not fun to read, it's not entertaining" we should respond, "you're missing the point, the author isn't trying to entertain you, he's trying to save your life. If you're drowning in the ocean, and someone throws you a float, would you say, 'I don't like the color blue, throw me a red float'?"

8. *Praise the Dead, Stone the Living* The creative individual opposes current intellectual fashions. He's usually neither understood nor appreciated by his contemporaries. He's ignored and greeted with silence, or condemned by a chorus of critical voices, or persecuted, sometimes to the point of execution.

Yet the very people who ignore him or condemn him or persecute him, strive to outdo each other in paying homage to the creative individuals of the past. "We would not have voted to poison Socrates," they say; "we would not have looked on approvingly as Bruno burned; we would not have thrown stones into Rousseau's house; we would not have mocked Kierkegaard for his skinny legs and his odd clothing; we would not have harassed and insulted van Gogh." But if you confront these same people with a contemporary version of Socrates, of Bruno, of Rousseau, of Kierkegaard, of van Gogh, if you confront them with a creative individual, they will ignore him or condemn him or persecute him.

9. *The Stranger's Reception* In rural areas, people are glad to see other people, they appreciate other people, they're disposed to like other people. In small cities, people take other people for

granted; they're disposed neither to like other people nor to dislike them. In big cities, people wish that there were fewer people; they're disposed to dislike other people and to fear them.

10. *Public Opinions*

Doing Well	Making a lot of money (see *Successful*).
Freud	Obsolete. All his theories have been disproven.
Law	The extension of politics by other means.
Living, To Make A	The essence of life; one who makes a good living is one who makes a lot of money.
Neurotic	Someone you don't get along with.
Nietzsche	Not a real philosopher.
Philosophy	Is there any market for it?
Politics	A dismal science.
Right	Something one desires, and thinks that one deserves. There's a right to have a job, a right to have housing, a right to have a TV, a right to be informed of your rights, a right to march in order to demand your rights, a right to invent new rights, etc., etc.
Samovar	In Russian novels, every house has at least one. One doesn't know what it is.
Sennet	Shakespearian stage direction. One doesn't know what it is. Does it have something to do with a hautboy?
Successful	Making a lot of money.
Television	Say that you don't watch it much.

11. *Happiest Days* They say that the two happiest days in the life of a boat owner are the day he buys his boat, and the day he sells it. Perhaps one could say the same thing about readers: the happiest days in a reader's life are the day he starts a new book, and the day he finishes it.

6. SUNDRY THOUGHTS 117

12. *Changing Fate* Lincoln foresaw that he would be assassinated. "Several times Lincoln publicly expressed the belief that he would not live through his second term as President. He often reported his 'presentiments,' fantasies, and even his dreams, not only to his intimate friends but to strangers as well."[1] One of Lincoln's friends said, "he always believed that he would fall by the hand of an assassin."

Let's assume that our unconscious can read the book of fate. Does that allow us to change fate? For example, if Lincoln believed his prophetic dreams, in which his assassination was a *fait accompli*, could he avoid assassination? If he dreamed that he had been assassinated, and if he told people about his dream, and if perhaps other people dreamed the same thing, is it possible that someone around him would say, "let's increase the guard that protects him, let's try to dissuade him from entering public places, let's try to change fate." Has this ever happened? Has our anticipation of the future ever enabled us to change that future?

Osama bin Laden was concerned that anticipation of the future could change the future, that is, he was concerned that anticipations of the September 11 attacks could prevent those attacks from succeeding. A video of bin Laden chatting with a Saudi cleric reveals that bin Laden and his cohorts were preoccupied with prophetic dreams and other harbingers of the future. (The *New York Times*, in an article on the video, dismisses this preoccupation with prophecy as "tribal superstition"; evidently the *Times* writer has the shallow rationalism, and the contempt for psychic phenomena, that is typical of the intelligentsia.[2]) In the video, bin Laden says "I was worried that maybe the secret would be revealed if everyone starts seeing it in their dream. So I closed the subject. I told him if he sees another dream, not to tell anybody."

Throughout history, man has tried to foretell the future, avoid misfortune, and seize good fortune. Even in recent times, this ancient habit can still be found. When Reagan was President,

---

[1] Wilson, George W., "A Prophetic Dream Reported by Abraham Lincoln," *American Imago*, June, 1940
[2] *New York Times*, December 14, 2001

his wife often consulted prophets and fortunetellers, asking them what days were safe for her husband to travel, appear in public, etc. Will mankind forever be divided into two groups, those who fall victim to gross superstition and those who fall victim to shallow rationalism? Or can we enjoy the benefits of rational, scientific thinking, and at the same time appreciate and utilize the mysterious powers of the unconscious? Did Lincoln manage to combine respect for reason with respect for the occult?

13. *Clausewitz and Chance*   In his famous treatise on war, Clausewitz said, "There is no human activity that stands in such constant and universal contact with chance as does war.... Of all branches of human activity, [war is] the most like a game of cards." It's characteristic of a rational thinker to emphasize chance, just as it's characteristic of a non-rational thinker to emphasize fate. Clausewitz was a product of the Enlightenment, and he has a rational-scientific worldview; he likes to use mathematical terms like "laws of probability," and scientific terms like "centers of attraction" and "the principle of polarity." Doubtless Clausewitz would be uncomfortable with the idea that a mysterious fate shaped the outcome of wars.

But Clausewitz's contemporary, Napoleon, felt that fate was leading him to victory early in his career, and he felt that fate had turned against him at Waterloo; Napoleon was more impressed by fate than by chance. Perhaps what we call "chance" doesn't really exist, but is shaped by fate, just as Freud argued that we can't think of a random number, because our choice of a number will be shaped by unconscious factors. The ancient practice of divination uses chance events to learn fate, and predict the future. The ancient Chinese text known as *The Book of Changes* (or *I Ching*) uses dice and other random events to get advice and predict the future; Jung said this book never erred.

Clausewitz said war was like a game of cards, but modern playing cards originated from Tarot cards, and Tarot cards were used (and still are used) for divination. Perhaps neither war nor cards are matters of pure chance, as Clausewitz thought.

14. *Titanic Prophecy* The *Titanic* disaster was prophesied 14 years before it occurred. "In 1898, Morgan Robertson published a book called *Futility* in which a ship called *Titan* sinks after colliding with an iceberg. There are striking similarities between the *Titan* and the *Titanic* disasters: both ships sank in the North Atlantic during April, both did not have enough lifeboats, both were travelling at an excessive speed, and both were considered the largest ships of their time."[1]

15. *The Art of Memory* When Greco-Roman orators wanted to memorize a long speech, they sometimes constructed an imaginary house, with images in each room. The images were linked, in their memory, to parts of their speech; as they delivered the speech, they would move through the house, and the images would help them remember their speech. The Hermetic philosophers of the Renaissance, such as Giordano Bruno, expanded this ancient mnemonic device into a way of committing the whole universe to memory. Bruno constructed "memory wheels," which used images to remind him of stones, metals, plants, animals, planets, and also to remind him of 150 historic figures, who in turn reminded him of world history, the history of science, and the history of ideas.

In Bruno's memory system, everything in the world was linked to everything else. Thus, Bruno's memory system symbolizes the basic Hermetic teaching that All is One, that the universe is an organic whole, that everything is connected to everything else. Not only are objects inter-connected, but also ideas, philosophies, religions. The Hermetists subscribed to a "perennial philosophy" that tried to synthesize philosophies and religions. In 1486, at the age of 23, Pico della Mirandola went to Rome with 900 theses drawn from various philosophies and religions, and offered to prove, in a public debate, that they were all compatible with each other. A later Hermetist, Athanasius Kircher, attempted an even grander synthesis; in 1652, Kircher

---

[1] Wikipedia, with some minor revisions.

attempted a "synthesis of all mystical traditions,"[1] including Mexico and Japan.

The Hermetic philosophers of the Renaissance believed that positive images would lead to positive thoughts; positive images possessed a kind of magical power, they were talismans that could mold personality. If we surrounded ourselves with Jovial and Venereal images, we could escape the influence of Saturn, and escape melancholy. Frances Yates argues that Botticelli's *Primavera* was a talisman designed to "transmit only healthful, rejuvenating, anti-Saturnian influences to the beholder."[2] Yates believed that an understanding of Hermetism and Hermetic magic was "necessary for the understanding of the meaning and use of a Renaissance work of art." Early Hermetists, like Marsilio Ficino, were content to use images to chase away melancholy, but later Hermetists, like Bruno, tried to use images to bring the whole universe into their mind, and develop various kinds of magical power:

> By using magical or talismanic images as memory-images, the Magus hoped to acquire universal knowledge, and also powers, obtaining through the magical organization of the imagination a magically powerful personality, tuned in, as it were, to the powers of the cosmos.[3]

Bruno's art of memory was a magic art that aimed, like other forms of magic, to bring about results.

Another Renaissance Hermetist, Tommaso Campanella, aimed at developing an ideal society rather than an individual Magus. In 1602, Campanella described this ideal society in a book called *City of the Sun*. In the middle of Campanella's ideal city was a temple that contained a map of the heavens, and another map of the world. On the walls of Campanella's city were depicted all plants and animals (and the stars that influenced them), and all arts and sciences (and the heroes who developed them). Campanella's religion is, like Bruno's, a religion of

---

[1] Frances Yates, *Giordano Bruno and the Hermetic Tradition*, ch. 21
[2] Ibid, ch. 4
[3] Ibid, ch. 11

6. SUNDRY THOUGHTS

the world, a religion that views the universe as an inter-connected organism. God is everywhere, life is everywhere.

The Renaissance attitude toward images has analogues in our own time. Jungians speak of images that represent wholeness. A Tibetan mandala, for example, or a Navajo sand painting, may depict psychological integration in a way that has beneficial effects for both the observer and the creator. Images of wholeness may come to us in dreams. Bruno admired the book *On Dreams*, by the Hellenistic writer Synesius; Synesius believed that "divine and miraculous images [were] impressed on the imagination in dreams."[1]

Are images more effective than words—more apt to enrich the personality, more easily stamped on the memory? Bruno and other Hermetists seemed to think so. Bruno thought that the best writing systems were image-based systems, ideogram systems— like Egyptian hieroglyphs, or Chinese characters. These ideogram systems (in Bruno's view) are in direct contact with reality (since they consist of pictures of actual things). Compared to these ideogram systems, sound systems (phonetic alphabets) like Greek, Latin and other European languages, are (in Bruno's view) a step backward.[2] Here, as elsewhere, Bruno (and many of his contemporaries) had a high opinion of the ancient Egyptians.

The Hermetic texts were ascribed to an ancient Egyptian, Hermes Trismegistus. The antiquity of Hermes enhanced his authority. The Bible and Greek philosophy were regarded as later, derivative works.

Turkish military power was a factor in popularizing the Hermetic texts in the West. Turkish pressure on the Byzantine empire prompted that empire to seek help from their fellow Christians in the West, and to resolve their religious differences with the West. At the Council of Florence in 1439, Byzantine scholars met Italian scholars, and they began lecturing on Plato, the Neoplatonic writers, and the Hermetic texts. In 1453, Constantinople finally fell to the Turks. Ficino began translating Plato into Latin. In 1463, Cosimo de Medici, Ficino's patron,

---

[1] Ibid, ch. 18. This is a quote from Yates, not from Bruno or Synesius.
[2] Ibid, ch. 14

asked him to lay aside his translation of Plato, and focus instead on the more important Hermetic texts.

The Hermetic texts remained influential for about 150 years. In 1614, a scholar named Isaac Casaubon demonstrated that the Hermetic texts weren't as ancient as people thought—they were later than the Bible, later than Greek philosophy. Casaubon's work undermined the authority of the Hermetic texts; philosophers like Descartes and scientists like Kepler further reduced the influence of Hermetism. But Hermetism didn't die out completely, and the debate between rational philosophy and non-rational philosophy continues to this day.

16. *Chinese Painting* In China, the most important type of painting was landscape painting. Like Western painting, Chinese painting began as figure painting. Not until around 900 A.D. did landscape become the dominant type of painting in China. In the West, landscape didn't become prominent until around 1800. Why was landscape a more important type of painting in China than in the West? And why did landscape painting develop much earlier in China than in the West?

1. In the West, cultural development was arrested during the long period known as the Dark Ages; during the Dark Ages, the accomplishments of the ancient Greeks and Romans were largely lost. In China, on the other hand, cultural development was more steady and continuous; China experienced nothing comparable to the Dark Ages.
2. The Chinese felt closer to nature than the West did. The Chinese saw man as part of the world, while the West saw man as the "master and proprietor of nature" (as Descartes put it); the West felt that it was man's task to "subdue the earth." The Chinese felt that the human spirit was akin to the spirit of the rest of the universe, while the West felt that man was special and different, that God had made only man in his own image, that God had endowed only man with an immortal soul.
3. The Chinese saw nature itself as divine, while the West felt that divinity was only in certain beings. The Western artist

concentrated on those divine beings (including man, who had a "divine spark," an immortal soul), while the Chinese artist concerned himself with all of nature.
4. The Chinese were more relaxed and more receptive to nature than Westerners were. Chinese religions like Taoism and Zen Buddhism encouraged quiescence and passivity. Westerners, on the other hand, were more active and busy, hence less receptive to nature, and less inclined toward landscape painting.

One can distinguish four types of Chinese landscape painting: Impressive Landscape, Appreciated Landscape, Plain Landscape and Quotation Landscape. Impressive Landscape is a product of the Northern Sung Dynasty (around 900 A.D.). In paintings of this school, nature is awesome and dramatic. The artist is inspired by nature itself, rather than by earlier painters. Impressive Landscape resembles the work of 19th-century Western artists like Turner.

Appreciated Landscape is a product of the Southern Sung Dynasty (around 1200 A.D.). In paintings of this school, nature is no longer awesome, and no longer towers over man. Man has become prominent. The artist depicts the cultured person who appreciates nature; the artist depicts not nature alone, but man's response to nature. This is rarely found in Western painting. Western painting, particularly the school known as Italian Landscape, often depicts a landscape that includes ruins. Such ruins inspire thoughts about past civilizations, thoughts about the march of time, etc. Far different are the thoughts of a person in a Southern Sung landscape. Such a person can appreciate nature because his head isn't full of thoughts. He's attuned to the present moment, not pondering past epochs. "I'd rather be here now" is a phrase that's sometimes used to epitomize Zen Buddhism. A person in a Southern Sung landscape is "here now"—in the present moment, not in the past or the future.

Plain Landscape is a product of the Yuan Dynasty (around 1300). Plain Landscape lacks the interesting details of Northern Sung landscape, and also lacks the sweetness of Southern Sung landscape. Plain Landscape makes no effort to please the viewer, no effort to attain popularity. Plain Landscape reflects the tranquillity of the artist's soul, and also his disdain for popularity, and his disdain for the tricks that lead to popularity.

Leading Chinese painters were rarely professionals; they often refused to accept money for their works, and they denigrated professionals as "artisan-painters." They were cultured people who practiced poetry and calligraphy, as well as painting—all on a non-professional basis. They had no respect for the technical devices of professional painters. They didn't take their painting seriously; they often spoke of a painter "playing with his brush, to amuse himself."

Plain Landscape is a type of painting that reflects these values. Chinese critics admire Plain Landscape because they admire the cultured person who creates it. They believed that, "the quality of the painting reflects the quality of the man." Likewise, in the literary sphere, Chinese critics believed that good prose could be written only by a good man. The creator is more important than the creation. Chinese culture was a humanistic culture in which man himself came first. The supreme value was a good man leading a good life. The Chinese believed that, "it is man who makes truth great, not truth which makes man great."

Quotation Landscape is the final phase of Chinese landscape painting, and it was produced during China's last dynasty, the Qing Dynasty. Artists no longer responded directly to nature; rather, they responded to earlier artists, and quoted earlier styles.

But Qing Dynasty artists were not entirely uncreative. Qing painters began to bend reality more than earlier Chinese painters had done; in the 1700's Chinese painters were bending reality as much as van Gogh and Gauguin did. But Chinese painting never took the step that Western painting took after van Gogh and Gauguin—that is, it never became entirely abstract, it always retained some connection to the external world. Some Qing painters, such as Shih-t'ao, achieved what great culture often achieves, namely, a synthesis of subjective vision and objective truth.

17. *Borrowed and Transplanted Cultures* Rome went to school in Greece, then produced first-rate poets, but never produced a

philosopher equal to the leading Greek philosophers. Japan went to school in China, then produced first-rate poets and imaginative writers, but never produced a philosopher equal to the leading Chinese philosophers. Russia went to school in Western Europe, then produced first-rate imaginative writers, but never produced a philosopher equal to the leading Western European philosophers. One can infer from these three examples that borrowed cultures can achieve great richness and creativity, but can't produce first-rate philosophers.

Transplanted cultures—such as those of the Americas, Australia, and other colonized places—are often less healthy than borrowed cultures. Transplanted cultures often fail to achieve the richness and creativity of borrowed cultures. The weakness of transplanted culture is apparent in both art and philosophy. Culture can't flourish in a raw, uncivilized land; when colonists arrive in such a land, they're preoccupied with survival, with practical matters, with exploring and taming the land. They have little interest in culture, which requires stability and leisure. As the land is gradually tamed, interest in culture grows; the finest fruits of American culture have grown in New England, where the land has been settled and civilized for the longest time.

Cultures don't remain immature forever; eventually both borrowed cultures and transplanted cultures reach maturity.

18. *Hitler and Ibsen* Hitler once told his secretary that he didn't want to have children, because the children of genius are often cretins. Hitler's comment shows not only that he was convinced of his own genius, but also that he was a student of genius, of the psychology of genius. Hitler's sense of identity, his sense of who he was, was determined in large measure by the Cult of Genius, a cult that he probably acquired from his favorite philosopher, Schopenhauer. Hitler felt that his genius made him the natural leader of Germany.

Hitler seems to have had Multiple Personality Disorder. Like most people who have this disorder, he was abused as a child. He later told his secretary how he coped with abuse by creating an alter ego, a second personality:

> [I] resolved never again to cry when my father whipped me. A few days later I had the opportunity of putting my will to the test. My mother, frightened, took refuge in the front of the door. As for me, I counted silently the blows of the stick which lashed my rear end.

That is, he dissociated a part of himself from the self that was being beaten—as if he were acting in a play, and at the same time watching the play.

As a teenager, Hitler was out of school and out of work, and he spent much of his time watching plays and operas. Later, when he became a politician, he would arrange his speaking schedule based on where his favorite operas were being performed. Multiple Personality Disorder is characterized by a disintegration of the ego, and by a facility for being hypnotized. One might say that Hitler didn't merely watch plays and operas, he was hypnotized by them. He identified with the characters, he lived their lives.

One play that Hitler attended was *The King*, by Hanns Johst. Hitler later met Johst, and told him that he had seen *The King* seventeen times, and that he himself would die in the same manner as the king in Johst's play. And in fact, he did.

But Hitler's strongest identification was with the protagonist of Ibsen's *Emperor and Galilean*, Julian the Apostate. Indeed, Hitler seemed to believe that he was Julian reincarnated. Hitler's identification with Julian had a profound influence on his life and career. It influenced the most dramatic events in his personal life, such as the suspicious death of his niece, Geli Raubal. It also influenced the most momentous events of his career, such as his decision not to aim for Moscow during his invasion of Russia.

It may seem odd that Hitler would regard himself as Julian reincarnated. It should be remembered, though, that Hitler was receptive to all forms of the occult. Furthermore, Hitler's guru, Dietrich Eckart, believed that he was the reincarnation of one of Ibsen's most famous characters, Peer Gynt. Unlike Julian, Peer Gynt is a fictional character, so the idea of being Peer Gynt reincarnated is even odder than the idea of being Julian reincarnated. Yet that's what Eckart believed, and Hitler revered Eckart. "He shone in our eyes like the polar star," Hitler said of Eckart.

The connection between Ibsen and Hitler remained unknown for half a century, until it was discovered by an American scholar, Steven Sage. Apparently, Hitler never told anyone that he was following Ibsen's scripts; he carried this secret to his grave. The Hitler that emerges from Sage's book is the most remarkable example of life imitating art.

After showing how Hitler followed Ibsen's plays, Sage compares Hitler to other examples of "mimetic syndrome," including John Wilkes Booth following Shakespeare, and the Unabomber following Joseph Conrad.

In Ibsen's *Emperor and Galilean*, it is said that Julian may be a reincarnation of Christ, and that another incarnation would take place in the future. Hitler seemed to feel that he was Christ reborn, as well as Julian reborn. Hitler said he began his political career at 30, just as Christ began his mission at 30. Hitler often carried a whip, and threatened to "enter Berlin like Christ in the Temple of Jerusalem and scourge out the moneylenders."[1] Like many other anti-Semites, Hitler viewed Christ not as a Jew, but as a Gentile; mixing the words "Gaul" and "Galilee," anti-Semites argued that Christ was born into a colony of retired Gallic soldiers.

Before Sage made his discovery about Hitler, some people realized that Hitler was fundamentally an actor playing various roles. The philosopher Emil Fackenheim said, "I don't think he knew the difference between acting and believing. Of course, it's a shocking thing to consider that six million Jews were murdered because of an actor." The Dutch writer Harry Mulisch said, "Perhaps Hitler, the man of the theater... had only played theatrically with toy soldiers, albeit of flesh and blood."[2]

19. *Wild Fruits* Thoreau said that wild fruits taste better than farm-grown fruits. Likewise, cutting-edge theories are more exciting, more tasty, than textbook theories. An example of a

---

[1] Steven Sage, *Ibsen and Hitler*, ch. 4
[2] Ibid, ch. 15

cutting-edge theory is The Ibsen-Hitler Theory. This theory isn't in any encyclopedia or textbook—it isn't even in Wikipedia. Cutting-edge theories are the wild fruits of the intellectual world.

20. *Kierkegaard* Kierkegaard's life is, in several respects, typical of the life of the intellectual, the literary person.

Kierkegaard's life was short, but filled with high drama. His life was even shorter than Oscar Wilde's (he died at 42, Wilde at 46), and his life was even more dramatic than Wilde's. The three pivotal events in Kierkegaard's life were his brief engagement to Regina Olsen, the ridicule poured on him by a Danish newspaper (*The Corsair*), and his public attack on the established church (Lutheran church). Kierkegaard anticipated that his dramatic life would be of greater interest to posterity than his writings: "Some day," he wrote, "not only my writings but especially my life will be studied and studied."[1]

Kierkegaard was born in Copenhagen, Denmark in 1813. Like Schopenhauer, Kierkegaard lived on inherited money. Kierkegaard's father was a hosier (a maker of socks and hose), who enjoyed a monopoly granted by the Danish king. Kierkegaard revered his father, all the more so after his father died; he dedicated many of his books to his father, describing him as "late hosier of this city." "My father's death," Kierkegaard wrote, "was a terribly harrowing event for me, I never told a single soul how terrible it was."[2] While Kierkegaard's books and journals are filled with references to his father, he never mentioned his mother, a servant girl whom his father had made pregnant, and then married.

As a boy, Kierkegaard spent his time with books, or with his father, he didn't play with other children or with toys. Sometimes his father would take him by the hand, and they would walk back and forth in the house, pretending that they were outside:

---

[1] *Kierkegaard*, by Walter Lowrie, I, 2
[2] *The Journals of Soren Kierkegaard*, edited by A. Dru, long version, Oxford University Press, 1938, #775. Freud said that a father's death was "the most important event, the most poignant loss, of a man's life."

6. SUNDRY THOUGHTS

They went out of doors to a near-by castle in Spain, or out to the sea-shore, or about the streets, wherever [Soren] wished to go, for the father was equal to anything. While they went back and forth in the room the father described all that they saw; they greeted passers-by, carriages rattled past them and drowned the father's voice; the cake-woman's goodies were more enticing than ever.[1]

Kierkegaard said that his father was a man of iron will, a trait that he passed on to his son. Few people have had more will power, more inwardness than Kierkegaard. Here's how Kierkegaard dealt with academic problems:

> if after an hour he was tired of the effort, he used to employ a very simple method. He shut himself up in his room, made everything as festive as possible and said then in a voice loud and clear, I will it. He had learnt from his father that one can what one will.... This experience had imparted to [Soren's] soul an indescribable sort of pride. It was intolerable to him that there should be anything one could not do if only one would.[2]

Even as a youth, Kierkegaard had his father's melancholy. "I was already an old man when I was born," Kierkegaard wrote. "I leapt completely over childhood and youth. I lived through the pain of not being like others. And of course at that period I would have given all to be able to be that, if only for a short time." Like most writers and artists, especially philosophers, Kierkegaard was highly introverted: "he never in his life confided in anyone or expected anyone to confide in him."[3] Introversion and melancholy often go hand-in-hand.

With his tremendous will power, and his tremendous talent, Kierkegaard felt that he could do whatever he set out to do, except for one thing: to cast off his melancholy. He had the enormous confidence in himself, in his genius, that one finds in Schopenhauer: "It never at any time occurred to me," wrote Kierkegaard, "that there lived a man who was my superior, or

---

[1] *Kierkegaard*, by Walter Lowrie, I, 2
[2] ibid
[3] ibid, II, 3

that in my time such a man might be born."[1] But he also had the melancholy that one finds in Schopenhauer: "I was the most miserable of all," wrote Kierkegaard. According to Aristotle, "all geniuses are melancholy." In the last year of his life, Kierkegaard discovered Schopenhauer, and read him with keen interest; perhaps he recognized in Schopenhauer his equal, if not his superior.

Though Kierkegaard had large eyes and a handsome face, he was very small, and had a misshapen spine. As a result, "one could never keep to a straight line in walking with him," said one of his friends; "one was constantly pushed against the houses or the cellar stairs or over the curb-stone. When at the same time he was gesticulating with his arms or his cane, it became still more like an obstacle-race. And one had to seize the opportunity now and then to get on the other side of him so as to gain room."[2]

Kierkegaard often walked the streets of Copenhagen, and while walking, he sometimes conducted "psychological experiments."

> With one glance at a passer-by he was able to put himself irresistibly *en rapport* with him, as he himself expressed it. The person who encountered his glance was either attracted or repelled, thrown into embarrassment, uncertainty, or irritation.... While he explained his theories he put them into practice with almost every person we encountered. There was not one upon whom his glance did not make an impression.

One is reminded of a remark by Proust's maid: "the look that was always so strong that you felt it watching or following you."[3]

During one walk, Kierkegaard encountered Goldschmidt, the editor of the *Corsair*. This newspaper had made fun of Kierkegaard's odd appearance, until finally Kierkegaard had become the laughing-stock of the entire nation; he couldn't go anywhere without people laughing at him. When Kierkegaard met Gold-

---

[1] ibid, II, 1
[2] ibid, II, 3
[3] *Monsieur Proust, a memoir*, by Celeste Albaret, ch. 28

schmidt in the street, he passed him (Goldschmidt later wrote) "with a staring embittered glance, without greeting or wishing to be greeted." Then Goldschmidt realized Kierkegaard's "lofty ideality," which lay beneath his witty surface, and which Goldschmidt had a "presentiment" of. Kierkegaard's lofty ideality "accused me and crushed me; before I had got to the end of the street on my way home it was decided that I should give up the *Corsair*."[1]

Goldschmidt was crushed by Kierkegaard's moral strength, by the power of Kierkegaard's inwardness, by the power of his silence. Though Kierkegaard was a master of language, of metaphor, of style, his greatest strength was his silence.

> Silence and action correspond to one another perfectly [Kierkegaard wrote]. Silence is the measure of the power to act. A man has never more power to act than he has power to be silent.... When a man talks about doing a thing, it is a sign that he is not sure of himself.[2]

When Kierkegaard was about 25, he met a 14-year-old girl, Regina Olsen, and fell in love with her at first sight. He waited for three long years before broaching the subject of marriage. She told him that she was fond of one of her former teachers, Fritz Schlegel. Kierkegaard said, "You could talk about Fritz Schlegel till doomsday—that wouldn't help you in the least, for I will have you."[3] And sure enough, Regina eventually agreed to become engaged.

The next day, Kierkegaard realized that he had made a mistake. As long as he was courting her, and trying to win her, he had no doubts, but once she said "Yes," he had second thoughts. He described the situation thus (referring to himself as "he"):

> So long as the contest lasted he did not observe any difficulty—then she surrendered, he was loved with a young girl's whole enthusiasm—then he became unhappy, then his melancholy was

---

[1] ibid, IV, 2
[2] ibid, I, 2
[3] ibid, III, 1

awakened, then he drew back, he could combat the whole world, but not himself.[1]

Like many intellectuals, Kierkegaard was ambivalent about marriage. Kafka wrestled for years with the question of marriage; "the idea of a honeymoon," said Kafka, "fills me with dread."[2] Kafka read about Kierkegaard, and saw similarities between his situation and Kierkegaard's. The idea of marriage filled Kierkegaard with dread. He said that his love made him indescribably happy in the moment, but as soon as he thought of time he despaired. He didn't have enough Zen to live in the moment, to live outside time. "I was a thousand years too old for her."

Kierkegaard decided that he would have to break the engagement. He later wrote, "I suffered indescribably in that period.... It is so hard, upon her I had set my last hope in life, and I must deprive myself of it."[3] He sent her back the ring. But she resisted, "beseeching him in the name of Christ and by the memory of his deceased father not to desert her." He decided that he must do something to wean her from him, to weaken her love for him. He pretended to be a scoundrel who was playing with her affections. Though he was busy with literary projects, he went to the theater every night for ten minutes. Since he was well known in Copenhagen, he knew that someone would tell Regina, "he goes to the theater every night."

After two months, she agreed to break the engagement. When Kierkegaard left her house, he went to the theater. There he was accosted by Regina's father:

> "May I speak with you?" I followed him to his home. She is desperate, he said; this will be the death of her, she is perfectly desperate. I said, I shall still be able to tranquillize her, but the matter is settled. He said, I am a proud man, this is hard, but I beseech you not to break with her. In truth he was proud, he touched me deeply. But I held to my own. I took supper with the family that evening. I talked with her, then I left.

---

[1] ibid, III, 2, i, a
[2] *Makers of the Modern World*, by Louis Untermeyer, "Kafka"
[3] *Kierkegaard*, W. Lowrie, III, 1

6. SUNDRY THOUGHTS

Next morning I got a letter from him saying that he had not slept all night, that I must come and see her. I went and talked her round. She asked me, Will you never marry? I replied, Well, in about ten years, when I have sown my wild oats, I must have a pretty young miss to rejuvenate me. She said, Forgive me for what I have done to you. I replied, It is rather I that should pray for your forgiveness. She said, Kiss me. That I did, but without passion.... In parting she begged me still to remember her once in a while.... I passed the night weeping in my bed. But in the daytime I was as usual, more flippant and witty than usual—that was necessary. My brother said to me that he would go to the family and show them that I was not a scoundrel. I said: You do that and I will shoot a bullet through your head.[1]

So Kierkegaard broke his engagement to Regina. The people of Copenhagen were scandalized, and regarded Kierkegaard as the scoundrel that he had pretended to be. Kierkegaard vowed to himself not to love another woman: "Thou art to know that thou dost regard it as thy happiness never to have loved another besides her, that thou dost make it a point of honor never again to love another."[2] He kept this vow. Regina later married her former teacher, Fritz Schlegel. Shortly before her engagement to Schlegel, she caught sight of Kierkegaard in church:

> I let her catch my eye. She nodded twice. I shook my head. That meant, you must give me up. Then she nodded again, and I nodded as kindly as possible—that meant, you retain my love.[3]

The impact of this relationship lasted for the rest of Kierkegaard's life; many of Kierkegaard's books and journal entries allude to this relationship. He summarized the relationship thus: "She did not love my well-formed nose, nor my fine eyes, nor my small feet—nor my high intelligence—she loved only me, and yet she did not understand me."[4]

Although Kierkegaard had been raised as a Christian, whatever faith he had diminished as he grew older. By the time he

---

[1] ibid
[2] ibid
[3] ibid, III, 2, i, B
[4] ibid, III, 1

was 23, he had fallen into nihilism, and he thought seriously of suicide. But when he was 25, his father died, and that shattering event started him on his climb back from nihilism. When he was 28, his engagement to Regina ended, and his attitude toward life became even more serious. He was no longer living apart from life, living against life.

When he was 35, he finally attained the Christian faith that he had long sought. He finally became whole, he finally overcame his melancholy and his nihilism. He confided to his journal, "My whole nature is changed.... Now by God's help I shall become myself, I believe now that Christ will help me to triumph over my melancholy."[1] He spoke of, "an unfailing and ever-fresh source of joy: that God is love."[2] He learned to love not only God, but himself as well: "it is required of me that I should love myself and renounce the melancholy hatred of myself which in a melancholy man can be almost a pleasure."[3]

Even when his health was good, Kierkegaard sensed that he would die young. Feeling that time was short, he worked hard, and wrote much. When he turned 36, he looked back on the previous year: "I produced more powerfully than ever before, but more than ever before like a dying man."[4] Just as he produced with a feeling that time was limited, so too he spent his inheritance with a feeling that time was limited, withdrawing the last of his money just before he died. When he entered the hospital, he said that his illness was psychic, and that he had come there to die. His race was run, his destiny fulfilled.

In his final years, when Regina was married to Fritz Schlegel, Kierkegaard wanted to re-connect with her, and become a friend of her family. But his overtures were rebuffed; the door was closed to him. Kierkegaard died in 1855, at age 42. The people who had touched him most deeply were his father and

---

[1] ibid, V, 1
[2] *The Journals of Soren Kierkegaard*, edited by A. Dru, long version, Oxford University Press, 1938, #752
[3] *Kierkegaard*, by Walter Lowrie, V, 3
[4] ibid, V, 1

6. SUNDRY THOUGHTS 135

Regina: "I owe everything that I am to the wisdom of an old man and the simplicity of a young girl."[1]

21. *In Sync: A Dialogue*

A What's the weather like in *Macbeth*?

B Stormy, isn't it?

A Not just stormy—violently stormy, unprecedentedly stormy. Not only is the weather stormy, but animals are behaving strangely. Nature is disturbed, and this disturbance goes hand-in-hand with the disturbance in the human sphere, in the political sphere. Nature and man are part of the same whole. But the disturbance in nature doesn't *cause* the human disturbance, nor is it *caused by* the human disturbance. They're linked together, but it's not a causal link. This linkage between nature and man is found not only in *Macbeth*, but also in *Hamlet, Julius Caesar*, etc. It's an important part of Shakespeare's worldview.

B But couldn't it be just a dramatic device?

A Perhaps, but you must admit that this aspect of Shakespeare is strikingly similar to Jung's idea of synchronicity. Jung defines synchronicity as an acausal connecting principle; synchronicity helps us to understand the linkage between nature and the human realm. The agreement between Jung and Shakespeare strengthens the argument that Shakespeare is depicting the world as he understands it, not just employing a dramatic device. Truth agrees with itself and confirms itself.

B Where did Shakespeare get this worldview?

A It seems to be a very ancient worldview, and very widespread. It's part of the folk wisdom of mankind, and it's probably found in every corner of the world. The Chinese have always believed in acausal linkage, in synchronicity. Instead of looking for causal relationships, linear relationships, they looked for clusters of things, for things that often

---

[1] ibid, III, 1

occur together. They felt that the death of an emperor often occurred in the same cluster as an earthquake. So now we have an agreement not only between Shakespeare and Jung, but between Shakespeare, Jung, the Chinese, and the folk wisdom of mankind.

B You've brought a lot of people into your "synchronicity synthesis." Who's left out?

A Left out is Western scientific-rationalism, which begins with Descartes in the early 1600s, and continues with Newton. This sort of rationalism sees the world in terms of linear causality instead of synchronistic clusters. And perhaps we should also leave out the ancient Greek rationalists.

B So the synchronicity worldview is at odds with science?

A Actually, no. Quantum physics has much the same worldview; it sees acausal connections, occult connections; it sees separate parts of the universe acting in sync with each other. So modern science has put its "seal of approval" on this ancient worldview.

22. *Team Player* It's great to be a team player—if the team is on track. But if the team is off track, if the team is "up to no good," then it isn't a virtue to be a team player, it's a vice. Of all the vices to which mortal flesh is liable, surely this is the most common: to be a team player when you shouldn't be, to "go with the flow" when you should stand alone.

23. *Group Loyalty* If we are loyal to ideals—cultural and spiritual ideals—we won't have much loyalty to nation/school/ business/institution; individual ideals will take precedence over group ideals. Most writers—Joyce, Nietzsche, Ibsen, etc.—had little national feeling; indeed, they were often sharp critics of their nation, just as the Hebrew prophets were sharp critics of their nation. "Self-culture," wrote Wilde, "is the true ideal of man"—self-culture, not group loyalty. If someone criticizes you for a shortage of loyalty to nation/school/business/institution,

6. SUNDRY THOUGHTS 137

remind him that a model of group loyalty is a Nazi rally at Nuremberg.

24. *Senatus Bestia* If someone talks to you about the importance of consensus-building, remind him of the Roman adage, *senatores boni viri, senatus bestia* (senators are good men, the senate is a beast). Conscience is in the individual, not in the group. Instead of trying to build a consensus, instead of basing your decisions on other people's views, base your decision on your own view of what's right.

25. *Individuals and Institutionals* There are two kinds of people in the world, individuals and institutionals. An individual is a person who has a mind of his own and a conscience of his own. An institutional is a person who is at home in an institution, who knows how to play the game, who knows what direction the tide is flowing in, whose mind and conscience are not his own, but belong to the world around him.

26. *Perfect Bureaucrat* Institutions are sometimes founded by idealists, but they're perpetuated by bureaucrats. The perfect bureaucrat is subservient toward superiors, ruthless toward inferiors. Kiss up, kick down.

27. *Professional* In recent years, "professional" has become one of the highest compliments that a person can receive. One who is "professional" draws a sharp line between his career and his personal life; he doesn't allow personal feelings to intrude on his work life. The aspiration to be "professional" makes people into masks.

While the model executive is a cool professional, the model retail worker is a "fun person." Restaurants advertise for "smiling faces" and claim to have "great food, fun people."

28. *Saturnine* "Hiring Smiling Faces" reads a sign at McDonald's, and doubtless many companies follow the same policy. What chance does a poor philosopher, who rarely smiles, have of landing a job? Don't melancholics deserve an equal opportunity?

Should we be discriminated against just because we were born under Saturn? Should doors be closed to us because we're saturnine, not jovial?

29. *The Leader* There is a cult of leadership in the U.S. Numerous books discuss leadership, and business schools teach classes in leadership. As one observer put it, "The 'romance of leadership' that is common in the business world tends to put top executives on a pedestal."[1]

The leader hides his feelings, and ignores the feelings of others. He is ruthless in pursuing his institution's interests, or his own interests. He makes rules, but he doesn't follow rules; to him belongs the privilege of violating both legal and moral rules. Is it surprising, then, that many of today's business leaders are in prison or under indictment? As the Good Book says, "Pride goeth before destruction, and an haughty spirit before a fall." The Leadership Disease is widespread in American society, and affects countless institutions.

One student of The Leadership Disease traced it to narcissism, which gives one "an unrealistic sense of one's importance and power.... Narcissism is an occupational hazard of the corporate world.... 'it's fairly prevalent in organizations.'"[2]

30. *Homo Homini Lupus* The abuse of Iraqi prisoners by American guards is further evidence (if any were needed) that evil is embedded in human nature. Long ago, the Romans said *homo homini lupus* (man is a wolf to man), but somehow we think that this doesn't apply to us, and we're surprised to find that it still applies, that the goblins have returned, and always will return.

Another Roman saying is also applicable to this incident: *senatores boni viri, senatus bestia.* People who are individually decent can become depraved when they're in a group; moral restraints that are effective when a person is alone become ineffective when the same person is in a group.

---

[1] *New York Times*, July 29, 2002
[2] ibid

6. SUNDRY THOUGHTS

31. *Merely Means* Kant said that man is an end in himself, while animals are merely means. As one grows older, one finds to one's sorrow that people often treat you like one of Kant's animals, that is, they treat you as merely a means—a means to their own ends. They use you and then, when you're no longer useful to them, they discard you. Every teenager is told by his elders, "Beware! People will mistreat you! People will use you for their own purposes!" But the teenager doesn't believe it, he must learn it from his own bitter experience. *Homo homini lupus.* This is a fundamental law of human nature, applicable to the relations between nations as well as to the relations between individuals.[1]

32. *Digital Malice* Philosophers and psychologists are agreed: man has a dark side, an evil side, a sadistic side, a shadow. We know this from history, from literature, from observing others, from observing ourselves. We find this dark side in primitive peoples and civilized peoples alike.

Now the world is changing, computers are becoming widespread, the Internet is expanding. And we're always on the lookout for viruses, worms, hackers, etc., we don't dare to boot up without our anti-virus program. We spend billions defending ourselves against digital malice. As the old saying goes, "the more things change, the more they stay the same."

33. *Moral Order* There seems to be a moral order in the universe. Evil—such as we find in Hitler, Stalin, Macbeth, etc.—eventually comes to grief. On the other hand, evil often brings many innocents down with it; one might say that the moral order punishes evil, but doesn't always reward virtue. Furthermore, if we look for the source of evil, we find that the universe itself

---

[1] John Stuart Mill: "How often, when smarting under some unforeseen misfortune or disappointment, does a person call to mind some proverb or common saying familiar to him all his life, the meaning of which, if he had ever before felt it as he does now, would have saved him from the calamity.... There are many truths of which the full meaning cannot be realized, until personal experience has brought it home."

produces Hitlers, Stalins, and Macbeths; in other words, the universe produces the very evil that it later destroys. Evil is almost as much a part of the fabric of the universe as good.

Evil allies itself with death and disintegration, while good fosters life. Evil is one-sided, extreme, monomaniacal, while good is balanced; "evil entails being swept away by one-sidedness, by only *one single* pattern of behavior."[1]

According to Freud, the great man is also one-sided. Evil figures, like Macbeth and Kurtz, often have a touch of greatness, and the great man often has a touch of evil. One who was acquainted with André Gide said, "There is no one more courtly... charming... amiable than Gide, and yet suddenly... he shows himself, just for an instant, as a real demon."[2]

34. *The Cost of Living* "Time is money", according to the old saying. This implies that you can make money in a given period of time. But what if the situation were reversed, what if it were necessary to *spend* money in order to exist for a given period of time? Imagine someone saying, "I plan to die at 75 because I can't afford to live any longer than that."

35. *The Young Intellectual* One of the biggest problems of an aspiring writer, a young intellectual, is that he doesn't get along well with people. One reason for this is that he doesn't respect anyone. "Is respect a feeling that's foreign to him?" No, quite the contrary. But he lavishes all his respect on those whom Keats called "the mighty dead," and he has none left for his contemporaries. This lack of respect for people is matched by a lack of respect for institutions: he respects neither academia nor the business world. Academia is, in his view, a pale imitation of the literary world to which his reading has introduced him, and business is a lot of sound and fury signifying nothing—or rather, signifying nothing except money.

The young intellectual's feelings, as well as his thoughts, cause him to clash with society. His feelings are often crude,

---

[1] Marie-Louise von Franz, *Shadow and Evil in Fairytales*, Part II, ch. 2
[2] *Conversations With Gide*, by Claude Mauriac, 7/1/39

primitive, unconscious. He is enlightened, and spreads enlightenment, but "the brighter the light, the darker the shadow." For every Faust, a Mephistopheles.

If one adds up all these factors—bad relations with people, lack of respect for people, an aversion for the academic world and the business world—it seems most unlikely that the young intellectual will have much success in the world.

36. *The intellectual in society* "[E. M. Forster] told me that, at parties, he always feels 'self-conscious *and* contemptuous.'"[1]

37. *Corners* On several occasions, he tried to fit into an institution, but he never succeeded, it was like fitting a square peg into a round hole—he had too many corners.

38. *Chiaroscuro* His wife could light up a room, and he could darken a room, so if the two of them were together, chiaroscuro effects were achieved that reminded some people of Rembrandt, and others of Caravaggio.

---

[1] *E. M. Forster: Interviews and Recollections*, by J. H. Stape; "The Diaries of Siegfried Sassoon", 4/28/22

7. Literature

1. *A good book* is the offspring of many fathers and the father of many offspring.

2. *From China* A sheet of paper contains the infinite.

3. *Writer's Goal* By art to attain simplicity.

4. *A good style* is simple and powerful, like a wave breaking on a beach.

5. *Simplicity* La Bruyère, knowing that many writers make the mistake of expressing simple things in a complex way, gave this advice to writers: "if you want to say that it is raining, say: 'It is raining'." Simplicity is the mark of good prose, and it's also a virtue in other branches of culture.
    The Greeks regarded simplicity as both a cultural virtue and a moral virtue. "Beauty of style," wrote Plato, "and harmony and grace and good rhythm depend on simplicity—I mean the true simplicity of a rightly and nobly ordered mind and character."[1] If

---

[1] Plato, *Republic*, 3

there is one quality that is lacking in modern culture, it is simplicity.

6. *Clarity* Serious writers strive to be understood, strive for clarity. Bad writers, on the other hand, aren't afraid of being obscure as long as they can make the reader think, "What an extensive vocabulary! What learning! What talent!" The surest sign of bad prose is the use of uncommon words where common words would suffice.

Clarity can be achieved by the repetition of certain words. Repetition is more comprehensible for the reader than variety. As Anatole France said, "You will find in my paragraphs a word that comes over and over again. That is the leit-motif of the symphony. Be careful not to delete and replace it by a synonym."[1] One of the most common stylistic mistakes is avoiding repetition, and replacing a previously-used word with a synonym.

But clarity alone doesn't make good prose; clarity must be combined with brevity. Good prose is so concise that every word has the importance of an italicized word.

7. *Henry James* As Henry James grew older, his style became more obscure. Here's a quote from James' *Turn of the Screw*: "My question had a sarcastic force that I had not fully intended, and it made her after a moment inconsequently break down."[2] My objection to this sentence (and to James' style in general) is that it is obscure. The word "inconsequently" is unnecessary, it muddies the water. Mark Twain said that if you see an adverb, kill it, and "inconsequently" is richly deserving of death. "But you just used an adverb yourself: richly." But "richly deserving" is a common expression, easily understood, while "inconsequently" is an unusual word, almost never heard in spoken English, and "inconsequently break down" is a strange, obscure phrase.

Here's another example of James' style: "It was impossible to have given less encouragement than he had administered to

---

[1] Jean Jacques Brousson, *Anatole France Himself*, "The Scissors"
[2] Ch. 16

such a doctrine."[1] This sentence would be clearer, easier for the reader to grasp, if James had written "it was impossible to have given less encouragement than he had given..." Repetition is easier for the reader to grasp than variety, and repeating the word "given" makes the sentence clearer than replacing "given" with "administered". Furthermore, who ever heard of 'administering encouragement to a doctrine'?

One final example: "I dare say I fancied myself in short a remarkable young woman and took comfort in the faith that this would more publicly appear."[2] This sentence is wordy, in my view, and could be improved by deleting the phrase "in short". "But the phrase 'in short' is needed for the sake of summing up and concluding." Then move 'in short' to the start of the sentence, and delete "I dare say", so the sentence would run: "In short, I fancied myself a remarkable young woman..."

James forfeits the right to use the phrase "in short" because he's never "short", he always chooses to take the long way around. James' prose has no music, no rhythm, no force. James' prose is obscure, and for a writer, obscurity is the sin against the Holy Ghost, the sin for which there is no forgiveness.

An Englishman once asked Tocqueville, "What do you consider your Golden Age?" Tocqueville responded, "The latter part of the seventeenth century.... Style then was the mere vehicle of thought. First of all to be perspicuous, and then being perspicuous, to be concise, was all they aimed at.... In the eighteenth century... ornament was added."[3] A writer should aim to be clear and concise, he should aim to communicate something to the reader. James, however, seems to regard style as an end itself, not as a vehicle of thought.

8. *Five Techniques* A good writer makes skillful use of five techniques: he addresses someone, gives orders, asks questions, makes exclamations, and repeats certain words. Addressing

---

[1] Ch. 13
[2] Ch. 3
[3] *Correspondence and Conversations of Alexis de Tocqueville With N. W. Senior*, 8/26/50

someone is sometimes described as the vocative case, while ordering someone, telling someone what to do, is sometimes described as the imperative case.

Shakespeare uses the vocative case, followed by the imperative case, when he makes Juliet say, "Romeo, doff thy name." Melville gives us an example of exclamation when he writes, "Nantucket! Take out your map and look at it." This passage also uses the imperative case. Thoreau gives us an example of the repetition of certain words when he writes, "Simplicity, simplicity, simplicity! I say, let your affairs be as two or three, and not a hundred or a thousand." This passage also uses exclamation. In one line of poetry, Virgil uses three techniques: he repeats a word, he addresses someone, and he asks a question: "Ah, Corydon, Corydon, what madness seized you?"[1] In a passage in his novel, *The Castle*, Kafka uses four techniques: he addresses someone, asks a question, makes an exclamation, and repeats certain words: "Do you hear that, Frieda? It's about you that he, he, wants to speak to Klamm, to Klamm!"

9. *Style*   Though it's possible to lay down rules for style, though it's possible to describe the ideal style, it's impossible to teach someone to write great prose. Style is an expression of personality. Great prose writers don't follow rules, they follow their taste. Great prose writers are born, not made.

Style and content are of equal importance; literature is a combination of style and content. Only a philistine would overlook style, and only a pedant would overlook content. If style is pursued for its own sake, it becomes artificial; style should be the vehicle of thought. In order to write well, one must have something to say. If one has something to say, if one has profound ideas and strong convictions, style comes naturally.

Great thinkers are great stylists, and great stylists are great thinkers. Plato, Kierkegaard and Nietzsche are considered models of Greek style, Danish style and German style respectively, and they're also the deepest thinkers that those three nations

---

[1] See Melville, *Moby Dick*, 14; Thoreau, *Walden*, 2; and Vergil, *Eclogues*, 2.

have produced. Emerson is the deepest thinker that America has produced, and also America's best prose writer.

10. *Everyday Poetry* Nicknames, store names, and advertising are the poetry of everyday life, and one finds in them many of the techniques that one finds in poetry.

11. *Reader and Writer* Reading is often a kind of friendship. The reader gets to know the author, and if he likes him, if he feels akin to him, a kind of friendship develops. (The saying "opposites attract" may apply to love, but it doesn't apply to friendship; friendship is based on kinship, on similarity of character.) Sometimes reading leads to actual friendship, friendship between living people; Emerson and Carlyle, for example, became friends after Emerson read Carlyle's writings. More often, however, reading leads to friendship at a distance—a distance in space or a distance in time.

The writer is sometimes a father figure rather than a friend. Shakespeare was a father figure to Goethe, and Schopenhauer was a father figure to Nietzsche. When a young reader idolizes a writer, he often wants to imitate the writer, to model his whole life after the writer. The young Victor Hugo, for example, said that he wanted to be "Chateaubriand or nothing." The young reader envies the accomplishments of the writer he admires, he wants to accomplish as much himself, and he's discouraged when he thinks of the great distance that separates him from the writer he admires. Like a hiker setting out to climb Mt. Everest, he feels that he must work hard, and strain himself to the breaking point, in order to reach his goal.

The sons of today are the fathers of tomorrow, and the youth who reveres a writer may someday become a revered writer himself. Nietzsche realized that he would someday be an idolized and envied father figure, just as Schopenhauer had been a father figure to him. Thus, Nietzsche makes the young man say to Zarathustra, "it is *envy* of you which has destroyed me."[1] While self-satisfaction makes life easy and pleasant, envy makes life

---

[1] *Thus Spoke Zarathustra*, "Of the Tree on the Mountainside"

difficult and painful. Greatness is forged in suffering. Dissatisfaction with oneself, coupled with reverence for someone else, spurs one to great accomplishments. Envy has positive effects when it aims not to lower someone else to your level, but rather to raise yourself to someone else's level. Every great man was once a youth who envied someone else, was dissatisfied with himself, and was spurred to great accomplishments by his envy and dissatisfaction. Every great man was once a youth who revered greatness.

12. *Two Worlds* There are two worlds: the literary world, and the world that's known as the "real world." A serious writer is consumed by literature, hence the literary world is more real for him than the "real world." As Kafka said, "My whole being is directed toward literature." When Thomas Wolfe was 22, he wrote,

> There is nothing so commonplace, so dull, that it is not touched with nobility and dignity. And I intend to wreak out my soul on paper and express it all.... I will know this country when I am through as I know the palm of my hand, and I will put it on paper and make it true and beautiful.... This is what my life means to me: I am at the mercy of this thing, and I will do it or die.... I will write, write, write. [1]

It's impossible for a writer to explain his attitude toward literature to someone who lives in the "real world." As Kafka said to his fiancée, Felice, "you were unable to appreciate the immense power my work has over me."

13. *What is the purpose of literature?* The purpose of literature, like the purpose of art in general, is to make life more palatable to people, more interesting, richer. Art provides pleasure, stimulation, inspiration. Art doesn't have to teach, it doesn't have to be moral or religious or political or philosophical. There are great imaginative writers who don't teach us anything, just as a composer of music doesn't teach us anything.

---

[1] Letter to his mother, written when he was 22.

14. *Is Beauty Universal?* Beauty is neither universal nor timeless, it fades with distance and time. An imaginative writer from ancient Greece has little appeal for most modern readers; ancient Greek writers appeal only to scholars. Westerners find little enjoyment in Eastern culture; the poets of China and Japan are enjoyed only by a few Western scholars.

Eastern painting is more enjoyable to Westerners than Eastern literature. The beauty of fine art reaches further, and lasts longer, than the beauty of literature. And the beauty of music lasts longer than the beauty of fine art. Music is the most universal, the most timeless, of the arts.

15. *Educated Laymen* A culture of scholars isn't a healthy culture. A culture that is preoccupied with recapturing the faded beauty of old classics isn't a healthy culture. But a popular culture that appeals chiefly to uneducated people is also unhealthy. The best culture is a culture that appeals to educated laymen. The best culture respects the old classics, but it also respects the pleasure that contemporary artists provide. The best culture avoids the sterility of scholar culture, and also avoids the barbarism of popular culture. Modern culture isn't healthy, it isn't a culture of educated laymen. Modern culture is divided between sterile scholar culture and barbaric popular culture.

16. *Goethe* Goethe's novels have little interest for modern readers. Gide described one of Goethe's novels as "unbelievably silly"; Gide said that Goethe "could not have written it at present."[1] Like Goethe's novels, Scott's novels strike modern readers as dull, though they were once considered immortal classics. There is a certain progression in the history of the novel, a progression that has relegated many early novelists, including Scott and Goethe, to obscurity. The history of the novel casts doubt on the old theory that art, unlike science, is timeless and never progresses.

---

[1] *The Journals of André Gide: 1889-1949* (edited and abridged by Justin O'Brien), 7/25/40

Goethe's poetry, like most poetry, holds little attraction for those who read it in translation. (As Robert Frost said, "poetry is what gets lost in translation.") Goethe's best works, for those who read him in translation, are his autobiography and his conversations, as recorded by Eckermann. His autobiography is as pleasurable to read as Rousseau's autobiography, and his conversations with Eckermann are more interesting than Boswell's *Life of Johnson*. Nietzsche said that Goethe's conversations with Eckermann was the best German book.[1]

17. *Letters* During the early 1500's, collections of Erasmus' letters were in greater demand than any other book. Voltaire's letters from Ferney were so lively and witty that they were handed around Paris. It is said that Voltaire's writing is at its best in his letters. Letter-writing affords writers a freedom that they aren't afforded by any other type of writing.

18. *Personal, Interesting* The most interesting literature is the most personal literature: biographies, autobiographies, diaries, letters and conversations.

19. *Reading*[2] When you read a quotation, you learn about the author and the quoter. Reading quotations is reading squared.

Wilde said that criticism (commentary on someone else's writings) is the highest form of autobiography.

"Next to the originator of a good sentence," Emerson wrote, "is the first quoter of it."

20. *Valuable Service* One of the most valuable services that a writer can perform for a reader is to call his attention to good writers. This isn't only a service to the reader, it's also a service to the writers—developing a reputation for an unknown writer, or reviving the reputation of a writer who is sinking into oblivion. Regarding his translation of Ruskin, Proust wrote, "I believe that each of us has charge of the souls that he particularly loves, charge of making them known and loved, of avoiding for

---

[1] *The Wanderer and the Shadow* , #109

them the slights of misunderstandings, and the night... of oblivion."[1]

21. *Maturing Taste* Psychologists often say that the individual repeats, in his own development, the development of the human race as a whole. The individual repeats the religious history of mankind by beginning life with the earliest forms of religion, animism and totemism; that is, he begins life by believing that inanimate objects and animals have feelings and thoughts similar to his own.

The individual repeats the literary history of mankind by beginning life with the earliest forms of literature, fairy tales and animal fables. By age ten, we've graduated from fairy tales to myths, just as mankind once graduated from fairy tales to myths. At fifteen, we're able to read early novelists like Defoe and Dumas. At twenty, we're able to read later novelists like Dostoyevsky and Tolstoy. Not until twenty-five are we able to read modern novelists like Proust and Joyce.

22. *Keats* is one of the most remarkable talents in English literature. His life was short (he died at 26), and his complete works would scarcely fill a thin volume. Though he is best known for his poetry, his letters are also literary works of considerable value.

Born into the working class, Keats had little formal education. At age 14, he fell in love with literature, and began to read voraciously. His enthusiasm for the classics, especially poetry, was such that, at age 21, he stayed up all night with his former teacher and read Homer in Chapman's translation. In the morning, still without sleep, he composed the immortal sonnet, "On First Looking Into Chapman's Homer."

Keats knew that poetry was his calling; he was determined to be a poet. He also knew that he would die young; "even while his health was good, Keats felt a foreboding of early death, and

---

[1] *The Cambridge Companion to Proust*, "Ruskin and the cathedral of lost souls", by Diane R. Leonard

applied himself to his art with a desperate urgency."[1] Keats asked

> for ten years, that I may overwhelm
> Myself in poesy; so I may do the deed
> That my own soul has to itself decreed.[2]

Keats said that his models (in life and in art) were the "mighty dead." Keats had confidence in his own work: "I think I shall be among the English poets after my death."[3]

All these traits are characteristic of a great writer: the enthusiasm for literature, the determination to be a writer, emulation of the "mighty dead," and confidence in one's own work.

23. *Chekhov* depicts people whose romantic visions are shattered by day-to-day living. No matter what they're doing, they always wish that they were doing something else, and no matter where they are, they always wish that they were somewhere else. They remind one of Socrates' comment about marriage: if you get married you'll regret it, and if you don't get married you'll regret that, too. Chekhov's characters also remind one of Flaubert's character, Madame Bovary, who found that reality never lived up to her expectations; Chekhov must have been influenced by Flaubert.

Layevsky, a character in Chekhov's story, "The Duel," is typical of Chekhov's characters. "Two years ago," Chekhov writes, "when [Layevsky] fell in love with Nadyezhda Fyodorovna, it seemed to him that he had only to join his life to hers, go to the Caucasus, and he would be saved from the vulgarity and emptiness of his life; now he was just as certain that he had only to forsake Nadyezhda Fyodorovna and go to Petersburg to have everything he wanted."

Like many modern writers and painters, Chekhov doesn't depict reality as it is, but reality as it is perceived. Instead of describing a woman's personality, Chekhov describes the

---

[1] *The Norton Anthology of English Literature*, Fourth Edition
[2] "Sleep and Poetry"
[3] letter of 10/25/18

impression that she made on people; he says of one of his characters that since she was always seen with her dog, people thought of her as "the lady with the dog."

Chekhov believed that art should be realistic and true to life; in this respect, he's similar to other late-nineteenth-century writers, such as Ibsen, Flaubert and Zola. Chekhov's specialty is detail; in Chekhov's stories, the parts are more important than the whole.

Chekhov depicts the absurdity of life, as Kafka does. But Chekhov is more realistic and less imaginative than Kafka. Chekhov composed his works from notes that he jotted down during the course of his daily life, while Kafka composed his works during inspired periods, periods in which he surrendered himself to his unconscious.

24. *Kafka* Philosophers often have one central idea around which their entire philosophy revolves. Likewise, imaginative writers often have one central theme that is expressed in all their work.

In the case of Kafka, this central theme is the overwhelming of the individual by huge institutions, by huge inanimate objects, by huge crowds, and by the absurdity of the world. This theme is especially evident in *The Trial* and *The Castle*. In Kafka's *Amerika*, and in some of Kafka's short stories, this theme, although it isn't as pervasive as it is in *The Trial* and *The Castle*, recurs again and again. Examples of huge institutions in *Amerika* are the Hotel Occidental and the Theatre of Oklahoma, which has "almost no limits." An example of a huge inanimate object is the ocean liner, with its "endlessly recurring stairs" and its "corridors with countless turnings."

While Joyce's prose is innovative and eccentric, and Proust's is precious, Kafka's prose is simple, pure and classical. Hence Kafka is more readable and popular than Joyce or Proust.

While many modern writers stayed close to reality, and drew on their own lives, Kafka created worlds that were far removed from the real world; Kafka's work has rare imaginative power. A book of aphorisms could be compiled from Shakespeare's philosophical comments, from Tolstoy's psychological observations, and from Proust's remarks on art. Kafka's work, however, doesn't contain any such comments or observations; Kafka is impossible to quote. Kafka doesn't try to understand reality, he creates fantasies that contain psychological truth.

One factor that shaped Kafka's work was the development, in recent times, of large institutions and bureaucracies; Kafka himself was a government bureaucrat. Another factor that shaped Kafka's work was Gogol's stories, which often begin with the protagonist finding himself in a strange and absurd situation, just as some of Kafka's stories—"The Metamorphosis," for example, and *The Trial*—begin with the protagonist finding himself in a strange and absurd situation. A third factor that shaped Kafka's work was that his father was an aggressive, dominating personality who instilled in him a feeling of guilt, inferiority and powerlessness. A fourth factor was that Kafka was Jewish; being Jewish increased Kafka's feeling of powerlessness.

Kafka found relief for his sufferings, his guilt and his powerlessness in humor. Kafka is an extraordinary writer because he had an extraordinary sense of humor. As Freud said, "It is not everyone who is capable of the humorous attitude: it is a rare and precious gift."[1]

25. *Flaubert* While the dominant note in Kafka's personality was humor, the dominant note in Flaubert's personality was pride. Flaubert was proud of his devotion to art, regardless of whether his books were acclaimed or not: "As for the outcome, or for success, who cares? The main thing in this world is to keep one's soul on the heights, out of the bourgeois noise and the democratic mire. The pursuit of Art makes one proud, and one can never have too much pride. That is my philosophy."[2]

Flaubert despised the materialistic values of the middle class; he satirized the middle class in his *Dictionary of Platitudes*, and also in the character of M. Homais. Like Ibsen, Flau-

---

[1] "Humor," 1928. "When Kafka read the first chapter of *The Trial* to his friends, everyone laughed, including the author."(Milan Kundera, *The Art of the Novel*, Harper & Row (paperback), V, 2, p. 104)
[2] *Letters*, 2/23/73

bert rebelled against the democratic trend of his time. Flaubert had little regard for universal suffrage or for equality: "I am grateful," he told Renan, "for your protest against 'democratic equality'; which is, to my mind, a seed of death in the world."[1]

Like other great writers, Flaubert studied the classics and scorned journalism. His scorn for journalism prompted him to wish that printing were banned: "If the Emperor were to abolish printing tomorrow, I'd crawl to Paris on my hands and knees and kiss his behind in gratitude."[2] Flaubert anticipated that democracy and the mass media would put the future of culture in doubt.

26. *Objective or Subjective?* Flaubert believed that literature should be impersonal, that literature shouldn't be a vehicle for the author's feelings and experiences. This was a widespread view in the late nineteenth century; it was a reaction against Romanticism, against the Romantic tendency to write in a personal, subjective way. Since Flaubert's time, the view that literature should be objective has been embraced by many writers and critics.

In support of the objective theory of literature, one could argue that some of the best literary works are objective; Homer's works, for example, don't express their author's feelings, or describe their author's experiences. In opposition to the objective theory of literature, one could argue that some of the best literary works are personal and subjective. Most of the outstanding Western writers since the Middle Ages have been subjective. Ibsen, for example, was subjective; Ibsen said, "If you want objectivity, then go to the objects. Read me so as to get to know me!"[3] Great literature can be objective or subjective, just as great literature can be realistic or unrealistic.

27. *Dostoyevsky* wrote in a subjective way; many of his characters are based on facets of his own personality. The main charac-

---

[1] ibid, 5/76
[2] F. Steegmuller, *Flaubert and Madame Bovary: A Double Portrait*, III, 4
[3] M. Meyer, *Henrik Ibsen*, ch. 15.

ters in *The Brothers Karamazov*, for example, are based on facets of Dostoyevsky's own personality: Dmitri is a losing gambler (like Dostoyevsky), Ivan a journalist tormented by religious doubts (like Dostoyevsky), Smerdyakov an epileptic (like Dostoyevsky), etc.[1] Many of Dostoyevsky's characters possess the sadistic and masochistic tendencies that Dostoyevsky himself possessed. The protagonist of "A Gentle Creature," for example, says, "I tormented myself and everybody else."

Masochism leads many of Dostoyevsky's male characters to love crippled women. The severe super-ego of these characters prevents them from loving normal women. Masochism also leads many of Dostoyevsky's characters to be buffoons, to make fools of themselves; such characters derive a certain pleasure from publicly humiliating themselves. One can compare Dostoyevsky with Johnson's biographer, Boswell: both had tyrannical fathers, both developed defective super-ego's, both experienced bouts of masochistic severity toward themselves, and both had tendencies to make fools of themselves.[2]

Dostoyevsky's greatest fault is that he carries his psychological analysis to an excessive and morbid point. This fault is particularly evident when Dostoyevsky is compared with Tolstoy. Tolstoy has Dostoyevsky's profundity and keen insight and, in addition, Tolstoy has a simplicity and serenity that Dostoyevsky lacks.

28. *Tolstoy* While Dostoyevsky is famous for his psychological insights, Tolstoy's greatness as a psychologist is sometimes overlooked. Dostoyevsky could understand others because he probed his own complex, neurotic personality. Tolstoy was less neurotic than Dostoyevsky, but he lived with exceptional inten-

---

[1] See "Dostoyevsky: Epilepsy, Mysticism, and Homosexuality," by J. R. Maze, *American Imago*, summer, 1981.
[2] On Boswell, see E. Hitschmann, *Great Men: Psychoanalytic Studies*, "Boswell: The Biographer's Character." Three of Dostoyevsky's characters who loved crippled women are Raskolnikov, Stavrogin and Alexei Karamazov; three who made fools of themselves are Fyodor Karamazov, Captain Snegirev and Semyon Marmeladov.

sity, energy and animal vitality. Tolstoy experienced many things, and was familiar with his own rich personality, hence Tolstoy understood others as few people ever have. Understanding of others comes from understanding of oneself; psychological insight comes from self-consciousness.

If one compares Tolstoy's observations on human nature with Freud's, one finds a striking agreement between them. Tolstoy said, "[Levin's] conception of [his mother] was for him a sacred memory, and his future wife was bound to be in his imagination a repetition of that exquisite, holy ideal of a woman that his mother had been." Likewise, Freud said, "A man... looks for [a woman] who can represent his picture of his mother, as it has dominated his mind from his earliest childhood."[1]

Tolstoy spoke of "the vindictive fury which can only exist where a man loves," and Tolstoy said, "where love ends, hate begins." Likewise, Freud said, "Love is with unexpected regularity accompanied by hate [and] in a number of circumstances hate changes into love and love into hate."[2]

In his case history of Dora, Freud said, "the usual sexual attraction had drawn together the father and daughter on the one side and the mother and son on the other." Tolstoy discusses this "usual sexual attraction" in the following passage: "The little girl, her father's favorite, ran up boldly [and] embraced him.... 'Good morning', he said, smiling to the boy.... He was conscious that he loved the boy less, and always tried to be fair; but the boy felt it, and did not respond with a smile to his father's chilly smile."[3]

Great thinkers often reach the same conclusions independently of each other. A thinker's ideas usually come from his own experiences, or from his observations of other people. Since human nature remains much the same in different times and

---

[1] See Tolstoy, *Anna Karenina*, I, 27, and Freud, *Three Essays on the Theory of Sexuality*, III, 5.
[2] See Tolstoy, *War and Peace*, VIII, 3, and *Anna Karenina*, VII, 30. The Freud quotation is from *The Ego and the Id*, 4.
[3] See Freud, "Dora: An Analysis of a Case of Hysteria," I, 2, and Tolstoy, *Anna Karenina*, I, 3.

places, the experiences and observations of different thinkers are often similar. Truth agrees with itself and confirms itself.

Just as great thinkers often agree with each other, so too one's own experience often agrees with the observations of great thinkers. Here again, truth agrees with itself and confirms itself. An idea drawn from experience is confirmed when one finds the same idea in a book. Likewise, the ideas in a book are confirmed when one finds that they agree with one's own experience.

29. *Joyce* While the novels of Tolstoy and Dostoyevsky express ideas and reflect their authors' struggles for spiritual peace, the novels of Joyce have a different purpose. Joyce said, "*Ulysses* is fundamentally a humorous work," and Joyce said that *Finnegans Wake* was "meant to make you laugh."[1] *Ulysses* and *Finnegans Wake* belong in the comic tradition of Petronius, Rabelais and Sterne. Joyce's short stories, on the other hand, remind one, by their simplicity and by their realism, of Chekhov's short stories.

Joyce had no interest in politics and little interest in philosophy. He disliked Shaw's plays, which set forth ideas. When World War II was breaking out, and his brother asked him what he thought about the political situation, Joyce said, "I'm not interested in politics. The only thing that interests me is style."[2]

Like many imaginative writers, Joyce observed and wrote about the occult. In *A Portrait of the Artist*, for example, Stephen Dedalus is lying in bed, thinking of his girlfriend, and he wonders what his girlfriend is doing: "Might it be, in the mysterious ways of spiritual life, that her soul at those same moments had been conscious of his homage? ....Conscious of his desire she was waking from odorous sleep." Joyce's interest in the occult sets him apart from Kafka; Kafka never discusses the occult or aesthetics or religion. Kafka stays in the world of fantasy, and never leaves it for a moment.

Like Joyce, Ibsen discussed telepathy, non-verbal communication. One of Ibsen's characters says, "If I happen to look at

---

[1] On *Ulysses*, see *Conversations With Joyce*, by Arthur Power, 11; on *Finnegans Wake*, see *James Joyce*, by R. Ellman, ch. 36
[2] *James Joyce*, by R. Ellman, ch. 36

her when her back is turned, I can tell that she feels it.... She believed I had said to her what I had only wished and willed—silently—inwardly—to myself."[1] Dostoyevsky was also fascinated by telepathy, by the power of the mind; one of his characters says, "I did not speak of it directly.... I spoke almost without words. And I am an old hand at speaking without words. I have spent all my life speaking without words. I have lived through whole tragedies without uttering a word."[2]

Sound is as important in Joyce's prose as it is in the work of modern poets. It isn't surprising that Joyce himself wrote poetry. Joyce erased, or at least blurred, the distinction between poetry and prose. Just as poetry is impossible to translate, so too Joyce's prose is impossible to translate. Just as poetry can be read over and over, so too Joyce's prose can be read over and over.

30. *Proust* One might describe Kafka as humorous, Joyce as comic, and Proust as nostalgic. Kafka's humor conceals suffering and seriousness; one cannot imagine Kafka telling the bawdy jokes that Joyce tells. Joyce's comic sense expresses not suffering but joy; Joyce said that literature "should express the 'holy spirit of joy'."[3]

Proust's nostalgia has two sources: his detachment from the present, and his attachment to his mother. Proust wrote his *magnum opus* while he was entombed in his cork-lined Paris apartment, isolated from the world. Such a detachment from the present has the effect of awakening memories of the past. Proust had an unusually strong attachment to his mother. After his mother had died, Proust told his maid that, "if I were sure to meet my mother again, in the Valley of Jehosaphat or anywhere else, I would want to die at once."[4] Proust's attachment to his mother, and his detachment from the present, combined to form the nostalgic tone of his work.

---

[1] *The Master Builder*, I
[2] "A Gentle Creature," I, 3
[3] ibid, ch. 2
[4] *Monsieur Proust: A Memoir*, by Celeste Albaret, ch. 12

One prominent theme in Proust's work is idealism, that is, the notion that the world is one's idea of the world. Proust isn't as concerned with depicting Balbec and the Duchesse de Guermantes as he is with depicting how the narrator perceives Balbec and the Duchesse de Guermantes. Proust's main subject is the narrator's mind, the narrator's thoughts and feelings. Thus, he's akin to Cervantes, whose main subject was not the world as it is, but the world as it is perceived by Don Quixote.

But while Don Quixote is always the same, Proust's narrator changes over time. The narrator's attitude toward Albertine, for example, changes over time; though the narrator is obsessed with Albertine, and is crushed by Albertine's flight, he eventually puts Albertine out of his mind and becomes indifferent to her. Proust depicts how time changes one's idea of the world, and also how time changes the world itself.

Proust's work contains much character analysis and little plot. His narrative ambles along at a leisurely pace, and often stands still; it reminds one of two people who go for a walk, and then become so involved in their conversation that they come to a stop.

Proust's peculiar style is related to his peculiar personality; the style marks the man. Proust's prose is precious, convoluted and obscure.

Proust created his own personal religion, a religion based on literature and art. Like all religions, Proust's religion justifies life, makes it possible to accept death, and holds out the hope of life after death, of immortality.

Proust is a profound thinker, and can teach one much about life, about the passage of time, and about death. But Proust isn't the sort of thinker that Tolstoy and Dostoyevsky were, and his work doesn't contain discussions about the existence of God. Proust's thinking isn't speculative, like a philosopher's thinking; Proust thinks with his heart (as Tolstoy said of Ruskin).

31. *Proust and Ruskin* One of Proust's favorite writers was John Ruskin, who wrote mostly about architecture and painting. Proust translated two of Ruskin's books into French, and when Ruskin died in 1900, Proust wrote an obituary. Proust took sev-

eral "Ruskinian pilgrimages," visiting cathedrals that Ruskin had written about. Proust even read Ruskin's *Stones of Venice* while sitting inside San Marco.

Ruskin believed that a craftsman shouldn't be just a laborer, like those who built the pyramids. A craftsman should express his creativity and individuality, he should have his heart in his work, like those who carved the ornaments on Gothic cathedrals:

> I believe the right question to ask [Ruskin wrote], respecting all ornament, is simply this: Was it done with enjoyment—was the carver happy while he was about it? It may be the hardest work possible... but it must have been happy too, or it will not be living.[1]

We can ask of a literary work, too, "Was it done with enjoyment?" And if we ask that about Proust's work, it's clear that the answer is yes, he wrote with great enjoyment. Hence he said it was easy to write his novel, and hence he wrote so much. Wilde said that Henry James wrote fiction as if it were a painful duty, but no one would say that about Proust. Proust wrote with a light heart, and with deep affection for his subject. Indeed, nothing was closer to Proust's heart than the childhood memories that he drew upon in his fiction. Proust's affection for his subject communicates itself to the reader, and helps to explain the reader's affection for Proust's work.

32. *Proust and Detachment* One part of spiritual growth is detachment—detachment from emotional entanglements, detachment from life in general. Detachment shouldn't be confused with pessimism, with turning against life. Meditating means practicing detachment; meditating doesn't mean turning against life. In a detached mind, wrote Jung, "the fullness of the world which hitherto pressed upon it has lost none of its richness and beauty, but it no longer dominates."[2]

---

[1] *The Seven Lamps of Architecture*, ch. 5, sec. XXIV
[2] *Psychology and the East*, "Commentary on The Secret of the Golden Flower", ¶65

Alchemy is about spiritual growth, about achieving detachment. Alchemists used the image of a "diamond body" to represent one who is detached, one who is unaffected by "emotional entanglements and violent shocks."[1]

Proust helps us to understand detachment by describing its opposite—the state of attachment, the state of unhealthy obsession. Swann is obsessed with Odette, and Proust's narrator is obsessed with his mother and later with Albertine. Proust's narrator escapes from his twin obsessions through the death of the two people he's obsessed with. These deaths bring him great suffering, but they also bring him wisdom, detachment.

Just as Proust's narrator detaches himself from people, so too he gradually detaches himself from places—the places that he has romanticized and longed for. Both forms of detachment prepare the narrator for death.

Detachment is a natural part of the process of aging and dying. As Jung put it, "A consciousness detached from the world.... sets in after middle life and is a natural preparation for death."[2] If this is so, then perhaps Proust's narrator would have eventually achieved detachment even if his mother and Albertine hadn't died. Conversely, if his mother and Albertine had died when he was young (say, twenty), their deaths wouldn't have led to detachment and wisdom, since he wasn't old enough to achieve detachment. Is wisdom a function of time?

One can interpret Proust's work as beginning with attachment, and ending with detachment, resignation, and an acceptance of death. In other words, one can interpret Proust's work as a study of spiritual growth.

33. *Shakespeare and Detachment* Like Proust, Shakespeare treats detachment as a part of spiritual growth. Shakespeare depicts detachment in the character of Horatio, who is steady and cool-headed. Hamlet says to Horatio,

> thou hast been
> As one, in suffering all, that suffers nothing,

---

[1] ibid, ¶68
[2] ibid

> A man that fortune's buffets and rewards
> Hast ta'en with equal thanks....
>   Give me that man
> That is not passion's slave, and I will wear him
> In my heart's core.

Shakespeare's portrait of Horatio reminds us of Jung's portrait of the detached personality that "suffers only in the lower stories, as it were, but in its upper stories is singularly detached from painful as well as from joyful happenings."[1]

34. *Blood and Judgment* While detachment is one part of spiritual growth, another part is balance—balancing mind and body, intellect and feeling, conscious and unconscious. Hamlet praises Horatio for balancing "blood and judgment," for mixing the "elements," rather than repressing some and favoring others. Antony praises Brutus in similar terms:

> His life was gentle, and the elements
> So mixed in him that Nature might stand up
> And say to all the world, "This was a man."

Elsewhere Shakespeare speaks of mixing "blood and virtue"; in *All's Well That Ends Well*, Bertram's mother says,

> Be thou blest, Bertram, and succeed thy father
> In manners, as in shape! thy blood and virtue
> Contend for empire in thee...

The phrase "blood and virtue" reminds one of "blood and judgment." "Contend" is in the imperative case (equivalent to "may your blood and virtue contend for empire in thee"). Shakespeare seems to have felt that "blood and virtue" can't coexist harmoniously, they can only coexist contentiously. The highest degree of harmony that we can achieve is a stand-off between "blood" and "virtue."

    A mix of contrary tendencies is as healthy for the individual as a system of "checks and balances" for the state. "Without contraries," wrote Blake, "is no progression. Attraction and

---

[1] ibid, ¶67

Repulsion, Reason and Energy, Love and Hate are necessary to human existence. The man who never alters his opinion is like standing water, and breeds reptiles of mind."

Just as Shakespeare's view of detachment resembles Jung's view, so too Shakespeare's view of balancing/mixing resembles Jung's view (though Jung used the term "functions" rather than "elements"). Shakespeare's view of spiritual growth is similar to Jung's, and is as relevant for our time as a book written yesterday.

35. *The Power of Thought* Thought alone can bring about results. Negative thoughts, though buried in secrecy and silence, can bring about negative results. Marie-Louise von Franz, a disciple of Jung, said "by nursing secret destructive attitudes, a wife can drive her husband, and a mother her children, into illness, accident, or even death."[1] Such destructive attitudes can also lead to self-destruction, suicide, which is sometimes concealed beneath the appearance of accidental death. Negative thoughts may be conscious or unconscious, or they may be semiconscious, occupying that borderland between conscious and unconscious.

Proust had a destructive attitude toward two people, his mother and his chauffeur, and when both of them died, he felt that he was guilty of a double murder. (Proust would have understood Oscar Wilde's paradox, "we always kill the thing we love.") Proust's love for his chauffeur, Albert Agostinelli, ended when Agostinelli left Proust, went to the south of France to learn flying, and died in an airplane accident.[2]

In Proust's *Remembrance of Things Past*, the narrator's love for Albertine follows the same pattern as Proust's love for his chauffeur. But the first draft of Proust's novel, including the death of Albertine, was written before the death of Agostinelli. Thus, the whole history of Proust's love for Agostinelli existed in Proust's mind, and in Proust's novel, before it existed in the external world. The mind shapes circumstances.

---

[1] *Man and His Symbols*, part 3, p. 191 of hardcover edition
[2] See *Marcel Proust: A Biography*, by George Painter, vol. II, ch. 10

Was Hamlet also a negative thinker, a person who committed thought-murders? The literary critic Wilson Knight argued that Hamlet is obsessed with death, infected with nihilism; Knight argued that Hamlet's nihilism spreads through the Danish court, and results in a pile of corpses.[1] Some critics reacted to Knight's argument with indignation, insisting that Claudius, not Hamlet, is the villain. But if we reflect on the importance of negative thinking, in life and in literature, we become receptive to Knight's argument.

If we accept Knight's argument, must we abandon the traditional view that Hamlet is an intellectual, a noble heart, etc.? No, Hamlet can be both an intellectual and a "negative thinker," both a sweet prince and a shadow prince. As Jung said, "The brighter the light, the darker the shadow. For every Faust, a Mephistopheles."[2] For every intellectual, a devil within. Doubtless Shakespeare himself, who resembles Hamlet in so many ways, was both a genius and a "negative thinker." The brighter the light, the darker the shadow.

"Shadow" is Jung's term for the dark side of human nature, the impulses that are hidden from society, and even from ourselves. The shadow arranges things, while the conscious mind is only partly aware of what the shadow is doing. In Ibsen's *Wild Duck*, Gregers gives a young girl, Hedvig, a gun, and she later shoots herself. Does Gregers consciously intend to cause Hedvig's death? No, his destructive impulses are below the threshold of consciousness. Sometimes, however, an event like Hedvig's death causes one to become conscious of impulses that have hitherto been unconscious.

Many writers, realizing the power of thought, have urged their readers to control their thoughts, organize their thoughts, focus their thoughts on a positive goal. This argument has spawned an entire literary genre: inspirational literature, self-help literature. One of the most well-known writers of inspira-

---

[1] G. Wilson Knight, *The Wheel of Fire*, "The Embassy of Death: An Essay on *Hamlet*"
[2] Jung, *C. G. Jung Speaking: Interviews and Encounters*, Princeton University Press, 1977, p. 165, "On Creative Achievement"

tional literature is James Allen, author of *As A Man Thinketh*. According to Allen, "Man is the cause (though nearly always unconsciously) of circumstances.... Circumstance does not make the man; it reveals him to himself.... He will find that as he alters his thoughts towards things and other people, things and other people will alter towards him."[1] The genre of inspirational literature is based on a deep truth—namely, that thoughts can bring about results in the external world.

36. *Shakespeare* depicts the shadowy world of semi-conscious impulses. Shakespeare goes beneath the surface, beneath external appearance, beneath the image that we present to the world and to ourselves. He deals with the passions that lurk beneath our character, our self-image. The word "personality" comes from persona, meaning mask; Shakespeare tears off the mask of personality, and depicts the primal drives that everyone shares.

Shakespeare's harshest critic was Tolstoy. Tolstoy excoriated Shakespeare for his vague characters and vague motives; Tolstoy spoke of "an obvious and glaring defect—particularly evident in *Hamlet*—namely, that the chief person of the play has no character at all."[2] Hamlet is universal—both good and evil, both a noble heart and a negative thinker. He lacks a clearly-defined character because he's universal, because he's Shakespeare's greatest creation. That is, he's Shakespeare's greatest creation for the very reason that Tolstoy criticized him—his lack of character.

Hamlet's world is upset, disturbed—"something is rotten in the state of Denmark." This disturbance extends to the heavens; Horatio says that Denmark has witnessed "stars with trains of fire, and dews of blood, disasters in the sun," and he points out that similar things were seen in Rome "a little ere the mightiest Julius fell."[3] In *Julius Caesar*, Shakespeare emphasizes the

---

[1] *As A Man Thinketh*
5. ibid, p. 33
[2] quoted in G. Wilson Knight, *The Wheel of Fire*, "Tolstoy's Attack on Shakespeare"
[3] I, i, 112

disturbance in the natural world that accompanies the disturbance in human affairs; as Knight put it, "we are confronted with things apparently beyond the workings of causality."[1] In *Macbeth*, the weather is stormy, birds behave strangely, horses eat each other, etc.

This is more than a literary device, this is a worldview. According to Jung's theory of synchronicity, there are meaningful coincidences between the human world and the natural world; synchronicity is an "acausal connecting principle."[2] For thousands of years, the Chinese noticed that certain events cluster together; instead of looking for causes, they looked for clusters. If an earthquake coincided with the death of an emperor, the Chinese saw this as a "meaningful coincidence." Shakespeare shared this worldview, and he describes all the "meaningful coincidences" at the time of Caesar's death; Shakespeare says, "when beggars die there are no comets seen."[3]

Are Shakespeare and Jung the only Western thinkers who had this worldview, who saw clusters rather than causes, synchronicity rather than causality? No, this was a widespread worldview in the West until the Age of Reason, until the Scientific Revolution, until Western man got into the habit of rational, cause-and-effect thinking, until Western man got into the habit of dismissing the occult, and dismissing "meaningful coincidences," as mere superstition.

In *Macbeth*, the future is predicted by the witches, and in *Julius Caesar*, the future is predicted by the Soothsayer. Shakespeare's plays are full of prophecies and hunches that anticipate future events. Again, this is more than a literary device, this is part of Shakespeare's worldview. Again, this is consistent with Jung's worldview, and consistent with the worldview that prevailed until rational-scientific thinking became dominant. Jung argues, following Kant, that space, time, and causality are merely categories of the intellect, they don't exist in the thing-in-itself; space and time are relative not absolute, the future is

---

[1] G. W. Knight, *The Wheel of Fire*, "Brutus and Macbeth"
[2] See Chapter 1, #15 and Chapter 6, #21
[3] *Julius Caesar*, I, iii, 128

embedded in the present. If prophecy has a long history in literature, it's because prophecy has a long history in the world itself; prophecy is more than a literary device, it's part of a worldview.

Shakespeare was content with a world that was mysterious and irrational. As Keats said, Shakespeare was "capable of being in uncertainties, mysteries, doubts without any irritable reaching after fact and reason." Keats called this capacity "negative capability"; he said that every great writer needed this, and Shakespeare possessed it in a high degree.

Modern thinkers like Jung are skeptical of the rational-scientific worldview, and are coming back to Shakespeare's worldview, coming back to a worldview that has long been dismissed as superstitious. Lichtenberg said, "There is a great difference between *still* believing something and believing it *again*. Still to believe that the moon affects the plants reveals stupidity and superstition, but to believe it *again* is a sign of philosophy and reflection."[1] Modern thinkers are *again* believing in the occult powers, and synchronous happenings, that Shakespeare believed in.

Those who are part of the rational tradition don't understand Shakespeare's Hermetic worldview. They think that Shakespeare was a skeptic, that he had no worldview, no philosophy. T. S. Eliot, for example, said, "Dante made great poetry out of a great philosophy of life... Shakespeare made equally great poetry out of an inferior and muddled philosophy of life."[2] Shakespeare's Hermetic worldview is beginning to be grasped, just as Shakespeare's identity is beginning to be grasped. The mystical works that Shakespeare wrote in his last years were scorned by a rational age, but are becoming increasingly popular today. Soon it will be said that Shakespeare made great poetry out of a great philosophy of life.

37. *Hamlet and Prospero*   Hamlet shapes circumstances by the power of his mind, by the power of his negative thoughts. Pros-

---

[1] *The Lichtenberg Reader* (Boston, Beacon Press, 1959), "Aphorisms", 1775
[2] See Eliot's Introduction to G. Wilson Knight's *Wheel of Fire*.

pero, the protagonist of Shakespeare's *Tempest*, also shapes circumstances by the power of his mind, but his thoughts are positive, and lead to a positive outcome, not to a pile of corpses. If magic is the power of the mind to affect the external world, both Hamlet and Prospero have magical power. Neither Hamlet nor Prospero are "characters"; they represent the universal rather than the particular or the characteristic.

38. *Growth from Disaster* Hamlet ends with a pile of corpses. Since Hamlet himself is part of this pile, he can't learn from the experience. Often, however, one learns from the disaster that one has created. Indeed, the unconscious arranges disaster in order to foster spiritual growth, in order to force a recognition of its own rights, in order to force the conscious mind to compromise, to share power. Once power is shared and wholeness is achieved, the unconscious no longer arranges disaster; it becomes a wise friend instead of a mischief-maker. One might say that we create disaster in our thirties in order to become wise in our forties.

When Max Weber was thirty, he was an aspiring academic. "He had an enormous load, working until very late. When [his wife] urged him to get some rest, he would call out: 'If I don't work until one o'clock I can't be a professor.'"[1] Clearly, this is a man ignoring his unconscious. If a healthy psyche has competing powers, a mix of elements, "checks and balances," Weber's mind was unbalanced, consciousness tyrannizing over the unconscious. And so the unconscious is aroused, seizes power, and begins to arrange Weber's life, trying to force Weber to come to terms with his unconscious, to become whole. In his early thirties, "Weber became fevered and ill with a psychic malady.... 'He could not read or write, speak, walk, or sleep without pain; all mental and part of his physical functions refused to work'... For hours he sat and gazed stupidly, picking at his finger nails, claiming that such inactivity made him feel good." Weber realized that his illness fostered his personal growth. "Such a disease [wrote Weber] has its compensations. It

---

[1] *From Max Weber: Essays in Sociology*, edited by H. Gerth and C. Wright Mills, Intro., 1

has reopened to me the human side of life, which mama used to miss in me."

Sometimes the unconscious leads one into a feeling of being stuck, into a situation that has no resolution. The conscious mind is baffled, consciousness is at its "wit's end," and the unconscious has a chance to express itself.

Since the feeling of being stuck can lead to spiritual growth, is it possible to create this feeling artificially? Zen tries to create this feeling by asking the student to solve a puzzle, a koan. The koan is insoluble by rational means, hence the student is baffled. When his conscious mind gives up, the answer comes by itself.

39. *The Hermetic Tradition* There are two competing traditions in Western thought: the rational-scientific tradition, and the Hermetic Tradition. These two traditions have left their mark on imaginative literature, as well as on philosophy.

The term "Hermetic" comes from Hermes Trismegistus, who was originally an Egyptian god (Thoth) and was later incorporated into Greek culture, and associated with Hermes. The god was called *megistos* (great), and he was addressed three times, hence tri-megistos, or Trismegistus; Milton calls him "thrice great Hermes." The term "hermetic" can mean "pertaining to alchemy and magic," but its more common meaning is "tightly sealed" (from a seal supposedly invented by Hermes Trismegistus).

About forty books are ascribed to Hermes Trismegistus. These books were written between about 200 BC and 200 AD; it appears that they were written in (or near) Alexandria. They deal with alchemy and astrology, and also with philosophy. The "Hermetic Tradition" isn't simply the Alchemical Tradition, it's a literary-philosophical tradition in which alchemy, astrology, the occult, and the philosophy of Plato are all interwoven. All European alchemists may be said to be part of the Hermetic tradition, but philosophers and poets with no interest in alchemy may also be considered part of the Hermetic tradition.

One of the basic tenets of the Hermetics is that the world is one (*unus mundus*), the world is an organic whole, and each part of the world is connected to all other parts. "Every human being, beast, plant or mineral is influenced... by one or more of the celestial bodies. It is the influence of Mars which distinguishes a wolf from a lion (the latter being a solar animal)."[1] Earthly things are connected to heavenly things, have affinities with heavenly things; "as above, so below" said the Hermetics. What the Hermetics refer to as "occult correspondences" is closely related to what Jung refers to as "acausal connections" and "synchronicity." Jung is part of the Hermetic Tradition.

The Hermetic Tradition can be traced from ancient Egypt, through Hellenistic times, then through the medieval alchemists, then to the Florentine Neoplatonists. The most famous of the Florentine Neoplatonists were Pico della Mirandola and Marsilio Ficino. The Neoplatonists were one of the most influential philosophical schools in Renaissance Europe. After the Neoplatonists had left the scene, the Hermetic Tradition was carried on by the Italian philosopher Giordano Bruno, a contemporary of Shakespeare. It isn't surprising that we find Hermetic thinking in the works of Shakespeare.

The Hermetic Tradition survived in the works of 17th century English poets—Marvell, Herbert, Donne, and the other "Metaphysical Poets." These poets were known for their elaborate metaphors, which connected things that seem far apart. These lines from a poem by George Herbert may serve as an example of Metaphysical poetry, Hermetic poetry:

> Man is all symmetry,
> Full of proportions, one limb to another,
> And to all the world besides.
> Each part may call the farthest, brother;
> For head with foot hath private amity,
> And both with moons and tides.

By comparing the world to the human body, Herbert argues that the world is an organic whole, an inter-connected whole, *unus mundus*.

---

[1] See Erwin Panofsky, *Studies in Iconology: Humanistic Themes in the Art of the Renaissance*, ch. 5

7. LITERATURE

Samuel Johnson complained that, in the poetry of the Metaphysicals, "the most heterogeneous ideas are yoked by violence together," and Johnson noted that the Metaphysicals were fond of the "discovery of occult resemblances in things apparently unlike."[1] Johnson was writing in the mid-1700s, when the Hermetic Tradition had fallen out of favor. In the 1700s, the mechanical worldview of Newton and Locke was more popular than the Hermetic worldview. The inter-connected world, the *unus mundus*, had been broken into pieces.

At the end of the 1700s, during the Romantic period, the Hermetic Tradition came back into favor, and again inspired poets. Coleridge and Blake rejected the mechanical, Newtonian worldview, and admired mystics and Hermetists like Boehme and Swedenborg. Coleridge argued that analogy and symbol could be used to make the world whole again.

New England Transcendentalism was a younger brother of English Romanticism. Emerson was influenced by Coleridge and other Romantics, and Emerson liked to look for correspondences between nature and man.

> Every appearance in nature [wrote Emerson] corresponds to some state of the mind.... Who looks upon a river in a meditative hour and is not reminded of the flux of all things? Throw a stone into the stream, and the circles that propagate themselves are the beautiful type of all influence.... The whole of nature is a metaphor of the human mind.[2]

Goethe, the most prominent of the German Romantics, was also in sympathy with Hermetism, and had a strong interest in alchemy and the occult.

In the mid-1800s, the Hermetic Tradition merged with the Spiritualist movement. A French writer named Éliphas Lévi published a study of the Hermetic tradition, a study that had wide influence, especially in France. Lévi probably influenced Baudelaire, one of the prominent Hermetics of the time. Baudelaire spoke of "universal correspondence and symbolism, that reper-

---

[1] S. Johnson, *The Lives of the Poets*, "The Life of Cowley"
[2] R. W. Emerson, *Nature*, ch. 4, "Language"

tory of all metaphor," and Baudelaire wrote a poem called "*Correspondances*."[1] Lévi also influenced Rimbaud and Mallarmé, the leading Symbolists; the Symbolist movement can be considered Hermetic.

By the late 1800s, the Hermetic Tradition enjoyed wide popularity among literary people. Ireland was a hotbed of Hermetism. The Irish poet Yeats joined various Hermetic societies, including the Theosophists, who were led by Mme. Blavatsky, and the Rosicrucians. Many of Yeats' works deal with Hermetic subjects, such as his stories "Rosa Alchemica" and "The Adoration of the Magi." Joyce was also deeply affected by Hermetism. Joyce's work abounds in analogies and correspondences; in *Ulysses*, chapters correspond to parts of the body, and also to branches of knowledge.

The Joyce scholar W. Y. Tindall argues that Joyce's "maze of correspondences" is merely a literary device, that Joyce was concerned with aesthetic unity, not cosmic unity, and that one must go all the way back to the Metaphysical Poets in order to find writers who believed in cosmic unity. In Tindall's opinion, Hermetism no longer survives as a worldview, but only as a literary technique.

It's true that some writers, including Joyce, are only concerned with aesthetic unity, but it isn't true that Hermetism is a thing of the past. Tindall fails to understand that Hermetic thinking has long flourished in China, not as a mere literary technique, but as a view of the world. Tindall also fails to understand that Jung has breathed new life into the Hermetic Tradition; Jung's theory of synchronicity revives the Hermetic search for occult connections, acausal connections. The Hermetic tradition will live again—not only as an inspiration to novelists and poets, but as part of an attempt to grasp reality itself. Thrice-great Hermes is not dead yet.

40. *Character Pairs* Fictional characters often come in pairs. The author seems to represent his bright side and his dark side in

---

[1] W. Y. Tindall, "James Joyce and the Hermetic Tradition", *Journal of the History of Ideas*, January, 1954

two separate characters. Combine these two characters, and you have a whole person. Don Quixote and Sancho Panza, for example, seem to be a pair—one idealistic, one earthy. The same is true of Faust and Mephistopheles, Othello and Iago, Adonis and the boar (in *Venus and Adonis*). If one views religion as literature, one can add another pair to this list: God and the devil. Since Hamlet represents both sides, bright and dark, we argued above that Hamlet is Shakespeare's most lifelike character.

According to Jung, each of us has a bright side and a dark side; he calls this dark side "the shadow." In light of Jung's idea, it isn't surprising that positive characters are often matched with a negative double, an evil twin.

Conrad creates paired characters, and explicitly refers to one member of the pair as a "shadow". In *Heart of Darkness*, Marlow refers to the savage Kurtz as a "shadow"; Conrad sometimes draws attention to the term "shadow" by capitalizing the S. Conrad uses the word "shadow" just as Jung uses it. This is a striking example of two great thinkers reaching the same insight independently. Perhaps the shadow is an archetype that both Conrad and Jung perceived.

In Conrad's *Secret Sharer*, there is a "character pair." As in *Heart of Darkness*, one member of the pair is a criminal, and is explicitly referred to as a "shadow." In Conrad's work, the encounter with the shadow helps the protagonist to grow and mature. Likewise, Jung says that encountering one's shadow, acknowledging one's dark side, is an important step in personal growth. One of Jung's disciples wrote:

> Until a year or so ago there lived among the Navajo a wise man who had to go on all fours because of a congenital lameness. His people called him "He-who-walks-close-to-his-shadow," a name that does indeed denote a wise one.[1]

41. *Kundera* Some writers start slowly, and write their best work in their old age. Others begin their career with a bang—their first book is their best, and they lose inspiration as they get

---

[1] "The Shadow," by Esther M. Harding, *Spring: A Journal of Archetype and Culture*, 1945

older. Milan Kundera began his career with a bang; his first novel, *The Joke*, was an international bestseller. His later works are somewhat contrived and uninspired.

Kundera deserves high marks for clarity and polish, for organizing and presenting his thoughts. He also deserves high marks for his non-fiction works, his works of literary criticism and philosophy; *The Art of the Novel* is excellent.

The chief inspiration for Kundera's fiction was Hermann Broch. Following Broch's example, Kundera wrote idea-novels, novels that fuse fiction and reflection, novels that interrupt the story with essays on philosophy, music, etc., novels that don't aspire to recreate life, don't aspire to create a realistic world. Kundera thinks that too much praise is lavished on Joyce and Proust; he prefers Central and Eastern European writers like Broch, Musil, Kafka, Hasek, and Gombrowicz. Kundera is also a fan of early novelists like Sterne and Fielding, who don't aspire to mimic reality, who precede the realistic trend of the 19th century.

One of the ideas that Kundera explores in his fiction is the idea of kitsch. Kitsch is a sentimental view of the world, a view that excludes everything dark and doubtful. Kundera says that Communist kitsch is exemplified by the May Day parade in which everyone smiles; "the unsung motto of the parade [was] 'Long Live Life!'"[1] Kundera avoids sugary sentiment, lest anyone accuse him of kitsch. Like many modern artists, Kundera dwells on the dark and morbid; an example is his fantasy of women forced to march around a swimming pool, being shot by a man suspended above the pool in a basket.[2] This preoccupation with the dark and morbid, this anti-kitsch, is a more common vice among today's artists than kitsch.

Another of the ideas that Kundera explores in his fiction is the idea of *litost*. Kundera tells us that *litost* is an untranslatable Czech word; "*litost* is a state of torment created by the sudden sight of one's own misery," a state of feeling miserable and

---

[1] *The Unbearable Lightness of Being*, VI, 6
[2] ibid, VI, 10

humiliated.[1] *Litost* awakens a desire for revenge, a desire to strike back at the cause of one's misery and humiliation. An example of *litost* can be found in the tale of Sleeping Beauty: the King and Queen have a baby, and invite everyone to the christening—everyone except one fairy, whom they forget to invite. This fairy feels slighted, humiliated; she crashes the party, and places a curse on the newborn child.

Another example of *litost* can be found in *Othello*. Iago seeks to be promoted to the rank of Othello's lieutenant, and several people intercede for him. But Othello gives the position to someone else. Many commentators have argued that Iago harms Othello out of "motiveless malignity," while others have said that Iago is consumed by jealousy, believing that Othello and others have slept with his wife. Many commentators have overlooked Iago's *litost*, overlooked the misery and humiliation caused by his failure to be promoted.

Litost can also help to explain animosities in the political sphere; an insulted nation may be as eager for revenge as one that is physically injured.

At the start of his *Unbearable Lightness of Being*, Kundera discusses Nietzsche's idea of eternal recurrence:

> The myth of eternal return [Kundera writes] states that a life which disappears once and for all, which does not return, is like a shadow, without weight, dead in advance, and whether it was horrible, beautiful, or sublime, its horror, sublimity, and beauty mean nothing.[2]

This is a misinterpretation of Nietzsche; in fact, it stands Nietzsche on his head. Nietzsche opposed the notion that life—everyday life, life as we know it—is meaningless. Nietzsche opposed nihilism, he was the champion of life, of reality, just as Zen is. Kundera converts Nietzsche's formula of affirmation into a formula of negation. It was because Nietzsche believed in life that he willed its repetition. If we accept the "lightness of being," it ceases to be "unbearable"; it's only unbearable if we want it to

---

[1] *The Book of Laughter and Forgetting*, Part V
[2] Part I, ch. 1

be other than it is. The message of Nietzsche and Zen is to perceive the lightness of being, to accept it as it is, and to celebrate it.

Some have argued that the novel, as a literary genre, is exhausted, dying. Kundera, however, is optimistic about the future of the novel, and one shares that optimism after reading Kundera's fiction and criticism.

One reason to be optimistic about the novel is that the Philosophy of Today, by being receptive to the occult, encourages novelists to explore the vast, mysterious realm of the occult, a realm that is fertile ground for imaginative literature.

42. *Whitman and Zen* Whitman often reminds one of Zen. Other 19th-century writers—including Thoreau and Pater—also remind one of Zen. The West first became acquainted with Zen around 1900. In the decades before 1900, there are signs of an Eastern drift in Western thought, as if the West might have developed Zen on its own, if it hadn't imported it from the East.

What first strikes the reader about Whitman's *Leaves of Grass* is its mystical quality, its feeling of union with all of nature, its love for all of nature—even something as humble as "a spear of summer grass." Thoreau noticed this mystical quality in Whitman's work, and when Thoreau met Whitman in Brooklyn, he said that Whitman's work was "wonderfully like the Orientals."[1] Thoreau asked Whitman if he had read the Oriental classics. No, Whitman responded, he hadn't. (Thoreau, recognizing a kindred spirit in Eastern literature, had obtained a card for the Harvard library in order to study Eastern literature.) Like Thoreau and Pater, Whitman had abandoned Christianity and the Christian worldview, and had begun to see the world in a new way.

Like Zen, Whitman has no use for moral judgments:

What blurt is it about virtue and about vice?
Evil propels me, and reform of evil propels me.... I stand indifferent,
My gait is no faultfinder's or rejecter's gait,
I moisten the roots of all that has grown.

---

[1] Walter Harding, *The Days of Henry Thoreau*, ch. 17, §5

Like Zen and other mystical worldviews, Whitman takes a positive attitude toward life:

It seems to me that everything in the light and air ought to be happy;
Whoever is not in his coffin and the dark grave, let him know he has enough.

Whitman sees the world as it is, accepts it, and celebrates it, instead of seeing the world as a preparation for something else, a tryout for the Afterlife. Whitman would have understood the Persian poet, Omar Khayyam who, when asked what he worshipped, pointed to a flower. And Whitman would have understood the story that Meister Eckhart liked to tell: when he met a peasant on the road, and said "good morning," the peasant said, "Every morning is a good morning."

Whitman often takes the passive attitude of meditation:

I think I will do nothing for a long time but listen,
And accrue what I hear into myself.... and let sounds contribute toward me....
I loaf and invite my soul,
I lean and loaf at my ease.... observing a spear of summer grass.

Whitman's work has the inspired, prophetic tone of Nietzsche's *Thus Spoke Zarathustra*. Like Nietzsche, Whitman saw himself as the prophet of a new religion. Whitman saw *Leaves of Grass* as the Holy Scripture of this new religion, and he planned to expand it into 365 chapters or psalms, one for each day of the year.[1]

43. *Milosz and Zen* While Whitman reached Zen on his own, the Polish poet Czeslaw Milosz studied and admired Eastern literature. "His reading of East Asian poetry confirmed Milosz in his preference for poems that 'honored the object, not the subject'.... He extolled 'the holy word: Is.' All that he required for a justification of existence was a description of existence."[2] In the

---

[1] *Leaves of Grass: The First (1855) Edition*, Penguin Classics, Introduction by Malcolm Cowley, p. xxviii
[2] See "Czeslaw Milosz, 1911-2004" by Leon Wieseltier in *The New York Times*, 9/12/04

darkest days of World War II, Milosz wrote "The World," a series of poems that describe the elements of a child's world: the road, the gate, the porch, the dining room, the stairs.

Milosz believed that the struggle against totalitarianism was a philosophical struggle, a battle of ideas, just as the current struggle against Islamic extremism can be viewed as a philosophical struggle.

While he was respectful of religion, Milosz was impatient with church orthodoxy; "wandering on the outskirts of heresy is about right for me," he wrote. He admired mystics like Swedenborg.

Like Whitman and Zen, Milosz took a positive attitude:

> You gave me gifts, God-Enchanter.
> I give you thanks for good and ill.
> Eternal light in everything on earth.
> As now, so on the day after my death.

44. Mark Twain Like Whitman and Thoreau, Twain broke with Christianity, referring to it as "an odious religion."[1] But while Whitman and Thoreau reached a mystical affirmation of life, there are dark streaks of pessimism in Twain.

Twain was fond of history, especially the French Revolution. His favorite book was Carlyle's history of the French Revolution, which gave Twain history with a literary flavor, and with philosophical depth. Twain probably read Carlyle's book more than twenty times; he was reading it on his death-bed. One might say that Twain didn't learn by reading, he learned by re-reading; he read Carlyle until his mind was saturated with him, until he could re-create Carlyle's scenes in his own fiction.

It was probably his study of Carlyle that gave Twain a sympathy for all his characters, even the "rapscallions." When Carlyle's villain, Robespierre, is finally brought to justice, Carlyle expresses sympathy for him. Likewise, when Twain's villains (the "King" and the "Duke") are finally brought to justice,

---

[1] *Twentieth Century Interpretations of* Adventures of Huckleberry Finn, "So Noble... and So Beautiful a Book"

Twain's narrator says, "I was sorry for them poor pitiful rascals."[1]

Twain was a keen student of Shakespeare, and Shakespeare had considerable influence on him. Like Whitman, Twain tried to rival Shakespeare, and was disappointed and jealous if he thought he didn't measure up. There are many echoes of Shakespeare in Twain's works. One of the most notable passages in all of Twain's works is the passage in *Huck Finn* where Huck considers whether to give up his slave-companion, Jim. This passage is modeled on Claudius's soliloquy in *Hamlet*:

Claudius	Huck
Pray can I not, though inclination be as sharp as will.	I about made up my mind to pray... But words wouldn't come.
And, like a man to double business bound, I stand in pause where I shall first begin.	I knowed very well why they wouldn't come ...it was because I was playing double.
I am still possess'd of those effects for which I did the murder.	I was letting *on* to give up sin, but ...I was holding on to the biggest one of all.
Bow, stubborn knees.	So I kneeled down.
My words fly up, my thoughts remain below. Words without thoughts never to heaven go.	I was trying to make my mouth *say* I would do the right thing ...but deep down in me I knowed it was a lie.... You can't pray a lie.... All right, then, I'll *go* to hell.[2]

Twain took a dim view of conscience, perhaps because he himself was troubled by an overly severe conscience. He felt that society and education could train conscience to approve of anything. When Huck decides to protect Jim, he does so not *because* of his conscience, but *despite* his conscience. As one critic wrote, "What is still sound in him is an impulse from the deepest

---

[1] Walter Blair, "The French Revolution and Huckleberry Finn," *Modern Philology*, Vol. 55, No. 1. (Aug., 1957), pp. 21-35
[2] James Hirsh, "Samuel Clemens and the Ghost of Shakespeare," *Studies in the Novel* 24, no. 3 (fall 1992): 251-72

level of his personality."[1] Twain himself described *Huck Finn* as "a book of mine where a sound heart and a deformed conscience come into collision and conscience suffers a defeat." In Twain's world, virtue is a matter of the heart, not the head, a matter of spontaneous feeling, not rational judgment. "In a crucial moral emergency," Twain wrote, "a sound heart is a safer guide than an ill-trained conscience."[2] We saw earlier how Macbeth makes the wrong choice by listening to his conscious thoughts rather than his feelings.[3] Conversely, Huck makes the right choice by listening to his feelings, his heart, "the deepest level of his personality."

When Shakespeare praises someone, he does so unstintingly; one might say that Shakespeare glorifies man. For example, Hamlet speaks thus of his father:

> He was a man; take him for all in all;
> I shall not look upon his like again....
> See, what a grace was seated on this brow;
> Hyperion's curls; the front of Jove himself;
> An eye like Mars, to threaten and command;
> A station like the herald Mercury
> New-lighted on a heaven-kissing hill;
> A combination and a form indeed,
> Where every god did seem to set his seal,
> To give the world assurance of a man.

Perhaps Shakespeare's penchant for unstinting praise inspired Twain, who lavishes praise on the aristocrat, Colonel Grangerford:

> He carried a mahogany cane with a silver head to it. There warn't no frivolishness about him, not a bit, and he warn't ever loud. He was as kind as he could be—you could feel that, you know, and so you had confidence. Sometimes he smiled, and it was good to see; but when he straightened himself up like a liberty-pole, and the

---

[1] Henry Nash Smith, "A Sound Heart and a Deformed Conscience," *Twentieth Century Interpretations of* Adventures of Huckleberry Finn
[2] See "Society and Conscience in *Huckleberry Finn*," Leo B. Levy, *Nineteenth-Century Fiction*, Vol. 18, No. 4 (Mar., 1964), pp. 383-391
[3] See Chapter 2, #2

lightning begun to flicker out from under his eyebrows, you wanted to climb a tree first, and find out what the matter was afterwards.

Another of Twain's hero-aristocrats, Colonel Sherburn, faces down a mob, and lashes it with his contempt. Sherburn may have been inspired by Shakespeare's Coriolanus, who defies the Roman mob, and says, "You common cry of curs... I banish you!"

45. *The Desire to Die* Tragedy depicts suffering, suffering that drives the tragic hero to desire death. Why do we derive pleasure from tragedy? Why do we derive pleasure from the depiction of suffering?

Suffering is a universal human experience; it is impossible to live without suffering. When suffering reaches a certain degree, one wants to die, one wants to commit suicide. Almost everyone, at one time or another, has thought of committing suicide. Suffering, and longing for death, deepen and strengthen one's character. "No man is educated," said William James, "who has never dallied with the thought of suicide." As the result of suffering and longing for death, one resolves to act decisively. Suffering and the desire to die make one fearless, and this fearlessness translates into decisive action. As Johnson said, "after a man has taken the resolution to kill himself... he has nothing to fear."

One decisive action that is often preceded by suffering and by the desire to die is a religious conversion. Tolstoy described his pre-conversion state thus: "Behold me... hiding the rope in order not to hang myself."[1]

Crime is another decisive action that is often preceded by suffering and by the desire to die. The criminal often resolves to commit a crime after suffering has driven him to ask, 'what have I got to lose? Since I no longer want to live, why don't I fulfill my criminal desire at the same time as I end my life?' Mass mur-

---

[1] On William James, see Louis Untermeyer, *Makers of the Modern World,* "William James"; on Johnson, see James Boswell, *The Life of Johnson,* Aetat. 64; on Tolstoy, see William James, *Varieties of Religious Experience,* VI, 7.

derers often end their killing sprees by killing themselves. When Stendhal was contemplating suicide, he thought of assassinating Louis XVIII, in order to "make something of your misery," instead of dying to no purpose.

Sex is a third decisive action that is preceded by suffering and by the desire to die. Sex is closely related to death; people often fear sex, just as people often fear death. Lower animals, such as insects, often die during the sexual act. Orgasm is sometimes called, "a little death." Rank said, "the compulsive neurotic... abstains from sexual intercourse in order not to die."[1] According to the Book of Genesis, sex brought death into the world.

In addition to religious conversion, crime and sex, many other decisive actions are preceded by suffering and by the desire to die. Suffering makes one fearless, and thus prompts one to act decisively.

Tragedy depicts suffering, suffering that drives the tragic hero to desire death. The tragic hero's suffering and his desire to die instill in him courage for decisive action. The spectator, empathizing with the tragic hero, vicariously suffers and desires to die. The spectator's suffering and desire to die, though they are vicarious, instill in him courage for decisive action, and an appetite for living.

46. *Deconstruction* Perhaps the best way to approach Deconstruction is by looking at its antecedents, its foundations.

Scientific truths (for example, that the earth is round, not flat) aren't really understood unless they're challenged and questioned. As Mill put it, "Both teachers and learners go to sleep at their post, as soon as there is no enemy in the field."[2] To understand a widely-accepted scientific truth, we need to look at the arguments for it and against it, we need to bring ourselves back to a time when it was fighting for acceptance. If we simply tell a young student, "the earth is round, though it appears to be flat,"

---

[1] On Stendhal, see his *Memoirs of an Egoist*, §1; on Rank, see his *Psychology and the Soul*, 6
[2] *On Liberty*, ch. 2

he won't understand it as well as someone who has to look at the evidence, make up his own mind, and defend his view against people who maintain a contrary view.

What is true in the intellectual sphere is also true in the religious sphere. A religion that is widely accepted receives passive assent, while a religion that is fighting for acceptance receives enthusiastic adherence. If people are born Christian, and raised in a predominantly Christian society, they passively accept Christianity. Kierkegaard asked, "how does one become a Christian in a country where almost everyone is born Christian?" How can we bring ourselves back to the time when Christianity was fighting for acceptance? How can we regain the passionate faith of early Christians, who suffered and died for their belief?

Kierkegaard tried to awaken people from their pseudo-Christian slumber, and make them realize what it meant to be a Christian. He wanted people to think for themselves, choose for themselves, not just receive the official religion of their nation. Kierkegaard argued that if we simply give people The Truth, they won't understand it; if we simply tell people, "the earth is flat," they won't understand it. They must reach it by themselves, fight for it.

In *Either/Or*, Kierkegaard presented two worldviews—the aesthetic worldview of a young art-lover, and the ethical worldview of a mature family man. Then he said to the reader, "you choose. You choose either the aesthetic or the ethical. Don't expect someone to tell you who you are, to tell you that you're a Christian. Don't expect someone to tell you what is The Truth. Find it for yourself. Choose." Kierkegaard opposed Hegel's approach because Hegel attempted to set forth The Truth. Kierkegaard felt that Hegel's approach would put the individual to sleep; Kierkegaard wanted to awaken the individual, present him with choices, insist that he fight his way to truth.

Kierkegaard admired Socrates because Socrates didn't claim to possess Truth; Socrates said, "the only thing I know is that I know nothing." Socrates questioned established views, and tried to rouse people to think for themselves; Socrates referred to himself as a midwife, because he tried to draw out of people what was within them, instead of handing them Truth on a platter, and saying "swallow." Socrates spoke not with authority but with irony. Socrates and Kierkegaard used an indirect approach, while Hegel used a direct approach. The Socratic method has long been respected as an educational technique because it stirs students to think for themselves, to earn truth instead of just passively receiving it. Kierkegaard created various pseudonyms to present various viewpoints, and force the reader to choose among them; he didn't want to build up his own authority as a author, he didn't want the reader to receive Truth from him. Existentialism, which Kierkegaard pioneered, says we must choose for ourselves, we can't rely on Truth—objective, absolute, universal Truth—to tell us what to do.

Kierkegaard's indirect approach has influenced Deconstruction, which believes that an author doesn't directly state The Truth. Deconstruction concerns itself with what an author doesn't directly state; Deconstruction reads between the lines, it interprets an author's silences. This enables critics to keep themselves busy, but it can lead to some wild and groundless interpretations. A commentator on Kierkegaard, for example, after pointing out that Kierkegaard never mentioned his mother in his writings, declares that "Kierkegaard's mother, who was not well educated, is represented in his writings by the mother-tongue (Danish)."[1] This without even a "probably" or a "perhaps"!

Most writers communicate directly, not indirectly; Kierkegaard is one of the few to employ an indirect approach. But Deconstruction assumes that all writers communicate indirectly, that all writers use Kierkegaard's approach. Furthermore, Deconstruction applies Kierkegaard's insights to a field they weren't intended for; Kierkegaard's goal was spiritual awakening, not literary interpretation. Surely Kierkegaard would disapprove of the use that is being made of his work.

Deconstruction is popular with academics, but of no interest to laymen. Deconstruction leads to over-reading and over-interpreting. Among modern critics, "simple" has become a

---

[1] McDonald, William, "Søren Kierkegaard", The Stanford Encyclopedia of Philosophy (Winter 2001 Edition)

pejorative term, and the most strained interpretation is considered the deepest. Modern critics have forgotten that simplicity has long been considered a sign of truth, an aesthetic virtue, a moral virtue—even a virtue for literary critics. One of the greatest critics praised Tolstoy for the "rock-like" simplicity of his literary criticism.[1] Modern critics have forgotten that simplicity is a characteristic of good prose; their prose is an obscure, technical jargon.

Surely the Deconstruction trend will fade away, just as earlier trends in literary criticism faded away. The next generation of critics will take a different tack; as Proust said, "the critics of each generation confine themselves to maintaining the direct opposite of the truths admitted by their predecessors."[2]

47. *LitSpeak* is the language of contemporary literary criticism, as ArtSpeak is the language of contemporary art criticism. The traditional rules of English style are discarded (one might say reversed) by writers of LitSpeak.

In the old days, simplicity was regarded as the hallmark of good prose; the French writer La Bruyère said, "if you want to say that it is raining, say: 'It is raining'." A writer of LitSpeak has nothing but contempt for simplicity. The rule for LitSpeak is, "if you want to say that it is raining, say: 'The expectation of precipitation has been realized, and pluviation is presently occurring.'"

---

[1] see G. Wilson Knight's *Wheel of Fire*, "Tolstoy's Attack on Shakespeare", §2. Deconstruction might be compared with the Straussian approach, developed by Leo Strauss. Strauss believed that philosophers don't say what they mean, that philosophers conceal their views from fear of persecution, and from fear that their views will have a harmful effect on society. Straussians argue, for example, that many philosophers, from Machiavelli on, were atheists, but concealed their atheism. Strauss looked for hidden meanings and secret codes; he even hired someone who had been a code-breaker for the U.S. Army to study Machiavelli! Like Deconstruction, the Straussian approach is very popular in academia, but of no interest to laymen.

[2] *The Guermantes Way*, Part II, ch. 1

Note the abundance of polysyllables in LitSpeak. The old rule was "Choose words of Anglo-Saxon origin [most of which are monosyllables] in preference to words of Greek or Latin origin [most of which are polysyllables]." LitSpeak has reversed this rule, too, and prefers polysyllables.

If you're able to write LitSpeak, and want to know if you've really mastered it, ask yourself whether you dream in LitSpeak or English. If your dreams contain words like polysemantically, epideictic, and ekphrasis, then you know you're a master of LitSpeak.

48. *Deconstruction and E. M. Forster* Now let's see how one of today's deconstructors deals with a classic of modern fiction, Forster's *Howards End*. Forster's genius shows itself in deep thought, as well as in sparkling wit and superb prose. Like many modern intellectuals, Forster realizes that Christianity has had its day: "I cannot believe that Christianity will ever cope with the present world-wide mess…. It was a spiritual force once, but the indwelling spirit will have to be restated if it is to calm the waters again, and probably restated in a non-Christian form."[1] Forster was a great admirer of Whitman, and read Whitman just before writing *Howards End*, which is suffused with the Zen spirit of Whitman. Here's an example of the Zen spirit in *Howards End*:

> The present flowed by them like a stream. The tree rustled. It had made music before they were born, and would continue after their deaths, but its song was of the moment. The moment had passed. The tree rustled again. Their senses were sharpened, and they seemed to apprehend life. Life passed. The tree rustled again. "Sleep now," said Margaret. The peace of the country was entering into her. It has no commerce with memory, and little with hope…. It is the peace of the present, which passes understanding. Its murmur came "now," and "now" once more as they trod the gravel, and "now," as the moonlight fell upon their father's sword.[2]

---

[1] *Two Cheers For Democracy*, "What I Believe"
[2] ch. 40

Notice the Zennish emphasis on the present moment, and notice the Zennish awareness of the world around us.

When Forster says, "the indwelling spirit [of Christianity] will have to be restated," it suggests that there is a kernel of truth in Christianity, a mystical core that deserves respect, a mystical core that is similar to (perhaps even identical with) the mystical core in Islam, Buddhism, and other religions. An example of the mystical spirit in Christianity is this passage from the New Testament:

> Take no thought for your life, what ye shall eat, or what ye shall drink.... Which of you by taking thought can add one cubit unto his stature?.... Consider the lilies of the field, how they grow; they toil not, neither do they spin.[1]

In *Howards End*, Forster often expresses a similar thought, often says that we shouldn't spend the Present preparing for the Future. When one character says, "'It's as well to be prepared,'" another character responds, "'No—it's as well not to be prepared'.... She could not explain in so many words, but she felt that those who prepare for all the emergencies of life beforehand may equip themselves at the expense of joy."[2]

Forster points out that the thought of death focuses us on the present moment, the thought of death leads us to Zen. If we lived forever, it might make sense to accumulate for the future, to

---

[1] Matthew, 6:25

[2] ch. 7. Forster expresses the same idea in Chapter 12: "Our national morality.... assumes that preparation against danger is in itself a good, and that men, like nations, are the better for staggering through life fully armed.... Margaret hoped that for the future she would be less cautious, not more cautious, than she had been in the past." Thoreau also speaks of the folly of spending your life preparing for the future, the folly of over-preparation: "Men say that a stitch in time saves nine, and so they take a thousand stitches today to save nine tomorrow."(*Walden*, ch. 2). A writer on Zen, Alan Watts, wrote a book on the folly of over-preparation (*The Wisdom of Insecurity*). Watts points out that "[Christ's] life was from the beginning a complete acceptance and embracing of insecurity. 'The foxes have holes, and the birds of the air have nests, but the Son of Man hath not where to lay his head.'"(ch. 1)

accumulate money, but since we can die tomorrow, we should experience today, we should appreciate the present moment. When Leonard Bast, plagued by poverty, says "The real thing's money and all the rest is a dream," Helen responds, "You've forgotten Death.... If we lived forever what you say would be true. But we have to die, we have to leave life presently.... I love Death—not morbidly, but because He explains. He shows me the emptiness of Money.... Death destroys a man: the idea of Death saves him."[1]

But today's deconstructors don't find any Zen in Forster, or any philosophical ideas except those that they discover "between the lines." They believe that Forster hides behind the narrator of *Howards End*, that Forster is being ironic, duplicitous, evasive, that Forster is "playing games with the reader," that Forster doesn't mean what he says, or say what he means, that the countless thoughts and feelings expressed by the narrator aren't those of Forster himself (though the narrator's thoughts frequently agree with the thoughts that Forster expresses in his essays, letters, etc.). "He winks at us as if to acknowledge that the beliefs he offers are only that—beliefs that can be played with and used to create a posture." In short, today's deconstructors regard this delightful novel as a complicated game of hide-and-seek—so complicated that generations of readers missed Forster's irony, and failed to join in the game.[2]

Even when Forster expresses his love for his native land, the modern critic finds ambiguity and irony. Forster writes thus of the Isle of Wight:

> Seen from the west, the Wight is beautiful beyond all laws of beauty. It is as if a fragment of England floated forward to greet the foreigner—chalk of our chalk, turf of our turf, epitome of what will follow. And behind the fragment lie Southampton, hostess to the nations, and Portsmouth, a latent fire, and all around it, with double and treble collision of tides, swirls the sea. How

---

[1] ch. 27
[2] see Paul Armstrong, "The Narrator in the Closet: The Ambiguous Narrative Voice in *Howards End*", *Modern Fiction Studies* 47.2 (Summer 2001): 306-28

many villages appear in this view! How many castles! How many churches, vanished or triumphant![1]

Though it may seem that here, surely, Forster is speaking from the heart, the modern critic speaks of "the irony of the extravagant prose," which calls for "critical scrutiny." The modern critic fails to see that writers usually mean just what they say; the modern critic is "too clever by half."

While Forster's humor entertains the reader, and his profundity impresses the reader, perhaps Forster's chief virtue as a writer is his taste. He treats the reader well, he treats the reader as a friend. Every sentence is clear, every page is a pleasure. Wit and wisdom is everywhere. Even Miss Avery, a minor character, expresses the deepest wisdom when she says that the world is better than nothing.[2] A pessimist can point out many flaws in the world—death, suffering, injustice, etc.—but only the most extreme pessimist could take issue with Miss Avery's view that the world is better than nothing. Forster makes the same argument in one of his essays: "Though I am not an optimist, I cannot agree with Sophocles that it were better never to have been born."[3] Though life has many flaws, it is better than non-existence.

Miss Avery's deep wisdom is completely missed by the modern critic, who is convinced that *Howards End* doesn't contain philosophical ideas, because it is a novel, and novels don't contain philosophical ideas. But Forster himself said that he had large ambitions; when he was asked what he had learned from Jane Austen, he replied, "I learned the possibilities of domestic humor. I was more ambitious than she was, of course; I tried to hitch it on to other things."[4]

Some critics complained that Forster's ambitions were too large. Virginia Woolf, for example, wished that Forster would "write comedy only," and Woolf said that when Forster "forgets

---

[1] ch. 19
[2] ch. 33
[3] *Two Cheers For Democracy*, "What I Believe"
[4] 1952 interview. See *Howards End*, Norton Critical Edition, edited by P. Armstrong

that he should solve the problem of the universe, he is the most diverting of novelists." Roger Fry made a similar criticism: "I wish [Forster] weren't a mystic, or that he would keep his mysticism out of his books."[1] Forster grasped the spiritual crisis of his time, and saw a solution to it. Naturally, he didn't want to hide his light under a bushel.

If Forster's chief virtue is taste, one may wonder, where does taste come from? Forster's taste probably stems from his sunny disposition, from his deep understanding of literature, and from his deep love of literature. He was suffused with literature, it ran through his veins. He knew that literature could take over one's life, hence he struggled against it. In *Howards End*, he often says that culture isn't an end, that great writers are only sign-posts, and we shouldn't "mistake the sign-post for the destination."[2] One of the novel's chief characters, Margaret, grows in wisdom as the novel proceeds, and at the end of the novel, she has little interest in new books, or in other forms of culture:

> As for theaters and discussion societies, they attracted her less and less. She began to "miss" new movements, and to spend her spare time re-reading or thinking, rather to the concern of her Chelsea friends.... She had outgrown stimulants, and was passing from words to things. It was doubtless a pity not to keep up with Wedekind or John, but some closing of the gates is inevitable after thirty, if the mind itself is to become a creative power.[3]

Of Nietzsche, too, it may be said that he was suffused with literature, it ran through his veins, and of Nietzsche, too, it may be said that he struggled against it. Nietzsche agreed with Forster that the mind can't be a "creative power" if one is continually reading and learning:

> Scholars who at bottom do little nowadays but thumb books... ultimately lose entirely their capacity to think for themselves.... They *respond* to a stimulus (a thought they have read).... They themselves no longer think.... Early in the morning, when day

---

[1] ibid
[2] ch. 14
[3] ch. 31. Wedekind was a German dramatist, John a British painter.

breaks, when all is fresh, in the dawn of one's strength—to *read a book* at such a time is simply depraved![1]

Great minds think alike, and whatever genre they choose becomes a vehicle for their thoughts.

Forster's view of love is similar to Schopenhauer's. In a journal entry, Forster wrote, "We like the like and love the unlike."[2] Friendship is based on similarity of character, while love is often based on difference ("opposites attract"). *Howards End* deals with 'loving the unlike', it deals with love between a Schlegel (Margaret) and a Wilcox (Henry), it deals with love between two opposite types. Schopenhauer also believed that opposites attract; Schopenhauer argued that a masculine man would love a feminine woman, and a feminine man would love a masculine woman. Jungians argue that people usually marry their opposites; for example, an extrovert-rational person will marry an introvert-feeling person. According to Jungians, marriage means seeking wholeness by joining with someone who complements you, someone who supplies your deficiencies. On the subject of love, as on other subjects, Forster shows himself to be a deep thinker, someone whose thoughts should be taken seriously, not dismissed as ironic.

Margaret speaks of "personal relations, that we think supreme."[3] Margaret is here expressing Forster's own view; in one of his essays, Forster wrote, "My books emphasize the importance of personal relationships and the private life, for I believe in them." [4] This suggests that Forster's novels are vehicles for Forster's own views, that Forster meant what he said, that he wasn't hiding his meaning, that he wasn't being ironic.

The epigraph of *Howards End* is "Only connect..." and connecting is one of its chief themes. The following passage deals with Margaret's attempt to guide Henry toward spiritual growth:

---

[1] *Ecce Homo*, "Why I Am So Clever," #8
[2] See *Howards End*, Norton Critical Edition, p. 269
[3] ch. 4
[4] See "The Challenge of Our Time"

She need trouble him with no gift of her own. She would only point out the salvation that was latent in his own soul, and in the soul of every man. Only connect! That was the whole of her sermon. Only connect the prose and the passion, and both will be exalted, and human love will be seen at its height. Live in fragments no longer. Only connect, and the beast and the monk, robbed of the isolation that is life to either, will die.[1]

Here, surely, Forster is giving us the best advice that he has to give. The theme of connecting complements the mystical theme. Eastern mysticism doesn't emphasize connecting since the opposites (conscious/unconscious, reason/feeling, etc.) aren't as far apart in the Eastern psyche as in the Western; there is no need to connect what was never disconnected. In the West, however, the opposites are far apart, and there is an urgent need to connect in order to reach wholeness. Forster sees this, and speaks frequently of the need to connect. But today's deconstructors insist that Forster is being "deeply ironic"[2] when he speaks of connecting. And if generations of readers thought that he meant what he said, and took his advice to heart, aren't the deconstructors forced to conclude that Forster has deceived generations of readers, has led them astray?

Margaret's attempt to foster Henry's spiritual growth is a brave attempt for "it was hard-going in the roads of Mr. Wilcox's soul. From boyhood he had neglected them. 'I am not a fellow who bothers about my own inside....'"[3] Henry is a "persona character"; he has a well-developed persona, plays his social role competently, and achieves success in the business world, but his inner life is undeveloped. One might compare him with Tolstoy's "persona character", Alexey Karenina (Anna's husband).

Henry's wife, Ruth Wilcox, is the opposite of Henry, and while Henry is depicted in a negative light, Ruth is idealized. One might compare Ruth to Prince Myshkin, the protagonist of

---

[1] ch. 22
[2] Paul Armstrong
[3] ch. 22

Dostoyevsky's novel, *The Idiot*. Myshkin is Dostoyevsky's attempt to depict an ideal person, Myshkin is Christ-like. But Forster's ideal person isn't Christ-like because Forster's ideals don't come from Christianity; Forster's ideal person is connected to nature and to herself, devoted to things rather than words, Zennish. Ruth and Myshkin both have undeveloped personas, they're somewhat naive, and somewhat awkward in social situations.

Forster himself aspired to live the quiet life that Ruth lived. "Let me not be distracted by the world," Forster wrote in his journal in 1910; "never forget nature and to look at her freshly. Don't advance *one step more* into literary society than I have."[1] But for today's critics, Ruth isn't Forster's ideal, she is merely the narrator's ideal. Today's critics, influenced by the deconstruction fad, rob *Howards End* of its ideals and its wisdom, and leave nothing behind but irony and humor.

49. *Queer Theory and E. M. Forster* Another modern literary theory that has been applied to *Howards End* is Queer Theory. This theory sees Forster as a "queer artist" who is trying "to pass for normal even while secretly rebelling against the normative."[2] Thus, instead of trying to communicate thoughts and feelings, Forster is playing another game of hide-and-seek, "a game so subtle and slippery that it can pass without notice."[3]

Queer Theory, Feminist Theory, Race Theory—all these theories view writers in terms of their group, rather than their individuality; these theories politicize the humanities. A great writer is highly individual, transcends his group, attains universality, and speaks to people in distant times and places. Shakespeare, for example, transcends his nation and class, and speaks to people in distant times and places.

Instead of speaking of a "queer writer," a "female writer," etc., we should speak of a writer who happens to be queer, a writer who happens to be female, etc. The mystical theme in

---

[1] see *Howards End*, Norton Critical Edition, p. 274
[2] Paul Armstrong
[3] ibid

Howards End is similar to the mystical theme in the work of Thoreau, who wasn't queer. Likewise, the connecting theme in *Howards End* is similar to the connecting theme in Jung, who wasn't queer. Forster's sexual orientation has little impact on the major themes of *Howards End*.

Today's colleges strive for racial diversity, gender diversity, etc. But diversity isn't about race and gender, it's about individuality. The Concord intellectuals—Emerson, Thoreau, Hawthorne and Alcott—were a diverse group, though not diverse in terms of race or gender. The diversity of the Concord intellectuals is real diversity, the diversity of individual thought and personality.

50. *Skepticism* The modern critic believes that Forster is hiding behind the narrator, playing games with the reader, and being ironic, not striving to discover truth, and communicate truth as clearly as he can. Likewise, the modern critic believes that Kierkegaard hides behind pseudonyms, he doesn't strive to discover and communicate truth. And the modern critic thinks that Nietzsche doesn't believe in truth; he describes Nietzsche as a "German philosopher who argued that truth is not absolute but varies with perspective."[1]

The modern critic is a skeptic, and doesn't believe in truth, hence he sees Forster, Kierkegaard and Nietzsche as skeptics. The modern critic overlooks the fact that Nietzsche explicitly rejected skepticism, and that Nietzsche's "perspectivism" is one more theory, one more attempt to discover and communicate truth. Nietzsche realized the popularity of skepticism: "Skepticism is the most spiritual expression of... nervous debility and sickliness.... Our present-day Europe [is] skeptical in all its heights and depths."[2]

Truth entails responsibilities, and affects one's life. Skepticism is alluring because it doesn't entail responsibilities, it lets one live as one wishes. Furthermore, truth is threatening because someone else may lay claim to truth, and may act on it. Hitler,

---

[1] see *Howards End*, Norton Critical Edition, p. 329
[2] *Beyond Good and Evil*, §208

7. LITERATURE

Marx, bin Laden—all lay claim to truth, and all act on it. Nietzsche wrote,

> When a philosopher nowadays makes known that he is not a skeptic... he is henceforth said to be dangerous. With his repudiation of skepticism, it seems to them as if they heard some evil-threatening sound in the distance, as if a new kind of explosive were being tried somewhere... perhaps a newly discovered Russian nihilism, a pessimism... that not only denies, means denial, but—dreadful thought!—*practices* denial.[1]

Since truth brings responsibilities and threats, today's intellectuals eagerly embrace skepticism, they turn to what Nietzsche called "the mild, pleasing, lulling poppy of skepticism."[2] Today's intellectuals are fond of saying, "there is no truth," or "all truth is relative," or "all truth depends on one's perspective." Skepticism corrodes the life of the mind. We should believe in truth, and strive to discover it and communicate it, though it may be elusive, though it may bring with it threats and responsibilities.

51. *Does Culture Matter?* Forster came of age before World War I, and lived through both World Wars. Forster came of age in a world that respected culture, and lived to see a world that had little use for culture, and little respect for tradition. Forster decried this change, and championed culture and tradition. "That clamor for art and literature," Forster wrote, "which Ruskin and Morris thought they detected has died down.... There is a hostility to cultural stuff today which is disquieting." Forster realized that, in the modern world, "there will be work for all and play for all. But the work and the play will be split; the work will be mechanical and the play frivolous. If you drop tradition and culture you lose your chance of connecting work and play and creating a life which is all of a piece."

---

[1] ibid
[2] Ibid. "There are two ways to slide easily through life; to believe everything or to doubt everything. Both ways save us from thinking."
--Alfred Korzybski

Forster argues that culture isn't a pastime for epicures: "The higher pleasures.... resemble religion, and it is impossible to enjoy them without trying to hand them on." Forster tried to "hand them on" through his criticism, his essays, and his lectures. The best way to champion culture, Forster argues, is to enjoy it, and let others see that you enjoy it:

> Let one's light so shine that men's curiosity is aroused, and they ask why Sophocles, Velasquez, Henry James should cause such disproportionate pleasure. Bring out the enjoyment. If 'the Classics' are advertised as something dolorous and astringent, no one will sample them. But if the cultured person [is] obviously having a good time, those who come across him will be tempted to share it and to find out how.[1]

Forster is one of the 20th century's great humanists; he reminds one of Bernard Berenson and André Gide. Forster was a champion neither of popular culture nor of scholarly culture, but rather of culture that is connected to life, that aims at The Good Life, that is as serious as religion and as playful as a child's game, that links our generation to previous generations in a great conversation.

52. *Edmundson* While many modern scholars insist that authors like Forster are subtle, slippery, and ironic, one modern scholar, Mark Edmundson, became famous by taking a different tack, by arguing that literature advises us how to live, and changes our life. Edmundson argued that studying literature doesn't mean learning to interpret, rather it means having one's life and personality challenged. According to Edmundson, an author advises us how to live either directly or indirectly, either by precept or by example, either by his works or by his life. Students should "measure themselves against what they've read."[2] The study of literature should be life-changing, inspiring.

---

[1] *Two Cheers For Democracy*, "Does Culture Matter?"
[2] "On the uses of a liberal education," *Harper's Magazine*, Sept. 1, 1997

Edmundson complains that today's students are too self-satisfied to be inspired: "some measure of self-dislike, or self-discontent... seems to me to be a prerequisite for getting an education that matters. The pervading view is the cool consumer perspective, where passion and strong admiration are forbidden." Edmundson's work struck a chord, since it was clear that the study of literature had become over-specialized, divorced from life, interesting to no one except academics. Indeed, many publishers had decided not to publish literary criticism because it didn't interest the public.

Edmundson takes a dim view of today's students and today's universities, but he thinks that literature will survive as long as the isolated individual finds a great book, and is inspired, transformed.

8. Education

1. *Academia* Culture is an organic whole, but academia divides it into departments. Culture should be bound to life, but academia separates it from life and turns it into a trade. Culture should be free of charge, but academia makes it a commodity to be bought and sold.

Before the printing press was invented, when students couldn't afford their own books, a professor was one who read aloud to a class; the word "lecture" comes from the Latin *legere*, meaning "to read." The invention of the printing press has enabled students to buy their own books, and thus has eliminated the professor's raison d'etre. Johnson said, "People have nowadays... got a strange opinion that everything should be taught by lectures. Now, I cannot see that lectures can do so much good as reading the books from which the lectures are taken."[1] Education takes place between an author and a reader, not between a student and a professor; one becomes educated by reading, not by listening to lectures.

2. *The Scholar* Academia is the home of the scholar, not of the true intellectual. For the scholar, culture is a job and a means of making a living. For the true intellectual, culture is a passion, a

---

[1] *Life of Johnson*, Aetat. 57

love affair, a mission. The true intellectual often makes a living from non-intellectual work; Kafka, for example, made a living as a bureaucrat, Thoreau as a surveyor, and Hoffer as a dockworker. To the scholar, culture is his career; to the true intellectual, culture is his life. The scholar wasn't born for intellectual work; he would be at home in another profession—in law, medicine, business, etc. The true intellectual was born for intellectual work, and couldn't live without it; if it didn't exist, he would invent it. The scholar has a respected position in society, the true intellectual is an outcast from society, a stranger in the world.

Classics aren't written by scholars. Not even one classic in a hundred was written by an academic. Classics contain personality and pathos and suffering and anger and humor, all of which scholarly books lack. Classics are written with passion, and arouse passion in those who read them. Scholarly books are dry, cold and impersonal, and don't arouse passion in those who read them. Classics have life and vitality; cut them and blood will come out. Scholarly books are lifeless; cut them and dust will come out.

3. *Reading vs. Writing* Students should read more than they write. The best way to learn how to write good prose is to read good prose. Students should read the classics—for their style as well as their content. Students today are often asked to write papers that deal with a narrow subject. This encourages them to read obscure authors who treat the narrow subject that they're writing about. Thus, students don't read the classics, and they don't become broadly educated.

Professors, like students, should concentrate on reading and on studying the classics, not on writing. Professors, like students, should follow Schopenhauer's advice, and read what is good rather than write what is bad. Today's professors spend their time either reading second-rate literature within their specialized field, or writing second-rate literature within their specialized field. They feel compelled to write; their motto is, "publish or perish." Academia debases literature and turns it into a trade.

4. *Literature vs. Journalism* Modern books aren't written to be read by future generations, they're written for the present generation. Thus, most modern books are mere journalism, not real literature. People in earlier cultures wrote books as if they were going to last forever, as if they were going to be carved in stone. Nowadays, people write books as if they were going to last one year, then be recycled. People in earlier cultures took more pains with their letters than we take with our books; their letters were closer to being literature than our books are. Literature is gradually sinking to the level of journalism, just as education is gradually sinking to the level of vocational training.

5. *What is a Classic?* This question must be answered anew by each generation; each generation must redefine the classics. The body of classics must be continually rejuvenated by the addition of new books. As new books are added to the body of classics, other books must be subtracted, lest the number of classics becomes excessively large. Old classics must make way for new classics, just as a tree's lower branches die off as it grows taller and puts forth new branches. The body of classics should be kept small enough to allow the average person to read them. In the modern West, almost no one has read the classics, since culture has been fragmented into specialized fields.

The classics should be a combination of old and new—Homer and Kafka, Shakespeare and Freud. There is a tendency, however, to regard only old books as classics. Academia is slow to recognize modern books as classics. Academia's clock is always a few centuries slow. In the argument of "Ancients Versus Moderns," academia usually sides with the ancients. Academia prefers old writers like Aristotle, Machiavelli and Hobbes to modern writers like Kierkegaard, Ortega and Jung.

Modern writers, other things being equal, are more important, more relevant, than old writers. Modern writers have experienced modern civilization, and can discuss the problems of modern civilization. And modern writers have benefited from the advances in knowledge that have taken place in modern times. Nietzsche, for example, benefited from the advances made by Schopenhauer and Darwin, while Plato couldn't benefit from those advances. Likewise, the philosophers of our time can benefit from the advances made by Freud and Jung, while Nietzsche couldn't benefit from those advances. Modern writers are also preferable with respect to language: Forster's language, for example, is easier to read than Chaucer's.

Recently, the old argument of "Ancients Versus Moderns" has been overshadowed by another argument, an argument against the classics in general. According to this argument, the classics were chosen by white Western males, who ignored works by women and works by people of color. This argument is an extension to culture of principles that have already become widespread elsewhere—principles such as preferential treatment for women and minorities.

6. *The Unpublished Classic* Everyone can appreciate a classic when it's established, but few can appreciate a classic when it's still an unpublished manuscript. Consider *Swann's Way*, for example: it was rejected by numerous publishers, and even Gide, the foremost critic of his era, failed to see any merit in it. Frustrated, Proust wanted to publish *Swann's Way* at his own expense. But a friend persuaded him to send his manuscript to one more publisher, who returned it with a note that read, "Dear friend: I may be thicker-skinned than most, but I just can't understand why anyone should take thirty pages to describe how he tosses about in bed because he can't get to sleep. I clutched my head." [1] So Proust published *Swann's Way* at his own expense.

The most difficult task for a critic is to appreciate an original work before it's established. Most people wait until a book is established before praising it, just as most people clap when others clap. Only a few people clap alone.

7. *Foreign Languages* Why do people study foreign languages? Nowadays people usually study foreign languages for the sake of business or travel. In earlier periods, however, people studied foreign languages in order to read in those languages.

---

[1] André Maurois, *Proust: A Biography*, 9, 1

They studied Greek and Latin, for example, in order to read Greek and Latin literature in the original.

There are several arguments against studying a foreign language for the sake of reading. One such argument is the amount of time that must be spent doing it, which is so large that one could, during the same amount of time, read a great deal in translation. Another such argument is that people who study a foreign language usually acquire only a rough and incomplete knowledge of that language.

There are, however, several reasons to study Latin, even if one doesn't want to read Latin literature in the original. Studying Latin improves one's knowledge of vocabulary and grammar, and thus enables one to write better in one's own language. Is it possible to have a firm knowledge of a Latin-based language if one doesn't know Latin?

Until recently writers assumed that their readers knew Latin, and sprinkled their works with Latin phrases. Thus, knowing Latin enables one to read many books with greater understanding and enjoyment.

8. *The Good Life* Montaigne complained that education in his day had no effect on a person's life, that it stuffed the brain without improving the person. Likewise, Nietzsche complained that the study of history diverted people's attention from their own lives; "we would serve history," wrote Nietzsche, "only so far as it serves life."[1] Nietzsche praised Greek philosophers for teaching through the example of their own lives, instead of devoting themselves to abstract questions that were remote from actual life. The goal of philosophy, like the goal of history, like the goal of education in general, should be The Good Life.

Just as Nietzsche complained that history had strayed too far from life, so too Ruskin complained that economics had strayed too far from life. Ruskin challenged the proud science of economics, and insisted that all its theories of wages, value, labor, etc. were worthless if they didn't make people's lives better. A nation that was wealthy in financial terms but not in

---

[1] *Untimely Essays*, "The Use and Abuse of History"

quality-of-life was a nation that was on the wrong track. Ruskin said, "There is no wealth but life."[1] The goal of economics, too, should be The Good Life.

9. *Bernard Berenson* Goethe was a great humanist because he never lost sight of man, never lost sight of the individual human life. Whether he was engaged in scientific studies, or painting, or political affairs, or literary projects, he never forgot that the greatest masterpiece is a human being, and the greatest achievement is self-culture, self-development, *bildung* (to use the German term). Goethe would have agreed with the Chinese humanists who said, "it is not truth that makes man great, but man who makes truth great."

If Goethe was a leading humanist of the early 19th century, Bernard Berenson was a leading humanist of the early 20th century. Goethe had said that visual art should be life-enhancing—that is, it should heighten our joy in existence, our love of the world. Berenson developed this idea, and applied it to the history of Italian painting. When he was in his thirties, Berenson began writing *Italian Painters of the Renaissance*, in which he argued that great art is life-enhancing. Berenson regarded the nude figure as the perfect subject for life-enhancing art; he praised Pollaiuolo's *Battle of the Nudes*:

> The pleasure we take in these savagely battling forms arises from their power to directly communicate life, to immensely heighten our sense of vitality.... The significance of all these muscular strains and pressures is so rendered that we cannot help realizing them; we imagine ourselves imitating all the movements, and exerting the force required for them.... While under the spell of this illusion [we] feel as if the elixir of life, not our own sluggish blood, were coursing through our veins.[2]

Throughout his long career, Berenson continued to believe that great painting is life-enhancing. In the late 1940s, when he was in his eighties, Berenson wrote *Aesthetics and History in the Visual Arts*, in which he argued that art should provide models

---

[1] *Unto This Last*, "Ad Valorem"
[2] *Italian Painters of the Renaissance*, "Florentine Painters," §8

for people, just as Nietzsche had argued that history should provide models for people. Berenson praises paintings that provide a vision of The Good Life, paintings that

> offer the noblest models for mankind to attain, models of realizable and never impossible states of being and ways of living.... Raphael's "Disputa," "School of Athens," and "Parnassus" seem now, as they did fifty years ago, the clearest and most convincing visions of the perfect existence for which we yearn, and which we hope to attain.[1]

Berenson was as fond of nature as he was of art, and he loved to walk in the hills around Florence. He believed that one of the chief benefits of studying art is that it heightens one's appreciation of nature.

Berenson's middle years were spent writing *Drawings of the Florentine Painters*, which was his most detailed, most scholarly book. He worked on this book for many years; day after day, he walked from Fiesole down into Florence, and pored over drawings in the Uffizi. Later, he felt that this book was a distraction from his true calling; he felt that he should have been a generalist, not a specialist; he felt that he should have applied the idea of life-enhancement to literature, and to other branches of culture.

As a young man, Berenson had aspired to be a generalist, a humanist, a second Goethe, and in his old age, he achieved this goal with books like *Aesthetics and History in the Visual Arts* and *Sketch for a Self-Portrait*. "All the arts," wrote Berenson, "poetry, music, ritual, the visual arts, the theater, must work singly and together to create the most comprehensive art of all, a humanized society, and its masterpiece, the free man: free within and free without, ready in Goethe's untarnishable words to live manfully in the whole, the good, and the beautiful."[2]

One of Berenson's greatest pleasures was conversation. He lamented the fact that, in the modern world, conversation is becoming a lost art, and is no longer taken seriously. Berenson

---

[1] *Aesthetics and History in the Visual Arts* (Pantheon Books, 1948, NY), ch. 3
[2] ibid, Conclusion. Goethe's original: "Im guten, ganzen, shönen resolut zu leben."

says that, like other arts, conversation should have no utilitarian purpose. Berenson met several experts at monologue, like Oscar Wilde, but his favorite conversation was dialogue—an exchange of thoughts that gave birth to new thoughts. The best conversationalist, according to Berenson, was a man who is famous not for his monologues, but for his questions: Socrates. One who often conversed with Socrates, Plato, said "it is the speech of the man who knows that is alive, the written word is really but its ghost."[1] And it was with his speech, not his pen, that Socrates made his mark on history, just as Jesus and Buddha made their mark with their speech, not their pen.

The art historian Kenneth Clark, who knew many eminent intellectuals, described Berenson's conversation thus:

> It was indeed a remarkable performance, of which the reader of his later journals can form a faint impression. The flow of ideas, the range of historical reference, the intellectual curiosity and unexpected human sympathy were certainly beyond those of anyone I have met.[2]

Berenson especially enjoyed conversing with women. He says that people of the same sex are often divided by "jealousy, envy, and spite."[3] Jungians tell us that the shadow causes conflict between people of the same sex, but between people of the opposite sex, the shadow causes merely annoyance.

Berenson was fond of conversation and reading, but not of writing; he always wrote with reluctance. He would have understood Wilde's remark, "I am too fond of reading books to care to write them."[4]

10. *Kenneth Clark* One of Berenson's disciples was Kenneth Clark. Like Berenson, Clark understood that culture could be life-enhancing, could strengthen our desire to live.

---

[1] See Berenson's *Sketch for a Self-Portrait*, Part 2, Ch. 3
[2] *Another Part of the Wood*, p. 156
[3] ibid, Part 1, Ch. 1
[4] Wilde, *Dorian Gray*, ch. 3

Clark became world-famous in 1969 as a result of a TV series called *Civilization*. When Clark had first been introduced to Berenson's writings, at the age of 16, he had been deeply impressed, and when a friend asked him what he wanted to do after leaving school, he replied, "Help Mr. Berenson to produce a new edition of his book on the drawings of the Florentine painters."[1] This from a teenager who had never met Berenson, and didn't even live in the same country as Berenson!

Six years later, Clark visited Italy, and was introduced to Berenson. As he was leaving, Berenson asked him if he would help with a new edition of his book on the drawings of the Florentine painters. The realization of his youthful ambition was (says Clark) "rather uncanny—like something out of a fairy-tale."[2] Thus began Clark's two-year apprenticeship with Berenson.

One of Clark's first loves in the world of art was Japanese prints. He felt that whatever misfortunes he suffered, whatever problems life presented him with, he could always enjoy his Japanese prints, and his other favorites. For Clark, art was a source of pleasure, art was something to live for.

Clark believed that the purpose of art criticism is to keep alive or revive one's enjoyment of an art work. Clark was an aesthetic hedonist. Academia often overlooks the "pleasure factor," and turns culture into a task. Academics were scornful of Clark's TV series, but laymen felt that Clark's series strengthened their desire to live. Clark says that he received forty or fifty letters a day, and he received nine letters "from people who said that they had been on the point of committing suicide, and that my programs had saved them."[3] Here we have a concrete example of the life-enhancing function of culture.

---

[1] K. Clark, *Another Part of the Wood: A Self-Portrait*, Harper & Row, 1974, p. 76
[2] ibid, p. 129
[3] *The Other Half* (the second volume of Clark's memoirs), Harper & Row, 1977, ch. 4, p. 223

11. *Zen Education* Zen is practical and doesn't try to stuff the brain with knowledge. Zen never strays from life itself. Zen touches a person deeply, it touches every breath he takes.

One facet of life to which Zen seems especially relevant is parenting. Zen teaches patience, of which a parent has great need since parenting involves a thousand little annoyances. Zen encourages perception rather than reflection, and thus develops in the parent a mental state akin to that of a child, and an appreciation of nature that can be transferred to a child. A Zen parent teaches his child not to regard the present as a preparation for the future, not to be preoccupied with himself, not to take himself too seriously, not to view life as a competition (for academic success, for wealth, for popularity, for moral virtue, etc.), and not to feel that he should be doing something at all times. A Zen parent instills in his child joy in existence, joy in the simplest, most ordinary things, a love of life, a love of the world.

The Good Life is not only a goal for the child, but also for the parent; a parent shouldn't be so preoccupied with his child's life that he forgets his own life.

A parent should remember that evil is part of human nature, there is a dark side in everyone, a shadow in everyone. The child's misbehavior shouldn't be countenanced, but it shouldn't astonish us either; the child's misbehavior should be met with understanding disapproval.

12. *Oxford vs. Stratford* When we hear how the theories of Copernicus, Galileo, and others were received, when we hear how those theories were ignored or ridiculed or suppressed, we think that such things couldn't occur in our age, that our age is free and open, enlightened and advanced. Actually, the progress of truth is as slow now as it was in the past.

Academia is supposed to pursue truth, but academia is often more concerned with defending established dogmas than with discovering truth. One established dogma that academia defends is that the works attributed to Shakespeare were indeed written by William Shakespeare of Stratford. There's little evidence supporting this dogma, and abundant evidence suggesting that these works were written by the Earl of Oxford. The evidence suggests that the Stratford man could barely write, let alone write plays, let alone write plays of extraordinary quality. But the Stratford theory still survives.

Academia suppresses the Oxford theory, just as the church suppressed heretics. When *Harvard Magazine* published a defense of the Oxford theory in 1974, Harvard professors were furious with the magazine's editor for allowing the Oxford theory to have a hearing. A proponent of the Oxford theory would have little chance of winning a position in academia. To succeed in academia, one must espouse popular opinions and defend established dogmas.

Beginning in the nineteenth century, many leading intellectuals rejected the Stratford theory. (The leading intellectuals of a given period often reach the same conclusions; academia reaches those conclusions, too, but not until many years have passed.) Whitman, for example, emphatically rejected the Stratford theory: "I am firm against Shaksper—I mean the Avon man, the actor." Mark Twain said he was "composedly and contentedly sure" that the Stratford man wasn't the real author. Henry James said, "I am 'sort of' haunted by the conviction that the divine William is the biggest and most successful fraud ever practiced on a patient world."

Criticism of the Stratford dogma prompted people to ask, "if the Stratford man didn't write those works, then who did?" Several candidates were suggested, but it was impossible to make a convincing case for any of them. Finally, an English schoolteacher, J. T. Looney, conducted a systematic search for the real author, discovered that it was the Earl of Oxford, and published his findings in 1920. Freud, after reading Looney's book, said "the man of Stratford... seems to have nothing at all to justify his claim, whereas Oxford has almost everything."[1]

But the views of leading intellectuals don't matter to English professors; they aren't the views of specialists. Specialists know better, specialists understand great writers better than great writ-

---

[1] See Charlton Ogburn, *The Mysterious William Shakespeare: The Myth and the Reality*, ch. 10. Nietzsche, Whittier, Galsworthy, Bismarck and others also rejected the Stratford theory.

ers do. Specialists can write fat biographies of the Stratford man—biographies built of straw, with a foundation of sand.

13. *Discoveries, Re-discoveries*   Looney's discovery was actually a re-discovery, since the identity of "Shakespeare" was known, at least to a few people, in Shakespeare's time. Likewise, Copernicus didn't discover the heliocentric theory, but rather re-discovered it centuries after a Greek astronomer discovered it. Columbus didn't discover America, but rather re-discovered it centuries after Vikings and other peoples had discovered it. How many "discoveries" are actually re-discoveries? Didn't Plato say that all knowledge is remembering?

14. *Twain and Shakespeare*   Near the end of his life, in 1909, Twain wrote an essay called "Is Shakespeare Dead?" in which he discusses the Shakespeare controversy. He tells us that he has been interested in this controversy for fifty years—ever since he read a book by the American writer Delia Bacon. Twain devotes most of his essay to attacking the Stratford Theory. Twain argues that the Stratford man's environment and education weren't the sort to produce *Hamlet*. Twain describes Stratford as

> a small back settlement which in that day was shabby and unclean, and densely illiterate. Of the nineteen important men charged with the government of the town, thirteen had to "make their mark" in attesting important documents, because they could not write their names. [Shakespeare's] father could not read, and even the surmisers surmise that he did not keep a library.

Twain notes that whoever wrote the works attributed to Shakespeare had a deep knowledge of law:

> At every turn and point at which the author required a metaphor, simile, or illustration, his mind ever turned *first* to the law. He seems almost to have *thought* in legal phrases, the commonest of legal expressions were ever at the end of his pen in description or illustration. That he should have descanted in lawyer language when he had a forensic subject in hand, such as Shylock's bond, was to be expected, but the knowledge of law in "Shakespeare" was exhibited in a far different manner: it protruded itself on all

occasions, appropriate or inappropriate, and mingled itself with strains of thought widely divergent from forensic subjects.[1]

The true author was steeped in the law; his legal knowledge was such as couldn't have been acquired by mere reading, mere socializing with lawyers. He had a "perfect familiarity with not only the principles, axioms, and maxims, but the technicalities of English law, a knowledge so perfect and intimate that he was never incorrect and never at fault."[2] Twain describes how Stratfordians have struggled to explain the poet's legal knowledge—how they've supposed that he was a clerk in a Stratford law office, etc.

Twain argues that the Stratford argument is based on conjecture:

> The historians "suppose" that Shakespeare attended the Free School in Stratford from the time he was seven years old till he was thirteen. There is no *evidence* in existence that he ever went to school at all. The historians "infer" that he got his Latin in that school—the school which they "suppose" he attended.... It is *surmised* that he travelled in Italy and Germany and around, and qualified himself to put their scenic and social aspects upon paper; that he perfected himself in French, Italian and Spanish on the road.

Stratfordians resort to conjecture because evidence is lacking. "We can go to the records," Twain writes, "and find out the life-history of every renowned *race-horse* of modern times—but not Shakespeare's!"

Twain describes the Stratford man's will as

> eminently and conspicuously a business man's will, not a poet's. It mentioned *not a single book*. Books were much more precious than swords and silver-gilt bowls and second-best beds in those days, and when a departing person owned one he gave it a high place in his will. The will mentioned *not a play, not a poem, not an unfinished literary work, not a scrap of manuscript of any kind*. Many poets have died poor, but this is the only one in history that

---

[1] Twain is quoting the anti-Stratford writer George Greenwood, who is quoting a lawyer named Lord Penzance.
[2] This, too, is a quote from Lord Penzance.

has died *this* poor; the others all left literary remains behind. Also a book. Maybe two.

Twain notes that the reaction to the Stratford man's death wasn't the sort of reaction that you'd expect to the death of an illustrious poet:

> When Shakespeare died in Stratford *it was not an event*. It made no more stir in England than the death of any other forgotten theatre-actor would have made. Nobody came down from London; there were no lamenting poems, no eulogies, no national tears— there was merely silence, and nothing more. A striking contrast with what happened when Ben Jonson, and Francis Bacon, and Spenser, and Raleigh and the other distinguished literary folk of Shakespeare's time passed from life!

In Twain's day, the Stratford man's chief rival was Francis Bacon. Twain doesn't try to build a detailed case for Bacon, he simply argues that Bacon had the wonderful education, and the amazing talents, that one would expect to find in the author of the works attributed to Shakespeare. Twain quotes from Macaulay's essay on Bacon:

> In a letter written when he was only thirty-one, to his uncle, Lord Burleigh, [Bacon] said, "I have taken all knowledge to be my province" ....The knowledge in which Bacon excelled all men was a knowledge of the mutual relations of all departments of knowledge.

Such vast ambitions, such vast knowledge, such an inter-disciplinary approach, is what one would expect to find in a first-rate philosopher. Bacon was the Aristotle of England, and he possessed an eloquence, a rhetorical gift, that we don't find in Aristotle. Twain points out that Bacon was fond of humor—as "Shakespeare" was.

Surely Twain is correct when he says that Bacon is a stronger candidate to be "Shakespeare" than the Stratford man. "It is evident," Twain writes, "that [Bacon] had each and every one of the mental gifts and each and every one of the acquirements that are so prodigally displayed in the Plays and Poems, and in much higher and richer degree than any other man of his time or of any previous time.... There was only one of him; the planet could not produce two of him at one birth, nor in one age. He could have written anything that is in the Plays and Poems." As Twain was writing these lines, Looney was building his case for Oxford, and soon Looney would show that the planet could produce two such geniuses in one age. What an age!

Twain understands how difficult it is to overthrow the Stratford Theory, weak though it is:

> I am aware that when even the brightest mind in our world has been trained up from childhood in a superstition of any kind, it will never be possible for that mind, in its maturity, to examine sincerely, dispassionately, and conscientiously any evidence or any circumstance which shall seem to cast a doubt upon the validity of that superstition.... It is the way we are made. It is the way we are all made, and we can't help it, we can't change it.... I haven't any idea that Shakespeare will have to vacate his pedestal this side of the year 2209.

15. *Whitman and Shakespeare* While Whitman's own work was eminently democratic, and championed the common man, Whitman regarded Shakespeare as the exact opposite, as eminently aristocratic. He said that Shakespeare's history plays were

> conceived out of the fullest heat and pulse of European feudalism—personifying in unparalleled ways the medieval aristocracy, its towering spirit of ruthless and gigantic caste, with its own peculiar air and arrogance (no mere imitation).... Everything possible is done in the Shakespeare plays to make the common people seem common—very common indeed.[1]

Whitman rejected the conventional view that Shakespeare was from the middle class. Stratfordians often accuse Oxfordians of snobbery, but surely Whitman, the arch-democrat, can't be accused of snobbery. Whitman remarked on the lack of evidence in support of the Stratford theory:

> It is remarkable how little is known of Shaksper the actor.... The record is almost a blank—it has no substance whatever: scarcely anything that is said of him is authorized.

---

[1] See "Walt Whitman on Shakespeare," by Paul A. Nelson, Newsletter of the Shakespeare Oxford Society, Fall, 1992

Who, then, wrote the works attributed to Shakespeare? "Only one of the 'wolfish earls' so plenteous in the plays themselves," said Whitman, "or some born descendent and knower, might seem to be the true author of those amazing works." A wolfish earl like Edward de Vere, the 17th Earl of Oxford. Surely Whitman would have been a passionate champion of the Oxford theory, if he had lived to hear about it. The Oxford theory was discovered about fifteen years after Whitman died.

Whitman was wise enough to remain an agnostic with respect to the Bacon theory—he neither accepted it nor rejected it ("as to Bacon, well, I don't know"). Twain was also an agnostic with respect to the Bacon Theory: "I only *believed* Bacon wrote Shakespeare," Twain said, "whereas I *knew* Shakespeare didn't."

Whitman was also wise enough to understand how difficult it would be to overthrow the traditional view of Shakespeare:

> The typical literary man is no more able to examine this question dispassionately than a priest is to pass on objections to the doctrine of the atonement, hell, heaven: not a bit more able: the scribblers are blind from the start.

Whitman said that Stratfordians used "dirty tricks" and *ad hominem* attacks to discredit their opponents; this is still true today.

If Oxford was the real author of the works attributed to Shakespeare, why didn't he publish under his own name? Why did he hide behind the pseudonym William Shakespeare? Writing plays wasn't considered appropriate for an aristocrat. Since Oxford was close to the Queen, and since he was the son-in-law of the Queen's chief minister, there may have been political reasons, or social reasons, to conceal his involvement with the theater.

Nothing could be printed without a government license, so the government had the power to conceal Oxford's authorship. The true identity of "Shakespeare" sank into oblivion because the Puritans closed the theaters, and because of the English Civil War. War always grabs people's attention, and causes them to forget matters that formerly held their attention. One of the casualties of the English Civil War was the truth about Shakespeare.

16. *Passing Singular* What sort of man was Edward de Vere, 17th Earl of Oxford (better known by his pseudonym "William Shakespeare")? He was much the sort of man that one would expect: he had a superb education (he entered Cambridge at age eight, and had private tutors before that), he was from a cultured family (two of his uncles, Surrey and Sheffield, were prominent poets, and another uncle, Arthur Golding, was a scholar and translator), he was exposed to drama at an early age (his father kept his own acting troupe), he began writing while still in his teens (he probably published an early version of *Romeo and Juliet* at age 13, and a translation of Ovid's *Metamorphoses* at age 17), he went to law school (his letters show legal knowledge), he participated avidly in the sports of the nobility (sports like falconry, which is mentioned often in Shakespeare's plays), he was an expert at jousting (he participated in several tournaments, and often emerged from the lists victorious), he had a temper, and perhaps a violent streak (when he was 17, he killed a cook with his sword), he was a passionate lover (his extra-marital affair with Anne Vavasor produced a son, and also angered the Queen, who clapped him and his mistress in the Tower of London), he was eccentric (Gabriel Harvey called him "a passing singular odd man"), he was close to the Queen, and close to the levers of power (scholars had wondered how Shakespeare was so familiar with politics), and he had a passion for travel, especially for travel to countries renowned for culture (he spent several months in Italy, and planned a journey to Greece).

While traveling on the Continent, Oxford may have encountered the poet George Chapman. In one of his plays, Chapman has a character say that he encountered Oxford in Germany, and that he found him to be

> ...the most goodly fashion'd man
> I ever saw: from head to foot in form
> Rare and most absolute...
> He was beside of spirit passing great
> Valiant and learn'd, and liberal as the sun,

Spoke and writ sweetly, or of learned subjects,
Or of the discipline of public weals.[1]

17. *Shakespeare and Goethe* There are many parallels between Shakespeare and Goethe—aside from the obvious one that they were both great poets. Both were "Renaissance men" with a wide range of interests: Goethe was a painter, actor and scientist, while Shakespeare was an expert in music, plants, sports, etc. Both were involved in politics, and lived in close proximity to the levers of power (Goethe, however, wasn't involved in military affairs as Shakespeare was). Both were Northern Europeans who had a passion for Italy; they flourished in Italy, they found themselves in Italy. Goethe called Rome, "the land where I was absolutely happy for the first time in my life."[2] Shakespeare's passion for Italy is evident in his plays, many of which are set in Italy. Both Goethe and Shakespeare were Hermetic thinkers; Goethe had a keen interest in the occult, and Jung said that Goethe's *Faust* was an alchemical work from top to bottom.

Goethe regarded Shakespeare as a father-figure, a second father. Just as a young child emulates his father, so a young adult emulates his second father. Doubtless the young Goethe emulated Shakespeare. Goethe would have had a keen interest in the identity of Shakespeare, just as he would have had a keen interest in the identity of his own father. Goethe would not have understood the common view that "it doesn't matter who Shakespeare was. We have the wonderful poetry, isn't that enough?" Shakespeare represents a high point of human achievement. If it doesn't matter who Shakespeare was, what does matter?

Goethe said, "Of what use are all the arts of a talent, if we do not find in a theatrical piece an amiable or great personality of the author? This alone influences the cultivation of the people."[3] Goethe is saying that the personality of the author not only mat-

---

[1] *The Mysterious William Shakespeare: The Myth and the Reality*, by Charlton Ogburn, 1984, Dodd, Mead & Co., ch. 19
[2] *Goethe: The History of a Man*, by Emil Ludwig, ch. 7
[3] *Conversations with Eckermann*, March 8, 1827

ters, it's the heart and soul of the drama. Goethe thinks the personality of the author (his "amiable or great personality") provides people with a model or ideal, and can guide people toward culture, toward personal growth. Goethe himself was such a model or ideal, and often appeared in the dreams of Germans as a father-figure, an ideal.

A critic of the Oxford Theory will say, "Oxford had many faults, he was neither 'amiable' nor 'great'." I don't deny that Oxford had faults. Goethe and Oxford both had a dark side, a shadow side. Goethe could depict Faust and Mephistopheles because he was acquainted with both, he had both within himself, he had the light and the shadow. Because of his contradictory nature, the impression Goethe made on people was contradictory. After Schiller met him, Schiller said, "it is a most peculiar mixture of love and hatred that he has inspired in me."[1] Goethe said that he knew a man "who, without saying a word, could suddenly silence a party engaged in cheerful conversation, by the mere power of his mind. Nay, he could also introduce a tone which would make everybody feel uncomfortable."[2] Doubtless this un-named man is Goethe himself. Goethe was acquainted with the occult power of the shadow.

But while Goethe and Oxford both had dark sides, they were, on the whole, great men, and impressed some of their contemporaries as such. Percival Golding said of Oxford, "I will only speak what all men's voices confirm: He was a man in mind and body absolutely accomplished with honorable endowments." Napoleon was more concise; after meeting Goethe, Napoleon said, "there is a man (*voilà un homme*)."

18. *Peer Review*   One of the cornerstones of academia is peer review, but peer review favors established ideas, and resists revolutionary ideas. Nicholas Negroponte, former head of the MIT Media Lab and current head of "One Laptop Per Child," said

---

[1] *Goethe: The History of a Man*, by Emil Ludwig, ch. 9
[2] *Conversations with Eckermann*, 10/7/27

I was always apprehensive of the peer review system. And I still am to this day, because, if your peers are reviewing you.... they're doing it from a point of view that is to some degree the establishment.... The peer review system suffers from often dismissing things, because they don't fit into what we're currently doing.[1]

Peer review frowns on new paradigms, like the Oxford Theory. Established scholars work within existing paradigms, they're concerned with "normal science," they resist revolutions. Wikipedia, on the other hand, allows new ideas to break through. A traditional encyclopedia is an organ of the establishment, and gives you the establishment view of Shakespeare. Wikipedia gives you both the Stratford Theory and the Oxford Theory.

If the Oxford Theory is true, then the academic establishment has failed miserably to understand the greatest of imaginative writers. Perhaps the establishment should re-think its methods, re-think the idea of peer review, and consider borrowing a page from Wikipedia. Perhaps Wikipedia has discovered a new approach to scholarly work, an approach that is especially well-suited to revolutionary ideas.

It's striking how many scholars have been taken in by the Stratford Theory, and it's also striking how many geniuses have rejected the Stratford Theory. Eissler said that, in the world of science, genius can be recognized by its discovery of new paradigms.[2] The same is true in the humanities: genius has a knack for discovering new paradigms, rejecting false paradigms, being receptive to paradigms discovered by others, etc.

We tend to believe that truth is discovered by careful research, by good methodology, etc. But perhaps genius—the vision of genius—is the best way to discover truth. Eissler said, "I doubt that the generally accepted principle of striving and searching as the means by which to accomplish the goal of finding the truth [is] correct. Freud made his great discoveries when he *let the truth come to him*."[3] Genius usually makes its discoveries through intuition, not through laborious research; genius

---

[1] Interview on C-SPAN's "Q & A," 11/25/07
[2] *Talent and Genius: The Fictitious Case of Tausk contra Freud*, ch. 7
[3] ibid

sees the truth. Decades of research may not be as effective in discovering truth as the vision of genius, as a flash of intuition. The Shakespeare case shows that academia is designed for the painstaking work of refining an existing paradigm; academia resists new paradigms, and thereby impedes the progress of truth.

9. Language

1. *How Languages Change* Europeans once believed that Hebrew was the first language, and that Greek and Latin were descended from Hebrew. After all, Hebrew was the language of the Old Testament, the language in which the creation of the world was described. Scholars labored mightily to find connections between Hebrew and Greek/Latin, but their labors bore little fruit. One scholar suggested that since Hebrew was written from right to left, and Greek from left to right, Greek words could perhaps be traced back to Hebrew by being read from right to left. But that suggestion, too, proved unavailing.

In the late 1600's, the philosopher Leibniz argued that Hebrew wasn't the first language. Leibniz urged missionaries and travelers to make notes on the languages they encountered; Leibniz inspired the scientific study of language. Travelers in North America noticed that American Indians spoke many different languages, and that these languages changed rapidly. Linguistic variety is caused by political fragmentation; rapid linguistic change occurs when a language is spoken by a small community, and when it isn't stabilized by a written literature.

The Chinese language has been remarkably stable, since China had a high degree of political unity and a long literary tradition. Since Chinese has changed little, it still has the characteristics of a primitive language. Like all primitive languages, Chinese is composed of nothing but monosyllables; it requires no effort to find the root of a Chinese word, because every word is a root. Chinese roots scarcely deserve to be called "roots" since they lie on the surface, in plain view. Take the days of the week, for example: Monday through Saturday are called Day One, Day Two, etc., up to Day Six. (Sunday is called Day of the Sun, or Day of the Sky.) Since Chinese names of days are so simple, one can't speak of the "roots" of these names. In English, on the other hand, the names of days are far more complex, and their roots are much deeper, stretching back to Roman and Germanic terms. Wednesday, for example, comes from the Germanic god Woden, and Friday comes from the god Frigga.

In Chinese, the names of months are also very simple; months are numbered one through twelve (Month One, Month Two, etc.). Something similar is found in English; September, October, November and December come from the Latin words for seven, eight, nine and ten. But these names aren't for Month Seven through Month Ten. Since two months were named in honor of the emperors Julius and Augustus (July and August), the remaining months are mis-named, mis-numbered. September, for example, which comes from the Latin word for seven, is actually the ninth month, etc. If you ask an English-speaker, "what is the root of September?" he isn't likely to know, whereas a Chinese-speaker would find the question so easy as to be meaningless.

A similar situation prevails with place names. Any Chinese-speaker can tell you that Beijing means "north capital," Nanjing "south capital," Sichuan "four rivers," etc., but how many English-speakers know that Connecticut means "long tidal river"? American Indian names (like Connecticut) are mixed with French names (such as Vermont, "green mountain), Spanish names (such as Arizona, "arid region"), etc. What confusion, what obscurity compared to Chinese!

Like all primitive languages, Chinese has no grammar. The plural form of a Chinese word is formed by adding a word that expresses plurality; the past tense of a Chinese word is formed by adding a word that expresses past time. In short, Chinese words don't change to express a certain grammatical form; rather, they're combined with other words that express number, tense, etc.

Unlike Chinese words, Greek and Latin words have many different forms, depending on their grammatical function. The Romans began studying grammar in order to facilitate the study of Greek. Soon grammar became a passion among educated Romans. Caesar wrote a book on grammar during his Gallic campaign; in fact, Caesar invented the grammatical term "ablative."

It would be wrong to suppose that grammar is a sign of growth, and that Greek and Latin are more advanced than Chinese since they have a more elaborate grammar. Actually, grammar is a sign of decay. All grammatical forms were once independent words, words that gradually decayed into mere endings. Take the English past tense, for example. In English, the past tense is usually formed by adding *ed* to a verb. This ending was once an independent word—the word *did*. Instead of saying "I loved," English-speakers once said "I love did."

The French adverb is another example of a grammatical form that was once two independent words. The French adverb is formed by adding *ment* to an adjective. This ending was originally a separate word, *mens* or *mente*, meaning mind. For example, *fortement* (strongly) was originally *forti mente* (with a strong mind, or strongly).

The process by which independent words coalesce into grammatical forms is sometimes called "phonetic corruption." Phonetic corruption allows native speakers to speak with less effort, but often makes it harder for foreigners to learn a language. For example, "I loved" is easier to say than "I love did," but a foreigner may find "I love did" more distinct. When Africans were brought to the U.S. as slaves, they often expressed the present tense with "do" and the past tense with "done"; for example, instead of saying "I love" and "I loved," they would say, "I do love" and "I done love."

2. *Sanskrit* Just as Europeans were puzzled by the lack of connections between Hebrew and Greek/Latin, so too they were

puzzled by the numerous connections between Sanskrit and Greek/Latin. In the late 1700's, a Scottish writer, Lord Monboddo, noted that "the words in the Sanskrit for the numbers, from one to ten, are, *ek, dwee, tree, chatoor, panch, shat, sapt, augt, nava, das*, which certainly have an affinity to the Greek or Latin names for those numbers."[1]

Sanskrit was an ancient literary language in India, just as Latin was an ancient literary language in the West. Sanskrit is as closely related to Greek and Latin as French is to Italian and Spanish. Some Europeans couldn't believe that a dark-skinned people in faraway India could have an ancient literary tradition, and a literary language as close to Greek and Latin as Sanskrit was; one scholar argued that Sanskrit, and Sanskrit literature, were a forgery, a modern attempt to imitate European languages and European literature.

In the early 1800's, the German writer Frederick Schlegel became the first to argue that Sanskrit, Greek and Latin were all part of the same language family, a family that also included German and Celtic languages; this language family has become known as the Indo-European family. The Indo-European language family originated among Aryan peoples, probably in Central Asia, and was spread to India, Iran and Europe by Aryan migrations.

Almost all European languages are part of the Indo-European language family. Hungarian, however, was imported by invading Huns, and is not an Indo-European language. Likewise, the language of the Basques isn't Indo-European; the Basques were in Europe before the Aryan migrations.

3. *Dialects* Every language is originally a collection of dialects. Each village has its own dialect, and the further apart villages are, the more their dialects differ. Once a dialect is written down, it becomes the standard form of a language, and may supplant other dialects. Latin, for example, was once merely one of the dialects spoken in Italy, but after it was written down, it

---

[1] Quoted in F. Max Müller, *Lectures On The Science Of Language*, ch. 4 (Longmans, Green, and Co., London, 1882).

became a standard language. Germany was home to many different dialects, but after Luther translated the Bible into a dialect known as High-German, High-German became the standard form of German.

If a written language becomes ossified, and fails to change and grow, it may become a "dead language"; instead of supplanting the dialects around it, it may be supplanted by those dialects. Thus, Latin was eventually supplanted by its dialects, the Romance Languages. This process may be termed "the revenge of the dialects."

English was originally a German dialect, one of the so-called "Low-German" dialects. English grammar is of German origin; English pronouns, prepositions, etc. are also of German origin. But while English is fundamentally a Germanic language, two-thirds of the words in an English dictionary are of Latin or Greek origin. English monosyllables can usually be traced to German, and polysyllables can usually be traced to Latin or Greek.

4. *Origin of Language* Language has its origins in sound. Language originated in primitive man's attempt to represent his thoughts and feelings by sounds. One can still see a connection between sound and meaning in such words as gloomy, cheerful, dark, light, sad, happy, fat, skinny, etc.

5. *Four Sources of Names* Surnames usually come from one of four sources: occupation, descent, locale or characteristic. Examples of surnames that come from occupation are Carpenter, Tanner, Fuller, Tinker, Sawyer, Smith, Wright, Mason and Weber, which is German for weaver. Examples of surnames that come from descent are Johnson (son of John), Robertson, Thompson, Davidson, Wilson, O'Brien (son of Brian), McDonald (son of Donald), Larsen, Ibsen and Fitzpatrick (natural son of Patrick). Examples of surnames that come from locale are Forest, Lake, Hill, Mount and Kierkegaard, which is Danish for churchyard. Examples of surnames that come from characteristic are Swift, Strong, Short, White, Brown and Black. Some surnames come from more than one of these sources; an example is Kleinschmidt, which is German for little smith.

6. *First Names* In the heyday of Protestantism, first names were often based on virtues, and names like Charity, Faith, and Prudence were common. When China was fervently Communist, children were given names like Hong-yu (Red Universe) and Kang-mei (Fight Americans). The character of our consumer culture is apparent in the popularity of names like Lexus, Chanel, Porsche, etc.

10. Modern Times

1. *After a Long Sleep* A century or two ago, many educated people in the Western world knew Greek and Latin, as well as some modern languages. They studied ancient literature and modern literature, the humanities and the sciences.

Some people thought that there was an excess of learning, that creativity was being stifled by learning. Lichtenberg was one who took that view; writing in 1775, Lichtenberg argued that the culture of his day needed, "the invigorating hibernation of a new barbarism." Nietzsche also thought that creativity was being stifled by learning; in 1878, Nietzsche spoke of an "oppressive cultural burden" and argued that there wouldn't be a second Renaissance until this burden was removed.[1]

Since Lichtenberg and Nietzsche made these remarks, the age of vast learning has given way to an age of moderate learning, and the age of moderate learning has given way to an age of almost no learning at all. Since the contemporary world pays little attention to literature, there is reason to fear that the West is losing contact with its literary heritage. But there is also reason

---

[1] See *The Lichtenberg Reader*, "1775" (Boston: Beacon Press, 1959), and Nietzsche, *Human, All-Too-Human*, §244 (Lincoln: Univ. of Nebraska Press, 1959, trans. M. Faber with S. Lehmann).

for hope: modern culture has done what Lichtenberg and Nietzsche prescribed, it has freed itself from excessive learning. After a long sleep, we will wake up refreshed and invigorated. We can rediscover the classics as if for the first time, just as the Renaissance humanists rediscovered the Greek and Roman classics. We're poised for a second Renaissance.

2. *Angry Isolation* What's remarkable about the golden age of Greek culture is that its best writers and artists were in harmony with the culture of their time; they were carried to greatness by the culture of their time. When one looks at the age of Pericles, one doesn't notice outstanding individuals, one notices the high level of culture in general.

What's remarkable about nineteenth-century culture is its outstanding individuals. The great writers of the nineteenth century weren't in harmony with the culture of their time, they angrily rejected the culture of their time. They insisted that to attain greatness in the modern world, one must isolate oneself.

What's remarkable about contemporary culture is that it combines a dearth of outstanding individuals with a low level of culture in general; contemporary culture has neither the virtues of Greek culture nor the virtues of nineteenth-century culture. The only hope for culture in our time is that a few individuals will be able to isolate themselves from contemporary culture, work in solitude, and draw strength from contact with earlier cultures. The best model for us to emulate is the individuals of the nineteenth century, not the high level of culture in the Periclean age. There's no hope for an improvement in the general level of culture; the general level of culture is far lower now than it was during the nineteenth century, and it's likely to decline still further.

3. *Modern Art* Every artist works within a religion, a worldview, a philosophy. In the late nineteenth century, the Western worldview was shaken by the decline of traditional religion and traditional morality; this decline is apparent in the philosophy of Nietzsche. The Western worldview was shaken further by World War I and World War II, which made people

think that civilization was bankrupt and the future bleak. Thus, the West fell into a deep spiritual crisis, into nihilism, and this crisis is reflected in Western art. As Solzhenitsyn said in 1993, "Our whole world is living through a century of spiritual illness, which could not but give rise to a similar ubiquitous illness in art."[1]

The modern artist is confronted by a world that seems devoid of meaning, and also devoid of beauty and poetry. Cities have lost much of their former beauty, and the countryside has been taken over by sprawling suburbs. The aristocracy, the leisure class, has disintegrated, and now everyone must work, everyone must earn money, everyone must do what it was once thought dishonorable to do. The splendor of the monarchy is gone, the lofty idealism of religion is gone, the glory of military service is gone, the simple life of the farmer is gone.

Confronted with a world in which there seems to be neither meaning nor beauty, a world in which nothing is glorious, and in which there are no heroes, modern artists have chosen to concentrate on the process of artistic creation. Instead of representing the world and glorifying the world, as artists often did in the past, modern artists turn their backs on the world, as if to say, "the world is ugly and depressing; I don't want to concern myself with the world; I want to concern myself with paint and with wood and with the process of artistic creation." Because it's concerned with process, modern art appeals only to a few initiates; it baffles and angers the layman.

Until recently, art always followed certain conventions and stayed within certain boundaries. The poet, the sculptor, the painter—all had to practice and study for years before they mastered the conventions of their art, and only after they had mastered these conventions could they call themselves artists and attempt something original. Modern art, on the other hand, has done away with all conventions and rules, and thus it has become possible for anyone to create something bizarre and then pretend that he's an artist, an original mind, a genius. Solzhenitsyn spoke

---

[1] "The Relentless Cult of Novelty and How It Wrecked the Century," New York Times Book Review, 2/7/93

of the "empty pursuit of novel forms as an end in itself."[1] Modern artists, knowing that many famous artists were controversial in their time, assume that controversy is a sign of originality, and strive to create something controversial themselves. Modern artists often remind one of people who run down the street naked in order to attract attention, and create a stir.

Kafka called one artistic movement (Dada) "a crime" and he said, "The spine of the soul has been broken. Faith has collapsed."[2] The current state of the fine arts is one of the clearest signs that Western civilization is in a crisis. But this crisis is only temporary. The Philosophy of Today can heal "the spine of the soul," and can have a positive effect on art. Art will be affected by the Zennish emphasis on tranquillity, the Zennish sympathy with nature, the Jungian respect for the unconscious, and the receptive attitude toward the occult.

4. *Imitation of Genius* Two characteristics of genius are that it draws on the unconscious and that it creates something new, something original. Modern art makes a deliberate attempt to draw on the unconscious, and it makes a deliberate attempt to be original. The disorder, the chaos, the madness of modern art stems, in part, from the insistence on expressing the unconscious, and the insistence on being original. What the genius does naturally and spontaneously, the modern artist does deliberately and by choice. Modern art is an imitation of genius.

During the Middle Ages, no one aspired to be a genius, because everyone felt themselves to be part of a larger whole. Nowadays, however, everyone aspires to be a genius, because no one feels himself to be part of a larger whole. Modern society is like an army made up entirely of generals.

5. *Swan Song* There are four kinds of cultural decline: psychological decline, spiritual decline, environmental decline, and biological decline. Psychological decline is an unconscious condition, a temporary weakening of the will to face life, a tem-

---

[1] ibid
[2] *Conversations With Kafka*, by Gustav Janouch

porary decline of the life-instinct. Even the healthiest cultures experience psychological decline periodically. Psychological decline is the least serious kind of cultural decline.

While psychological decline is unconscious, spiritual decline is conscious. Spiritual decline is the erosion of the prevailing belief-system, the prevailing religion. If psychological decline is a synonym for decadence, spiritual decline is a synonym for nihilism. Mankind has passed through numerous periods of spiritual decline. Just as psychological decline usually leads to a fresh outbreak of energy and health, so too spiritual decline usually leads to growth and progress, to the construction of a new belief-system that improves on the old belief-system.

Environmental decline is a social environment that isn't conducive to culture, a low level of popular culture, and a lack of healthy cultural traditions. Environmental decline is more serious than psychological decline or spiritual decline.

Biological decline is the extinction of genius, a society's inability to produce geniuses. Just as the existence of mankind on earth is an accident, and is neither a necessary nor a permanent feature of the universe, so too mankind's ability to produce genius is an accident, not an essential attribute of human nature. Biological decline is as serious as environmental decline.

Western culture now suffers from a combination of psychological, spiritual and environmental decline. Psychological decline never lasts forever, and the more extreme it is, the sooner it will turn into its opposite, a healthy, renaissance-type culture. Hence the West has little to fear from psychological decline. Nor does the West have much to fear from spiritual decline. The current spiritual decline of the West is gradually passing away as the West replaces traditional monotheism with new approaches to religion.

What is most threatening to the West is environmental decline: a low level of popular culture, an absence of healthy cultural traditions, a mode of life that consists of the feverish pursuit of wealth, and an educational system that is moving from bad to worse. But the West is not yet threatened by biological decline. During the last two centuries, the West has given ample evidence that it's capable of producing geniuses.

In conclusion, the outlook for Western culture during the next century is bright. But the outlook for Western culture after the next century isn't bright, since psychological decline will inevitably return, environmental decline will almost certainly continue, and biological decline may eventually set in. Will the next century be the swan song of Western culture?

6. *The Revolt of the Masses* In an earlier chapter, we discussed the current cult of leadership.[1] This is the kind of leadership that one finds in corporations and schools; one might refer to it as "leadership by position." This kind of leadership should not be confused with spiritual or intellectual leadership. A spiritual leader is one whom people look up to, one who provides people with a model or ideal.

In the last two centuries, many philosophers have argued that modern society has an aversion for spiritual leadership. This aversion for spiritual leadership is sometimes referred to as "the revolt of the masses." The classic expression of this idea is Ortega y Gasset's book, *The Revolt of the Masses.*

Ortega argues that the majority should listen to the privileged few, but they no longer do, and this is a grave threat to civilization. Ortega argues that ancient civilization perished because the masses attained power: "The history of the Roman Empire is also the history of the uprising of the Empire of the Masses, who absorb and annul the directing minorities and put themselves in their place."[2]

The masses no longer look up to the gifted few, and no longer look down on themselves. Ortega writes thus: "*The characteristic of the hour is that the commonplace mind, knowing itself to be commonplace, has the assurance to proclaim the rights of the commonplace and to impose them wherever it will.*" The masses have not only ceased listening to the elite, they are often hostile to the elite: "The mass crushes beneath it everything

---

[1] see ch. 6, #29
[2] ibid, ch. 2

that is different, everything that is excellent, individual, qualified and select."[1]

Freud reached a similar conclusion independently of Ortega. Freud witnessed the transition from aristocratic culture to popular culture, and he was horrified by popular culture. Like Ortega, Freud believed that the revolt of the masses could be found in its purest form in the U.S.:

> The danger of a state of things which might be termed "the psychological poverty of groups" [is] most threatening where the bonds of a society are chiefly constituted by the identification of its members with one another, while individuals of the leader type do not acquire the importance that should fall to them in the formation of a group. The present cultural state of America would give us a good opportunity for studying the damage to civilization that is thus to be feared.[2]

This passage is from Freud's *Civilization and Its Discontents*, which was published in 1930, the same year as Ortega's *Revolt of the Masses*. Freud's argument did not influence Ortega. Who, then, influenced Ortega's concept of "the revolt of the masses"?

The writer who influenced Ortega most was probably John Stuart Mill. Mill advocated individual liberty because it prevents the masses from suffocating the elite few, the few who think and act from their own mind, the few who are capable of innovations that will improve mankind as a whole. "These few are the salt of the earth," Mill writes; "without them, human life would become a stagnant pool."[3] Government and society will stagnate in mediocrity, says Mill, unless the masses listen to the elite few:

> No government by a democracy or a numerous aristocracy, either in its political acts or in the opinions, qualities, and tone of mind which it fosters, ever did or could rise above mediocrity, except in so far as the sovereign Many have let themselves be guided (which in their best times they always have done) by the counsels and influence of a more highly gifted and instructed One or Few.[4]

---

[1] ibid, ch. 1
[2] *Civilization and Its Discontents*, ch. 5
[3] *On Liberty*, ch. 3
[4] ibid

Mill venerated Alexis de Tocqueville, and Mill's *On Liberty* contains echoes of Tocqueville's *Democracy in America*. *Democracy in America* was published in 1835, 24 years before *On Liberty*. *Democracy in America* is one of the earliest expressions of the concept of the revolt of the masses. In the U.S., according to Tocqueville, a writer can't criticize The People, the majority: "No writer, no matter how famous, can escape from this obligation to sprinkle incense over his fellow citizens. Hence the majority lives in a state of perpetual self-adoration."[1]

Like Tocqueville and Mill, Nietzsche noticed "the revolt of the masses." Nietzsche spent much of his career attacking the egalitarian trend of his time. Nietzsche preferred aristocracy to democracy. He loathed Christianity because it was anti-aristocratic, and he loathed the French Revolution because it, too, was anti-aristocratic.

Nietzsche praised "those *noble* natures who do not know how to live without reverence." Nietzsche excoriated modern man, democratic man, because he had lost the feeling of reverence. When a young person reveres a hero-figure, he looks down on himself, since he thinks that he is far beneath the hero-figure. Mass man (to use Ortega's term) no longer reveres, and no longer looks down on himself. Nietzsche wrote,

> Alas! The time of the most contemptible man is coming, the man who can no longer despise himself. Behold! I shall show you the *Last Man*.... The earth has become small, and upon it hops the Last Man, who makes everything small.... No herdsman and one herd. Everyone wants the same thing, everyone is the same: whoever thinks otherwise goes voluntarily into the madhouse.[2]

John Ruskin is the most Nietzschean writer in the English language; in Ruskin's work, one often finds the same ideas, and the same tone, that one finds in Nietzsche's work. Both Ruskin and Nietzsche lapsed into madness in the 1890s, and both died in 1900. Ruskin and Nietzsche developed independently; they never mention each other, and almost certainly never read each

---

[1] *Democracy in America*, vol. I, part ii, §7
[2] *Thus Spoke Zarathustra*, Part I, "Zarathustra's Prologue," §5

10. MODERN TIMES

other. Here's a passage from Ruskin that is strikingly similar to Nietzsche:

> For us of the old race—few of us now left—children who reverence our fathers, and are ashamed of ourselves; comfortless enough in that shame, and yearning for one word or glance from the graves of old, yet knowing ourselves to be of the same blood, and recognizing in our hearts the same passions, with the ancient masters of humanity... the few of us now standing here and there, alone, in the midst of this yelping, carnivorous crowd, mad for money and lust... it is impossible for us, except in the labor of our hands, not to go mad.[1]

So there is Ruskin, ashamed and miserable, loathing the masses because they're neither ashamed nor miserable, but rather shameless and self-assured. If there's any difference between Ruskin and Nietzsche, it is that Ruskin is more strident in his scorn for the masses, and more pious in his reverence for "the ancient masters of humanity."

No one analyzed the revolt of the masses in a more penetrating manner than Soren Kierkegaard, perhaps because no one had such a painful experience of it. Like Nietzsche, Kierkegaard makes frequent use of the French term *ressentiment*, meaning resentment or envy. Kierkegaard argues that the masses feel *ressentiment* toward anyone who is distinguished, who is above them, and they try to drag down anyone outstanding, they try to level.

> No single individual [wrote Kierkegaard] will be able to arrest the abstract process of leveling.... that self-combustion of the human race.... All that is low and despicable comes to the fore, its very impudence giving the spurious effect of strength, while protected by its very baseness it avoids attracting the attention of *ressentiment*.[2]

As one reads these words, one thinks of the brash, coarse behavior that has become popular on American television. Though

---

[1] see John D. Rosenberg, *The Darkening Glass: A Portrait of Ruskin's Genius*, ch. 10
[2] Kierkegaard, *The Present Age*

we may believe that the greatest danger to mankind is terrorism or nuclear weapons or pollution, Kierkegaard believed that the greatest danger to mankind is the revolt of the masses, the leveling process, which he calls "that self-combustion of the human race."

The mass media fosters the revolt of the masses, while higher culture discourages it. In the 19th century, the primary form of mass media was newspapers. Mill noticed that newspapers were becoming more influential, while books were becoming less so:

> The mass do not now take their opinions from dignitaries in Church or State, from ostensible leaders, or from books. Their thinking is done for them by men much like themselves, addressing them or speaking in their name... through the newspapers.[1]

All the thinkers whom we've discussed in this section were born in the 1800s. One of the few thinkers born in the 1900s who discussed the revolt of the masses is Joseph Campbell.

> It's characteristic of democracy [Campbell said] that majority rule is understood as being effective not only in politics but also in thinking. In thinking, of course, the majority is always wrong.... The majority's function in relation to the spirit is to try to listen and to open up to someone who's had an experience beyond that of food, shelter, progeny, and wealth.[2]

Campbell was born in 1904, and his outlook was shaped by 19th-century writers.

The idea of "the revolt of the masses" has a long history, beginning in the early 1800s with Tocqueville and Kierkegaard, continuing in the late 1800s with Mill, Nietzsche, and Ruskin, culminating with Freud and Ortega in the early 1900s, and surviving into the late 1900s with Campbell. Nowadays, few writers discuss "the revolt of the masses," perhaps because it's so much a part of modern life that people are no longer aware of it (we're more aware of transitions than of steady states). No one

---

[1] *On Liberty*, ch. 3
[2] *The Power of Myth*, ch. 4

alive today has seen an aristocratic culture with their own eyes, hence no one notices "the revolt of the masses."

7. *Other-directed* The idea of "inner-directed, other-directed," which was first set forth by the sociologist David Riesman in 1950, resembles the idea of the "revolt of the masses," and makes our picture of modern society more complete. Riesman argues that, in our time, people are "other-directed," that is, they take their cues from the people around them. In an earlier time, people often had an ideal, a hero-image in their own mind, and they would take their cues from this ideal; they were "inner-directed." The inner-directed person has an "internalized set of goals," goals that are often instilled by books. The inner-directed person often keeps a diary in which he records whether his behavior lives up to his ideals.

The other-directed person is molded by the peer group, and is "sensitized to the expectations and preferences of others."[1] An other-directed person is chiefly concerned with people—not with God, not with lofty ideals, not with great men from previous centuries. Education, which once consisted of Reading, Writing and Arithmetic, is now concerned with how the child gets along with other children, and how the child listens to social cues. As education has changed, so too work has changed; the economy is now a "personality market." While the inner-directed person was concerned with self-improvement and character-building, the other-directed person is concerned with relating to others. As Riesman put it,

> Instead of referring himself to the great men of the past and matching himself against his stars, the other-directed person moves in the midst of a veritable Milky Way of almost but not quite indistinguishable contemporaries.... To shine alone seems hopeless, and also dangerous.[2]

---

[1] David Riesman, *The Lonely Crowd: A Study of the Changing American Character*, I, 1
[2] ibid, ch. 6, §2. Just as Kierkegaard noticed "the revolt of the masses," so too he noticed the trend toward "other-direction": "People's attention is no longer turned inwards," Kierkegaard wrote, "they are no

The phrase "almost but not quite indistinguishable contemporaries" reminds one of Nietzsche's comment, "everyone wants the same thing, everyone is the same."

Although the trend toward other-direction is still strong, some contrary trends have emerged since Riesman first published his theory. There is a trend toward introspection and stress-reduction; meditation and yoga are popular. An aristocratic culture may be a thing of the past, and "the revolt of the masses" may be here to stay. But the "inner-directed" personality may not be a thing of the past. Though modern man doesn't match himself against heroes and Great Men, he may listen to what his own soul and body are telling him.

---

longer satisfied with their own inner religious lives, but turn to others and to things outside themselves."(*The Present Age*)

11. Politics

1. *My Land*   Many political disputes begin with "That's my land, and it was stolen from me." But history teaches us that every country has been overrun by a series of invading peoples. Take England, for example: The Celts occupied the British Isles around 600 B.C., the Romans occupied England around 50 B.C., the Angles and Saxons occupied England around 500 A.D. (when the Romans had left), the Vikings occupied about half of England around 800 A.D., and finally the Normans occupied England around 1100 A.D. (after winning the Battle of Hastings in 1066).

Though Irish nationalists may see themselves as indigenous, and therefore as Ireland's rightful rulers, their Celtic ancestors aren't indigenous to Ireland or to any European country. The Celts came to Ireland quite recently (about 500 B.C.), dispossessing the previous inhabitants. Celtic languages are part of the Indo-European language family. The Celts have their roots in or near India, as do almost all European peoples.

Who is really indigenous? Are we not all usurpers?

2. *Rationalism in Politics*   I argued above that the most fundamental distinction in philosophy is the distinction between rational philosophy and non-rational philosophy. Does this distinction have any political import? Do rational philosophers,

for example, tend to be liberal? Do non-rational philosophers tend to be conservative?

Traditional conservatives tend to be wary of reason, but today's conservatives tend to be fond of reason. One traditional conservative who was wary of reason was Edmund Burke. Burke criticized the French revolutionaries for following reason, and for ignoring customs and traditions. In Burke's day, The Left followed reason, and advocated revolution to overthrow regimes that didn't live up to the dictates of reason. Burke cautioned against revolution, and the bloodshed that accompanied the French Revolution seemed to vindicate Burke's attitude.

Like the French revolutionaries, Marx and his disciples followed reason, and advocated revolution. The bloodshed that accompanied Marxist regimes in Russia, China, Cambodia, etc. seemed to vindicate the conservative view that reason was a dangerous guide in the political arena.

The English Radicals of the early 1800s—Jeremy Bentham, James Mill, etc.—were fond of reason, and advocated radical change.

In our time, however, a new tendency has emerged. The Straussian School, which includes prominent conservatives like Bill Kristol and Harvey Mansfield, is fond of reason but takes a conservative approach to politics. While Burke cautioned against revolution, today's conservatives advocated regime change, revolutionary change, in Iraq. Now it's The Right that talks about Universal Principles (as the French revolutionaries once did), and The Left that talks about respecting customs and traditions (as Burke once did).

Should we conclude that rationalism doesn't necessarily lead to a particular approach to politics, that rationalism can be conservative or liberal? Or is the current situation an anomaly? Will the long-standing link between rationalism and The Left reassert itself, and relegate the Straussian position to the status of a footnote?

3. *Rationalism in Theology* The views of the Straussians are strikingly similar to those of Pope Benedict, as expressed by the Pope in a speech delivered on September 12, 2006. The chief

organ of the Straussian school, Bill Kristol's *Weekly Standard*, hailed the Pope's speech as "astonishing.... moving and heroic."[1] Like the Straussians, the Pope believes in reason, and admires the rational Greek philosophers. The Pope argues that God Himself is rational. The Pope quotes the Gospel of John: "In the beginning was the Word, and the Word was with God, and the Word was God." The Pope notes that "Word" is *logos* in the original Greek, and "*logos* means both reason and word." The Pope applauds John for underlining the importance of reason: "John thus spoke the final word on the biblical concept of God."

The Pope says that the goal of theology is to correlate faith and reason, and he says that most Western theologians have worked toward this goal. The essence of European civilization, according to the Pope, is the convergence of Greek philosophy and Christianity. This convergence wasn't the result of chance, says the Pope; doubtless he thinks that God arranged this convergence. Why God would choose to enlighten Europe, and leave the rest of the world in darkness, the Pope doesn't explain.

According to the Pope, we must approach religion and morality as the Greek philosophers did—in a rational way. Otherwise, morality becomes merely subjective, and this is a dangerous situation. Like the Straussians, the Pope thinks that morality must be rational and objective, and that without such a morality, civilization is vulnerable to the worst excesses of decadence and despotism.

Strauss's work was a response to Hitler and Stalin. Strauss tried to build a "philosophical firewall" against nihilism and genocide. He felt that modern philosophers had failed to build such a firewall—indeed, Heidegger had even supported the Nazis. Strauss argued that modern philosophy had gotten on the wrong track, so we must go back to Plato and Aristotle.

Strauss didn't realize that we can go forward instead of backward, we can develop new approaches to religion with the help of Eastern philosophy, Jungian psychology, and the Hermetic tradition. Strauss wouldn't admit that, if subjectivity can

---

[1] "Socrates or Muhammad? Joseph Ratzinger on the destiny of reason," by Lee Harris, 10/2/2006

lead anywhere, so too reason can lead anywhere. Who respected reason more than the French revolutionaries, more than the Russian communists? "'Tis not contrary to reason," said Hume, "to prefer the destruction of the whole world to the scratching of my finger."[1] As Kierkegaard said, "'On principle' one can do anything."[2] The Philosophy of Today is a better firewall against nihilism than Plato, Strauss, or Pope Benedict because it strikes a chord with modern man, it strikes a chord with the man on the street, not just the professional scholar, it speaks to the soul, not just the intellect.

4. *Banfield and Kedourie*   Liberals view human nature as a *tabula rasa*, and believe that government policy can mold society, while conservatives believe that human nature is shaped by cultural factors, and government policy can do little in the face of these cultural factors.

At the start of his career, the American conservative Edward Banfield studied a poor village in southern Italy. He argued that its poverty was due, not to a shortage of government assistance, but to cultural factors—a devotion to relatives, and an uncooperative attitude toward non-relatives. Banfield also studied Mormon communities that had become wealthy, that had "made the desert bloom," not as a result of government assistance, but as a result of a culture of trust and cooperation.

A critic of President Johnson's War on Poverty, Banfield thought that many social programs harmed those whom they were intended to help. "Do no good," Banfield advised, "and no harm will come of it." Social programs, Banfield argued, are designed to satisfy the conscience of the upper classes, to satisfy their longing for service and progress, their longing to *do something* and to *do good*.

According to Banfield, urban poverty can't be relieved by government spending because poverty is caused by cultural factors, especially the inability to sacrifice present pleasure for future good. "The lower-class individual," Banfield wrote, "lives

---

[1] *Treatise of Human Nature*, Book II, Sect. III
[2] *The Present Age*

from moment to moment.... He belongs to no voluntary organizations, has no political interests, and does not vote unless paid to do so."[1] He noted that immigrants from Catholic countries were more present-oriented than immigrants from Protestant countries. He argued that the peasant cultures of Ireland, southern Italy and eastern Europe sent immigrants to America who lived for today, not for the future:

> The idea of self-improvement—and even more that of community improvement—was unfamiliar and perhaps even unintelligible to them. They were mainly concerned about survival, not progress; how to get food, drink, and shelter for the day was what preoccupied them. Their motive in coming to this country was apparently less to improve their general condition than to escape the threat of immediate starvation.[2]

Banfield chided liberals for refusing to admit that "some children simply cannot be taught much in school,"[3] for believing that any child can be educated if only enough government money is spent.

As Banfield was a leading conservative on domestic issues, Elie Kedourie was a leading conservative on international issues. Third World poverty, in Kedourie's view, wasn't caused by external factors such as colonialism, but rather by cultural factors—a tradition of despotic government, etc. Kedourie argues that colonialism was beneficial rather than harmful:

> Colonial rulers... as much in response to their own political traditions as because they were accountable to home governments, established in these territories a *Rechtstaat*, in which judges and courts did not obey the whim of the ruler, and administration operated according to publicly-known rules which were designed to eliminate favoritism and corruption, and to a large extent succeeded in doing so.[4]

---

[1] *The Unheavenly City*, ch. 3
[2] Ibid
[3] Ibid, ch. 11
[4] See Kedourie's essay, "The Prospects of Civility in the Third World," in a book called *Civility and Citizenship in Liberal Democratic Societies*

When colonial rulers departed, disaster ensued. Kedourie blames Western nations not for colonialism and imperialism, but rather for de-colonizing too rapidly; he blames the French for leaving Algeria too rapidly, the British for leaving India too rapidly, the Americans for leaving Iraq too rapidly (after the 1991 war), etc.[1]

Kedourie doubted that democracy could work in Third World countries. He felt that democracy required an electorate that wasn't accustomed to passive obedience, an electorate that would sometimes put the public interest over private interest. Without such an electorate, Kedourie argued, public power would remain what it always had been in these countries: the private property of those who held office.

Kedourie grew up in the Jewish Quarter of Baghdad in the 1930s. He felt that the Ottoman Empire's government of Iraq was preferable to Iraqi self-rule, and that the British Empire's government of Iraq was preferable to Iraqi self-rule. When the Ottomans and British left Iraq, there was little respect for private property; Kedourie speaks of, "the utter defencelessness of property in the face of official greed and willfulness.... 'Large estates were distributed among government officials and their friends.'" In Kedourie's view, Iraqi self-rule meant rule by Baathist thugs. Kedourie felt that the dismantling of the Ottoman and British empires, coupled with the rise of nationalism, had made the Middle East "a wilderness of tigers."

As a student at Oxford, Kedourie was asked to modify his Ph.D. thesis. Believing that it didn't need modification, Kedourie left Oxford rather than modify it; his admirers called this his "defiance" of his thesis.

Kedourie's books lack the ironic, sophisticated tone that is popular among the intelligentsia. One reviewer complained that Kedourie's work gave him "a sense of having been held by the lapels and screamed at."[2] Kedourie was a man of strong character, strong convictions, and vast erudition.

---

[1] Kedourie didn't live to see the American invasion of Iraq in 2003.
[2] A review in the *New York Review of Books* by a Mr. Geertz

5. *Chaudhuri*   Nirad Chaudhuri, a writer from India, lived under British rule for many years. He criticized the British for their rude, contemptuous behavior toward Indians. He also criticized the British for decadence. This decadence, Chaudhuri wrote, "consists in the refusal to acknowledge great achievements of great individuals. Disrespect for great achievements is a result... of the lack of courage to attempt them."[1]

Though he criticized British shortcomings, Chaudhuri nonetheless believed that the British governed India better than it had ever been governed before. Chaudhuri was opposed to Indian independence; "I thought that power in Indian hands," he wrote, "would be a calamity for the Indian people." In Chaudhuri's view, Gandhi's independence movement had no positive content, it was based on hatred and xenophobia. Like Kedourie, Chaudhuri blamed the British for leaving India too quickly. In the 1930s, when Fascism and Communism were popular, Chaudhuri remained pro-British. Like Nietzsche, Ibsen, and other intellectuals, Chaudhuri wasn't a patriot, but rather a citizen of the world. Inside India, Chaudhuri's writings were controversial, and he was subjected to "raucous hatred."

As a student at the University of Calcutta, Chaudhuri failed his Master's exam, then refused to take it again—an episode reminiscent of Kedourie's defiance of his thesis. For much of his life, Chaudhuri depended on hand-outs from reluctant relatives.

6. *September 11*   Political problems often have a religious dimension.

The 20th century was scarred by two movements, Communism and Fascism. Since Fascism is a subset of Nationalism, I should perhaps have said, "Communism and Nationalism." Both Communism and Nationalism originated around 1800, when religious faith was crumbling in the Western world, and atheism was spreading. Communism and Nationalism were new religions, filling the void left by the decline of Christianity.

---

[1] This is a quote from Edward Shils, *Portraits: A Gallery of Intellectuals*, ch. 3, "Nirad C. Chaudhuri"

In the 20th century, the West's crisis of faith became a worldwide crisis of faith; the sickness in the Western soul spread to other regions of the world, as Western civilization came into contact with other civilizations. Toynbee, the British historian, said that the key development in world history in the last two centuries was the coming together of the world. Civilizations that once had no contact with each other began to interact, often as a result of Western exploration and Western expansion.

Non-Western countries were faced with a choice: embrace Western influence, or slam the door against it. Until about 1860, Japan chose to slam the door against Western influence, then it did an about-face, and embraced Western influence. In the 1970s, the Shah of Iran attempted to Westernize, but he was driven from power by Islamic fundamentalism, which slammed the door against Western influence.

Many non-Western nations had living, functioning religions before they came into contact with the West. These religions had developed over thousands of years, they were well suited to the people that had developed them, and they embodied a deep wisdom. As a result of Western influence, however, many non-Western nations witnessed a disintegration of their age-old religions. Communism and Nationalism spread around the world, and Christianity made some converts, too.

Some non-Western nations, especially in the Muslim world, clung to their ancient religions, determined not to succumb to Western influence. In Iran, Islamic fundamentalism reached fever pitch, and became a state religion. Eventually, however, the pendulum swung in the other direction, and many Iranians now feel a deep aversion for Islamic fundamentalism, and a deep longing for Western ways. In Iran, fundamentalism is collapsing under the weight of its own success.

The current conflict between Islam and the West is part of the collision of civilizations that Toynbee discussed sixty years ago. During the first half of the 20th century, the collision of civilizations was overshadowed by the World Wars, which were essentially civil wars—wars within Western Civilization. When the World Wars ended, the Cold War overshadowed the collision of civilizations. When the Cold War ended, however, the Civilization War came to center stage.

In 1993, Samuel Huntington, who had studied Toynbee, predicted a "clash of civilizations." Huntington argued that future conflicts will usually occur between civilizations. Huntington quoted an Indian Muslim writer named M. J. Akbar: "The West's next confrontation is definitely going to come from the Muslim world."[1] Like Toynbee, Huntington argued that non-Western countries can embrace the West or reject the West. Huntington also mentioned a third possibility: steer a middle course, become a "torn country" like Turkey or Pakistan, in which the elite tries to Westernize, and the masses remain un-Westernized.

Those who carried out the September 11 attacks, and those who supported them (bin Laden's Al Qaeda group), and those who supported Al Qaeda (the Taliban), and those who supported the Taliban (Islamic fundamentalists in Pakistan) are examples of non-Western people who have chosen to reject Western influence, to slam the door against the West. Are they as deeply religious as they seem? Or is their fundamentalism a desperate attempt to establish an identity distinct from the West? Is their fanaticism an effort to suppress their own doubts? Are they afraid that, if they begin to question the Koran, their questioning will acquire momentum, and sweep away their ancient faith, leaving them without a religion, and without an identity?

Islamic fundamentalists have a narrow-minded, brittle, bookish religiosity, a religiosity that sticks to the letter of the law rather than the spirit. Religion should be an inner experience, an inner feeling, and it shouldn't matter who controls Jerusalem. "Render unto Caesar the things that are Caesar's," said Jesus; the kingdom of God is not of this world, it is within you. The Muslim poet Rumi often visited the temples of Jews and Christians, believing that all three religions are fundamentally akin. The religious spirit unites, the mystical spirit unites, but a narrow religiosity clings to the book, clings to the past, clings to the holy place, instead of finding God within oneself. A narrow religios-

---

[1] Huntington's essay appeared in *Foreign Affairs*, Summer, 1993

ity often has a political dimension, often becomes nationalistic. Shouldn't we give priority to spiritual and cultural pursuits over political goals, and treat politics as a necessary evil, rather than as the road to salvation?

It won't be easy for Muslims to achieve a genuine religiosity, nor is it easy for Jews and Christians to achieve a genuine religiosity. We all find it easier to obey a clear-cut law (eat fish on Friday, don't eat pork on Saturday) than to find God within us, and develop our inner life. The West is certainly not a model of genuine religiosity. Indeed, the West has experienced a collapse of spiritual values, a collapse evident in world wars, in the Holocaust, in Stalin's Gulag, in recent mass-murders by American students, in violent movies, etc. Is it any wonder that Muslims want to slam the door against the West? Is it any wonder that Muslims believe that salvation/happiness/the-good-life cannot be found by embracing Western influence, but only by following ancient traditions and ancient books?

The quest for spiritual values, spiritual peace is a quest for all peoples in the modern world. Religions must change and evolve, just as individuals must change and evolve, hence we can never achieve perfect, permanent spiritual peace. All of us, therefore, should regard the spiritual values of others with a measure of toleration and respect, and all of us should be receptive to change in our own spiritual values.

7. *Mutual Arising* Was the 9/11 attack the cause of the Iraq War? The 9/11 attack created a mood, a political climate, in the U.S. that contributed to the invasion of Iraq; the 9/11 attack made many Americans feel that we couldn't be passive toward terrorist threats, we had to be pre-emptive. There were, however, many other causes of the Iraq War:

1. Bush's personality, his worldview, his religious and moral views, etc.
2. Saddam's personality, his penchant for military adventure, his penchant for cruelty and torture, etc.
3. The previous Iraq war, the ending of which was viewed by many people as incomplete.

4. Saddam's history of developing WMD (Weapons of Mass Destruction), and his reluctance to allow international inspectors into Iraq.
5. The conclusion of the CIA (and other intelligence organizations) that Iraq possessed (or was on the brink of possessing) WMD.

This is just a partial list; the causes of the Iraq War are innumerable. And each of these causes has behind it innumerable causes. For example, the 9/11 attack was one cause of the Iraq War, and there are innumerable causes of the 9/11 attack.

Events can rarely be traced to just one cause; close examination usually reveals a vast network of causes—innumerable causes. As Joseph Campbell said,

> A great number of things round about, on every side, are causing what is happening now. Everything, all the time, is causing everything else. The Buddhist teaching in recognition of this fact is called the Doctrine of Mutual Arising.[1]

Perhaps the old puzzle, "which came first, the chicken or the egg?" can illustrate the Doctrine of Mutual Arising. If one sees causality in a linear way (A causes B, B causes C, etc.), then the puzzle of the chicken and the egg seems insoluble (there can be no eggs without chickens, but how can there be chickens without eggs?). But if one sees causality in terms of Mutual Arising, then chickens and eggs are no longer puzzling—chickens and eggs arose together, "mutual arising." The philosophers of India don't see linear causality, they see everything as part of a huge net, everything inter-connected, everything causing and being caused by everything else.

If you look back at your own life, you can probably find events that resulted from Mutual Arising. When you look at such events, you see a vast number of causes, each of which contributed to the outcome. If you focus your attention on any one of these causes, it appears that this was The Cause—without this the event wouldn't have happened. In truth, however, nothing is The Cause because everything is causing everything else.

---

[1] *Myths To Live By*, ch. 7, p. 144

Let's look at an event from Proust's life: the death of his beloved chauffeur, Albert Agostinelli, who died in an airplane crash in the south of France, on May 30, 1914. Proust felt responsible for Agostinelli's death, he felt that he had "willed" or "arranged" Agostinelli's death—unconsciously or semi-consciously. (One is reminded of Proust's character, Swann, who longs for the death of his beloved Odette, in order to free himself from the bondage of passion.) But though Proust felt responsible, there were many causes of Agostinelli's death besides Proust's "will":

1. Agostinelli was something of a daredevil, who liked fast cars, etc.
2. Agostinelli didn't know how to swim, and could have survived his accident if he had known.
3. Agostinelli's wife seems to have encouraged him to pursue his flying ambitions.
4. Agostinelli's accident might have been averted if his training had been a little better, his plane a little better, etc.

Like the Iraq War, Agostinelli's death has infinite causes, and many people, besides Proust, could say, "it was my fault."

12. Physics

1. *Physics and the Occult*   There is a striking agreement between modern physics and modern philosophy/psychology. To summarize modern physics is to review the ideas we've discussed earlier in this book; instead of calling this chapter "Physics," I could have called it "Summary of the Previous Chapters."

In an earlier chapter, I wrote,

> Mind and matter overlap; there is no 'pure spirit', divorced from matter, and there is no 'dead matter', lacking all spirit and energy. The whole universe is suffused with energy, with a kind of consciousness.[1]

This conclusion was based on philosophy and psychology, but it agrees with the conclusions of physics. Einstein's famous equation, $e=mc^2$, says that there is enormous energy in all matter. "Mass is only a form of energy.... Even the tiniest, the very tiniest particle of matter has within it a tremendous amount of concentrated energy."[2]

But Einstein's theory isn't the only way in which modern science confirms what I wrote earlier; quantum mechanics also confirms it.

---

[1] Ch. 1, #15. A similar argument can be found in ch. 3, #16.
[2] Gary Zukav, *The Dancing Wu Li Masters: An Overview of the New Physics*, "Special Nonsense"

> The astounding discovery awaiting newcomers to physics is that the evidence gathered in the development of quantum mechanics indicates that subatomic 'particles' constantly appear to be making decisions! More than that, the decisions they seem to make are based on decisions made elsewhere. Subatomic particles seem to know *instantaneously* what decisions are made elsewhere, and elsewhere can be as far away as another galaxy! ...."The central mystery of quantum theory," wrote Henry Stapp, "is, How does information get around so quick?" ....The philosophical implication of quantum mechanics is that all of the things in our universe (including us) that appear to exist independently are actually parts of one all-encompassing organic pattern, and that no parts of that pattern are ever really separate from it or from each other.[1]

Stapp's question, "How does information get around so quick?" is also a key question in occult studies. If someone is killed in a car accident in New York, and their mother, who is in California, senses that something is wrong with them, the question arises, "How does information get around so quick?" One wonders if physicists like Stapp realized that students of the occult were asking the same questions they were asking. Physics is merging with philosophy/psychology, just as Western thought is merging with Eastern thought. Are we on the brink of a grand synthesis—a philosophy that will unite the sciences and the humanities, West and East?

How does information get around so quick—in the world of subatomic particles, and in the human world? It seems that particles and people can exert some sort of influence from a distance (action-at-a-distance). Newton was a rational thinker who sought clear causes and effects, hence he angrily rejected the possibility of action-at-a-distance:

> That one body may act upon another at a distance through a vacuum without the mediation of anything else, by and through which their action and force may be conveyed from one to another, is to me so great an absurdity that, I believe, no man who

---

[1] ibid, "Living?"

has in philosophic matters a competent faculty of thinking could ever fall into it.[1]

Newton tried to show that the whole universe was like a pool table, with objects influencing each other by their momentum and contact. Now, however, physicists are finding that a ball on one pool table can influence a ball on a different table, without coming into contact with it. Newton's mechanical worldview is breaking down, and the old concept of action-at-a-distance is coming back into favor.

How does information get around so quick? How can particles "know" what other particles are doing? Some physicists are reaching for Jung's concept of synchronicity.[2] Physicists are unable to explain quantum phenomena in physical terms, Newtonian terms, so they're reaching out to psychology, to the occult, for explanations. They're reaching out to an "acausal" principle (synchronicity). They're moving away from the bedrock of rational-scientific thinking: causality. (Wouldn't Newton be horrified?) Niels Bohr said that quantum mechanics entails, "the necessity of a final renunciation of the classical ideal of causality and a radical revision of our attitude toward the problem of physical reality."[3] Newton's world is crumbling!

Here's an experiment that troubles Newtonians: two paired particles, with opposite spin, are sent in opposite directions. The spin of one of the particles is changed. The other particle's spin also changes, at the same instant, without any apparent cause.

> Somehow the particle traveling in area B "knows" that its twin in area A is spinning *right* instead of *up* and so it spins *left* instead of *down*. In other words, *what we did in area A... affected what happened in area B*. This strange phenomenon is known as the Einstein-Podolsky-Rosen (EPR) effect.... Physicists realized that this peculiar situation raises a critical question: "How can two of anything communicate so quickly?"[4]

---

[1] ibid, "Einstein Doesn't Like It"
[2] ibid, "Living?"
[3] ibid, "The Role of 'I'"
[4] ibid

Experiments like this inspired Bell's Theorem. Bell's Theorem is a mathematical proof, first published in 1964; it demonstrates that action-at-a-distance is possible, and that "our commonsense ideas about the world are profoundly deficient."[1]

Bell's Theorem develops the EPR effect into a mathematical proof, applicable to the macroscopic world as well as the microscopic world. One prominent physicist said, "Bell's Theorem is the most profound discovery of science."[2] Bell's Theorem was confirmed and refined by the Clauser-Freedman experiment (1972) and by the Aspect experiment (1982). Bell's Theorem suggests communication between particles that is "superluminal"—that is, faster than the speed of light. Bell's Theorem suggests that the principle of local causes (also known as "locality") is false, and action-at-a-distance is possible.

Bell's Theorem is not only difficult for Newton to swallow, it's also difficult for modern physicists to swallow; doubtless Einstein would be uncomfortable with Bell's Theorem, as he was with the EPR effect. But Bell's Theorem wouldn't be difficult for alchemists or Jungians to swallow; alchemists would say, "nothing new, just another example of action-at-a-distance," and Jungians would say, "nothing new, just another example of synchronicity."

Can any particles communicate at a distance, or only particles that were once intimately connected? A similar question arises in the study of the occult: can any two people communicate telepathically, or only people who were once intimately connected, such as a mother and her child? Gary Zukav speculates that

> when "separate parts" interact with each other, they (their wave functions) become correlated (through the exchange of conventional signals).... Unless this correlation is disrupted by other external forces, the wave functions representing these "separate parts" remain correlated forever.[3]

---

[1] ibid, "The End of Science"
[2] ibid, quoting Henry Stapp
[3] ibid, "The End of Science"

12. PHYSICS

Could this reasoning provide a basis for astrology? Could a particular planet become "correlated" to a person at the time of his birth, as a result of its position, its proximity to the earth? Could there be correlations between many seemingly-separate things? "If the Big Bang theory is correct, the entire universe is initially correlated."[1] Is anything really separate, or is everything part of one inter-connected world?

According to James Frazer, the famous student of primitive religion, primitive man believed that "things which have once been in contact with each other continue to act on each other at a distance after the physical contact has been severed."[2] Frazer was a rational thinker, so he dismissed this belief as a primitive superstition, but now we find that primitive thinking is strikingly similar to modern science and modern philosophy. Like the modern physicist, primitive man believed that the world was an organic whole, a whole in which all parts were connected. Many primitive beliefs that were once dismissed as superstition now appear to be based on a deep understanding of reality.

2. *One Inter-Connected World*   Earlier we quoted Zukav's remark that, "all of the things in our universe (including us) that appear to exist independently are actually parts of one all-encompassing organic pattern." This reminds us of the Hermetic philosophy. One of the basic tenets of the Hermetics is that the world is one (*unus mundus*), the world is an organic whole, and each part of the world is connected to every other part. What the Hermetics refer to as "occult correspondences" is closely related to what Jung refers to as "acausal connections" and "synchronicity." Jung is part of the Hermetic Tradition.

When physicists first became familiar with the baffling and irrational world of quantum mechanics, they fell into despair. These men were scientists, rational thinkers; Hermes Trismegistus was no friend of theirs, and neither was Carl Jung. Heisenberg said,

---

[1] ibid
[2] *The Golden Bough*, vol. 1, ch. 3, #1

> I remember discussions with Bohr [in 1927] which went through many hours till very late at night and ended almost in despair; and when at the end of the discussion I went alone for a walk in the neighboring park I repeated to myself again and again the question: Can nature possibly be as absurd as it seemed to us in these atomic experiments?[1]

The world of quantum mechanics may be new, strange, and irrational, but it isn't pessimistic, any more than Jung is pessimistic, any more than Eastern thought is pessimistic. There's no reason why quantum mechanics should throw us into despair, except that it alters our worldview, it shakes the ground under our feet (if we're rational thinkers). Doubtless Newton's worldview was unsettling when it first appeared. Even in the Romantic period, intellectuals were depressed by Newton's cold determinism, and one Romantic lamented that the world lay in pieces at his feet; he hoped that these separate and disconnected pieces could be put back together again. Now they have. If the world is "one all-encompassing organic pattern," then we're connected to nature, connected to the universe, and even death can't sever this connection. The new worldview should raise our spirits, not throw us into despair. A world that's full of mysteries is more exciting than a mechanical, Newtonian world. Paranormal phenomena are like an unexplored continent. Shouldn't we rejoice that in this old world of ours there are still unexplored continents?

3. *Beginner's Mind*   Zukav says that a scientist should accept reality as he sees it, even if that lands him in contradiction and nonsense; he says that a scientist must have "a beginner's mind.... a childlike ability to see the world as it is, and not as it appears according to what we know about it."

A beginner's mind is valuable in art as well as science. The English painter Turner was once criticized for painting a ship that had no portholes. Turner responded, "I paint what I see, not what I know." Impressionism is about trusting what you see, painting what you see, even if it contradicts what you know.

---

[1] Zukav, "The Role of 'I'"

12. PHYSICS

Turner knew that ships have portholes, but he didn't see them, and he wanted to paint what he saw—this is the Impressionist creed. We know that ocean and atmosphere are different, but when we look out to sea, they sometimes appear indistinguishable, hence Impressionist painters sometimes depict them as one.

Scientists and artists must trust what they see, though it contradicts what they "know", what they think is possible. An artist must trust what he sees in his own soul, as well as what he sees in the outside world. The novelist Henry Miller said, "I obey only my own instincts and intuition.... Often I put down things which I do not understand myself, secure in the knowledge that later they will become clear and meaningful to me."[1]

People are often blind to occult phenomena because they clash with our worldview, because we regard them as impossible. If a psychic communicates with the dead, we say, "that's impossible, he must be a fraud." An intellectual should use the word "impossible" very rarely, if at all. Zukav quotes Suzuki (a Zen writer): "in the beginner's mind, there are many possibilities, but in the expert's there are few."[2] The Philosophy of Today sees the world as full of possibilities, and full of mysteries.

4. *Dancing Energy* Classical physics, Newton's physics, saw the world existing "out there,", independently of us. But modern physics says there's no ultimate substance, and nothing exists without us perceiving it. Our position has changed from spectator of the world to creator of the world. (Like other new ideas in physics, this is an old idea in philosophy. Has modern physics given us any new ideas? Hasn't it just confirmed the ideas we had already?)

Depending on which experiment we choose to perform, we can demonstrate light's particle nature, or its wave nature. In other words, the nature of light depends on our choice of experiment. Or rather, we can't know the nature of light in itself (as Kant would say, "we can't know the thing-in-itself"), we only know about our interaction with light.

---

[1] ibid, p. 133
[2] ibid, "Beginner's Mind"

> Since particle-like behavior and wave-like behavior are the only properties that we ascribe to light, and since these properties now are recognized to belong... not to light itself, but to our interaction with light, then it appears that light has no properties independent of us! To say that something has no properties is the same as saying that it does not exist. The next step in this logic is inescapable. Without us, light does not exist.[1]

Each of us creates the world, each of us creates light, each of us says "Let there be light!" Without us, there is no light, no world. As Berkeley would say, if a tree falls in a forest, and no one is there to hear, it makes no sound.

A quantum is a quantity of something. A quantity of what? We don't know. Quantum mechanics is a science that 'doesn't know what it's talking about.' (Is this true of every science?) But even though physicists don't know what a quantum is, quantum mechanics helps physicists to make sense of appearances, so they regard it as useful.

If we try to determine the ultimate stuff of the universe, we never succeed. Democritus and his school said that the ultimate stuff was the atom, the "uncuttable" thing. But later thinkers asked, "what is the atom made of?" and they found that the atom wasn't really uncuttable, it was made of subatomic particles. But subatomic particles have proven to be very elusive. We can't seem to find the ultimate stuff of the universe.[2]

Modern physics tells us that mass changes into energy, and energy into mass—they're interchangeable. "According to particle physics, the world is fundamentally dancing energy; energy that is everywhere and incessantly assuming first this form and

---

[1] ibid
[2] Nietzsche applauded Boscovich (an 18th-century scientist) for exploding the notion that atoms are the ultimate substance: "Boscovich has taught us to abjure the belief in the last part of the earth that 'stood fast'—the belief in 'substance,' in 'matter,' in the earth-residuum and particle-atom: it is the greatest triumph over the senses that has been gained on earth so far."(*Beyond Good and Evil*, #12) Did Nietzsche anticipate the revolution in physics, as he anticipated the revolution in psychology?

then that."[1] This sounds much like Eastern philosophy; the physical world is only clothing that god (or energy) puts on—ever-changing, ever-new. There is no ultimate substance, and nothing that exists independently. The physical world is "not a structure built out of independently existing unanalyzable entities, but rather a web of relationships between elements whose meanings arise wholly from their relationships to the whole."[2] Nothing is independent, everything is mutual.

In an earlier chapter, I discussed the idea that the mind, the ego, the "I", has no permanent, independent existence, it's part of the whole.[3] A tree isn't an independent thing, you and I aren't independent things, everything is part of the whole. Here again, modern physics has confirmed the ideas of philosophy in a most interesting and forceful way, but one can't say that modern physics changes our ideas, or leads us to new ideas.

5. *Time* Modern physics has changed our view of time, and here again, there is a striking parallel between physics and philosophy. Einstein's theory of relativity views time differently than Newton viewed it, and quantum mechanics also views time in an un-Newtonian way. In Newtonian physics, time is one-dimensional, it moves forward. According to modern physics, however, "it is preferable, and more useful, to think in terms of a

---

[1] Zukav, "The Particle Zoo"
[2] ibid, "What Happens". This view has a parallel in literary criticism—specifically, in Wilson Knight's interpretation of Shakespeare. "Einstein's relativity theory," Knight wrote, "served to shift emphasis from individual entities to their observable 'relationships'; just as, in my early essays on *Hamlet*, I tried... to see that hero not merely as an isolated 'character' rigidly conceived, but in direct and living relation to his own dramatic environment.... The belief in rigid particles with predictable motions has been replaced by concepts of form, pattern and symmetry.... For 'particles' put 'characters' and we have a clear Shakespearean analogy." (*The Wheel of Fire*, Preface, pp. viii, ix, x)
[3] see ch. 2, #14

static, nonmoving picture of space and time.... Events do not develop, they just are."[1]

Jung also viewed time in an un-Newtonian way. Jung felt that both the past and the future exist in the present, in the unconscious. Jung felt that, in the unconscious, time doesn't flow in a Newtonian way, it doesn't flow from A to B to C.[2] Shakespeare was a Hermetic thinker who viewed time in an un-Newtonian way. In *Macbeth*, for example, the plot doesn't unfold from A to B to C; rather, the atmosphere of evil is present at the start, pervading both the natural world and the human world. The witches anticipate the future. As in the theory of relativity, "events do not develop, they just are." Shakespeare Time is different from Newton Time, and similar to Jung Time, Einstein Time, Quantum Time.[3]

Just as Kant, Jung and other philosophical thinkers have long argued that space and time aren't absolute, so too modern physics argues that space and time aren't absolute. Particles that are spatially separate have been seen to communicate with each other, just as the future has been found embedded in the present. As Stapp wrote, "Everything we know about Nature is in accord

---

[1] ibid, "Special Nonsense", p. 168. The physicist de Broglie put it thus: "in space-time, everything which for each of us constitutes the past, the present, and the future is given in block.... Each observer, as his time passes, discovers, so to speak, new slices of space-time which appear to him as successive aspects of the material world, though in reality the ensemble of events constituting space-time exist prior to his knowledge of them."(ibid, "The Dance", p. 245)

[2] "There are indications," Jung said, "that at least a part of the psyche is not subject to the laws of space and time. Scientific proof of that has been provided by the well-known J. B. Rhine experiments."(*Memories, Dreams, Reflections*, ch. 11)

[3] For more on Jung's view of time, and Shakespeare's view of time, see ch. 7, #36. Many Shakespeare critics have been baffled by the lack of sequence in Shakespeare. Perhaps the only critic who understood "Shakespeare Time" and Shakespeare's worldview is G. Wilson Knight.

with the idea that the fundamental process of Nature lies outside space-time."[1]

On numerous points, modern physics agrees with the Eastern worldview, the Hermetic worldview, the Jungian worldview, and the primitive worldview. A grand synthesis is within our reach.

---

[1] Zukav, "The End of Science", p. 328

13. Life- and Death-Instincts

1. *Part Animal, Part God* From the beginning of philosophy until recent times, from Socrates to Kant, it was believed that reason was the essence of man, reason was distinctively human, reason made man different from the rest of the animal world. Philosophers said that man had a rational soul, and therefore man was akin to God; man was the king of nature, he was halfway between animals and God. Many philosophers said that man should listen to his rational soul, not to his animal passions; man should let his rational part rule his animal part. Kant, for example, said that man should follow moral principles that were untainted by emotions or inclinations. Kant also said that man should seek knowledge—pure, disinterested knowledge. Like earlier philosophers, Kant separated man from the rest of the animal world; Kant said that man was an end in himself, while animals were merely means.

Schopenhauer freed himself only partially from these ideas. Schopenhauer traced most human actions to the unconscious, the "will"; thus he reduced the importance of the rational soul, of reason. But Schopenhauer thought that man could deny the will, that is, sever himself from his unconscious. This, according to Schopenhauer, was the goal of life: deny the will, and thus become a saint or a genius. The greatest achievements in the moral sphere and in the intellectual sphere were, in Schopenhauer's view, the products of pure intellect, of the mind separated from the unconscious.

Nietzsche and Freud went further than Schopenhauer. They agreed with Schopenhauer that man had much in common with animals, that consciousness was merely a skin over the unconscious, and that people were driven by unconscious forces, especially by a powerful sexual drive. But they disagreed with Schopenhauer about the possibility of denying the will, of breaking away from the unconscious. Schopenhauer had said that the saint and the genius attained a higher level of being, transcended their animal nature, and reached the realm of pure intellect. Nietzsche and Freud argued that all men, including the saint and the genius, were driven by unconscious forces.

Nietzsche and Freud said that pure intellect didn't exist, that the intellect was always influenced by the body and by unconscious forces, and that even great artists and philosophers were influenced by unconscious forces. According to Nietzsche and Freud, man wasn't halfway between animals and God, man was part of the animal world, and couldn't transcend his animal nature. Even man's loftiest flights in the sphere of culture and religion were attempts to live better, to make life pleasanter, to organize life better.

Nietzsche and Freud were rational thinkers, with little respect for Eastern philosophy, for occult powers, or for spiritual impulses. Their view of human nature is reductive; they tend to reduce human nature to "nothing but" biological impulses. It must be admitted, however, that Nietzsche and Freud made important innovations, and that their thoughts on man's instincts can contribute to our understanding of human nature. The biological viewpoint may not be the whole truth, but it is a part of the truth. To explore this part of the truth, to explore the life- and death-instincts, is the purpose of this chapter.

2. *Freud's View* Schopenhauer said that all organic life has the same basic "will" or instinct, a will to life. Nietzsche said that all organic life tries to do more than just live, it tries to enhance itself, to increase its power. Nietzsche replaced Schopenhauer's

theory of a "will to life" with his own theory of a "will to power."

But Nietzsche's theory of a will to power has some weaknesses. Though it can explain mankind fairly well, Nietzsche's theory has difficulty explaining animals and plants. One must distort the meaning of the word "power" before one can say that animals and plants have a will to power. Furthermore, the theory of a will to power exaggerates the importance of the egoistic drives, and overlooks the non-egoistic drives, the altruistic drives. These altruistic drives are found throughout the organic world—among plants, animals and human beings. They're especially evident among social animals, such as ants and bees.

Freud's theory of life- and death-instincts doesn't have the weaknesses of Nietzsche's theory. Freud's theory unites man with the rest of the organic world. According to Freud's theory, all organic life has descended from the earliest organic life, and therefore all organic life is related. Plants, animals and humans have the same basic instincts, a life-instinct and a death-instinct. According to Freud's theory, the life-instinct impels every organism to promote not only itself but also its family, its group or its species. Every organism has some altruistic drives.

3. *Tai Chen's View* While Western philosophy moved from an emphasis on reason to an emphasis on instinct, Chinese philosophy followed a similar course. The neo-Confucian school had stressed the importance of reason, but the eighteenth-century thinker Tai Chen stressed the importance of instinct. According to Tai Chen, there is no pure reason, no reason divorced from passion and instinct. Tai Chen traced morality not to an abstract sense of good or reason or justice, but rather to man's basic drives and instincts. These basic drives, in his view, were not merely egoistic. Virtue consists not in repressing these basic drives, but in making use of them in a balanced way.

4. *Pleasure and Sex* are often put forward as the goals toward which human nature strives. Early in his career, Freud expounded his "pleasure principle": man's primary goal was pleasure, and man's primary pleasure was sex. But late in his

career, Freud expounded his theory of the life- and death-instincts, and argued that pleasure and sex weren't man's primary goals.

Sexual pleasure is the bait by which man is induced to reproduce. By rewarding man with sexual pleasure, the life-instinct induces man to accomplish its purpose, which is reproduction. According to Freud, man is a creature of the life- and death-instincts, just as animals and plants are, and the life-instinct prompts man to reproduce, just as it prompts animals and plants to reproduce. Reproduction is the end, pleasure and sex are merely the means. According to Freud, when human nature is stripped of its trappings, and reduced to its essence, man's basic motives are the same as those of animals and plants. The life- and death-instincts are the driving forces of all organic life.

5. *Death Instinct* The influence of the life-instinct can be seen in many of our actions; indeed, the influence of the life-instinct can be seen in our very existence. The death-instinct, on the other hand, remains backstage and usually escapes attention. A few observers, however, have detected the existence of the death-instinct. Jung, for example, said, "it is as if the libido were not only a ceaseless forward movement... like the sun, the libido also wills its own descent." When Tolstoy was about fifty, he felt a death-instinct within himself: "An invincible force impelled me to get rid of my existence. It cannot be said exactly that I *wished* to kill myself, for the force which drew me away from life was fuller, more powerful, more general than any mere desire."[1] Seneca, the Roman philosopher, also noticed the death-instinct; "one must avoid that emotion," wrote Seneca, "which has seized many people—the lust for dying." And Dickens wrote thus of the death-instinct: "In seasons of pestilence, some of us will have a secret attraction to the disease—a terrible passing inclination to die of it." Nietzsche spoke of "those death-seeking mass deliria

---

[1] See Jung, Collected Works, vol. 5, ¶680, and William James, *Varieties of Religious Experience,* VI, 7.

whose dreadful cry *'evviva la morte'* [long live death] was heard all over Europe."[1]

6. *Balance of Power* Every organism is a combination of the life-instinct and the death-instinct. Since the death-instinct shares power with the life-instinct, it usually doesn't bring about the death of the organism to which it belongs. The death-instinct doesn't prevent one from living, but it does put a brake on activity, just as ankle weights don't prevent a runner from running, but they do reduce his speed.

7. *Anticipating Death* People can often foresee the time of their death. Is this because their own urge toward death, their own death-instinct, helps to bring about their end?

Lincoln anticipated that he would be assassinated during his second term as President. Though many people advised him to take precautions against assassination, he declined to do so; rather than avoid assassination, he seemed to invite it. At age thirty, van Gogh predicted that he would be dead in six to ten years; he died at age thirty-seven. At age twenty-nine, Kierkegaard, though his health was sound, wrote: "I have not long to live (I have a feeling) and I have never expected to"; he died at age forty-two. Keats, when his health was still intact, foresaw that he would die young; he died at age twenty-five. When Byron was preparing to go to Greece, he foresaw that he would die there; Byron died in Greece at age thirty-six.

Perhaps people will their own death once they've done all that they're capable of doing, once their work is finished. Lincoln, for example, may have felt that, having won the Civil War, his work was finished, and Byron may have felt that his creative power had reached its limit.[2]

---

[1] See Jung, Collected Works, vol. 5, ¶680, Seneca, *Epistles to Lucilius*, Loeb Classics, vol. 1, §24, Dickens, *A Tale of Two Cities*, III, 6, and Nietzsche, *Genealogy of Morals*, III, 21.
[2] On Lincoln, see G. Wilson, "A Prophetic Dream Reported by Abraham Lincoln," *American Imago*, June, 1940; on van Gogh, see *Dear Theo*, p. 227; on Kierkegaard, see W. Lowrie, *Kierkegaard*, III, 2.

8. *Not A Cannonball* Looking at the accomplishments of a writer who has died young, people often make comments such as, "In view of what Keats accomplished at twenty-three, which is far greater than what Shakespeare or Milton accomplished at twenty-three, I've calculated that if Keats lived to be seventy-five, he would have written seven plays better than *Hamlet*, and three epic poems better than *Paradise Lost*." Such reasoning assumes that the accomplishments of genius can be plotted on a graph, like the speed of a cannonball dropped from a rooftop. But genius is fickle, moody and unpredictable; it has an ebb and flow that can't be expressed in an equation. Genius defies mathematics.

A genius who lives to a ripe old age doesn't usually accomplish much in his twenties; he works slowly and paces himself, anticipating that he'll have time to work later. Conversely, a genius who dies young usually works with great intensity, anticipating that death is near. Genius anticipates how much time it has to do its work, and paces itself accordingly.

It's useless to speculate on what Keats would have accomplished if he had lived to be seventy-five. His early death was an expression of his personality, just as his poetry was; to say, "if Keats hadn't died young" is like saying, "if Keats hadn't been a poet." Keats was destined to die young, just as he was destined to be a poet. To say that Keats would have accomplished more than Shakespeare if he had lived to be seventy-five is like saying, "since John ran a mile in 4 minutes, he can run 26 miles in 104 minutes, which means he can easily win a gold medal in the marathon."

9. *Indirect Suicide* Sickness often affects those who want to be sick, while those who don't want to be sick can often overcome sickness. Accidents, like sicknesses, often come to those who desire them. The desire to have an accident is sometimes conscious, sometimes unconscious. Abraham spoke of,

> the frequent cases of suicide, or attempted suicide, arising from unconscious motives. Persons suffering from depressive moods

may often fail to take the most elementary precautions.... Into the category of unconsciously motivated suicide fall, for instance, many of the accidents so frequent in mountains.

Oscar Wilde was the cause of his own trial, conviction, and imprisonment; Wilde's decline and early death was a prolonged and disguised suicide. Wilde was aware of his own self-destructive impulses, and was puzzled by them; Wilde asked, "Why is it that one runs to one's ruin? Why has destruction such a fascination?"[1]

Death in war, like execution, sometimes comes to those who desire it. An unconscious desire to die impels a soldier to act in a way that brings about his death. Conversely, a soldier who is determined to survive can fight courageously, yet still manage to avoid death. Napoleon, for example, was in the thick of numerous battles, and had nineteen horses killed from under him, yet managed to avoid death.

Insanity, too, sometimes comes to those who desire it. Nietzsche, for example, seemed to desire insanity as a way of escaping from the pressures of life. Just as many writers anticipated death, Nietzsche anticipated insanity. Hence Nietzsche wrote his autobiography, and summed up his life and work, when he was just forty-five. When Nietzsche finally became insane, one of his friends said that he acted as if he were glad at how things had turned out.

10. *Will to Live* A long life, like a premature death, is often voluntary; just as some people die as a result of their own desire to die, so too others have a long life as a result of their own desire to have a long life. Thomas Mann was one such person. At age thirty-five, Mann wrote thus of the protagonist of "Death in Venice":

> he deeply desired to live to a good old age, for it was his conviction that only the artist to whom it has been granted to be fruitful on all stages of our human scene can be truly great, or universal.

---

[1] See Karl Abraham, "Giovanni Segantini: A Psycho-Analytical Study," 1911; Nietzsche, *Assorted Opinions and Maxims*, §94, and R. Ellman, *Oscar Wilde*, ch. 22.

Mann lived to be eighty. George Bernard Shaw, who discussed the desirability of a long life, and speculated about prolonging life indefinitely, lived to be ninety-four.

11. *Welcoming Death* If people have a death-instinct, why do they fear death? When people fear death, they sometimes fear not death itself, but their own unconscious desire to die. The fear of death is sometimes the result of discord between consciousness and the unconscious; man's consciousness cannot reconcile itself to his unconscious desire to die, and tries to repress this desire. Repression causes fear of that which is repressed, in other words, fear of one's own desire to die. An analogous situation is the fear of heights, which Freud thought might conceal an unconscious desire to fall to one's death.

The psychic evolution of man, which eliminates the repressions of primitive man and produces concord between consciousness and the unconscious, may eliminate the fear of death. Man's whole being, including his consciousness, may someday welcome death, or at least accept it, just as now man's unconscious often welcomes death.

12. *Tagore and Tolstoy on Death* Alan Watts wrote:

> When the body is worn out and the brain is tired, the whole organism welcomes death.... The body dies because it wants to. It finds it beyond its power to resist the disease or to mend the injury, and so, tired out with the struggle, turns to death. If the consciousness were more sensitive to the feelings and impulses of the whole organism, it would share this desire, and, indeed, sometimes does so.[1]

In Eastern writers, one sometimes finds an acceptance of death, even a welcoming of death. Rabindranath Tagore, one of India's most famous poets, embraced death with a kind of ecstasy. Tagore was a mystic who affirmed existence in general, affirmed both life and death.

---

[1] *The Wisdom of Insecurity*, ch. 4

Tagore's attitude toward death contrasts sharply with Tolstoy's; Tolstoy said that, throughout his life, he "feared and hated death."[1] As Tagore represents an extreme of accepting death, so Tolstoy represents an extreme of fearing death. Are these just individual reactions, or are they typical of the Indian and the Russian?

A non-Western writer, like Tagore, is more in harmony with his body, with his feelings, than a Western writer; in the words of Alan Watts, the non-Western writer is "more sensitive to the feelings and impulses of the whole organism." When the "whole organism" is ready for death, a person like Tagore senses that readiness, and 'goes with it' instead of struggling against it.

A Western writer, on the other hand, is apt to sharpen his consciousness by repressing his unconscious, his feelings, his body. A Western writer is apt to be insensitive to the "feelings and impulses of the whole organism." Though his body may desire death, he resists this desire, he doesn't 'go with it.'

If this is true of the West in general, it's even more true of the northern European than the southern European, since the northern European is more apt to repress his unconscious. When Christianity was brought to northern Europe, northern Europeans were still living at a primitive, barbarous level. They weren't ready for Christianity, which was the fruit of an older, more civilized society. They could only receive Christianity through a kind of violence, a violence that pitted the mind against the body, a violence that repressed feelings and impulses.[2]

Just as the inner conflict was more intense in northern Europe than in southern Europe, so too it was more intense in Russia than in northern Europe, since Russia was more primitive than northern Europe—more precisely, Russia in 1700 was more primitive than northern Europe in 1700. Russia had its "middle ages" later than northern Europe did; Russia had its period of violent inner conflict later than northern Europe did. Just as European culture was stimulated by its inner conflict, so too Russian culture was stimulated by its inner conflict; this inner

---

[1] *Reminiscences of Tolstoy*, by Maxim Gorky, ch. 2
[2] See also Chapter 1, #5

13. LIFE- AND DEATH-INSTINCTS

conflict, this tension, doubtless contributed to the flourishing of Russian literature in the 19th century.

If the West was conflicted, Russia was more so; if the West was rational, Russia was more so. Tolstoy is a rational thinker who tried to strip the irrational elements out of Christianity; he tried to make Christianity rational. Tolstoy loathed Shakespeare because Shakespeare had a Hermetic worldview, not a rational worldview. The inner conflict in Tolstoy (and other Russians) caused him to lose touch with his feelings and his body, and to fear death.

Tagore felt that the thought of death made everything precious—every life, every blade of grass, every day. Tolstoy, on the other hand, felt that the thought of death made everything worthless; nothing in life had any value, Tolstoy thought, because it would all end in death.

13. *Riddle* Bring yourself back to the time when there was no life on earth. No life could arise that wasn't controlled by the life- and death-instincts, since organic life is a manifestation of these instincts. But how could the life- and death-instincts themselves arise? And what do the life- and death-instincts actually consist of?

These are questions we can't answer. We must be content to state the laws that describe the behavior of the life- and death-instincts, though we're ignorant of what these instincts actually are, just as Newton was content to state the laws of gravity though he was ignorant of what gravity actually was, just as quantum physics doesn't know what a quantum actually is. As Schopenhauer said,

> At the end of every investigation and of every exact science the human mind stands before a primary phenomenon.... This primary phenomenon explains everything that is comprehended under it and follows from it, but it itself remains unexplained, and lies before us like a riddle.[1]

---

[1] *On the Basis of Morality*, §21

14. *One, Many* The metaphysician tries to find the one in the many, the one constant factor in a world of different things, the thing-in-itself that lies underneath the variety of phenomena. Schopenhauer thought that he had discovered the one in the many, the one constant factor, the thing-in-itself; Schopenhauer said that the "will" was the thing-in-itself, and that at the core of all individual things was the will. The will was true being, and true being must be one and undivided. Since the will was true being, it had to underlie everything, hence Schopenhauer ascribed the will even to inanimate objects, such as rocks.

The life- and death-instincts, like Schopenhauer's "will," can be viewed as the one in the many, the thing-in-itself. Instead of speaking of two separate instincts (a life-instinct and a death-instinct), one could speak of two versions of one instinct: a strong, healthy version of the life-instinct, and a weak, tired version of the life-instinct.

But whether one speaks of one instinct or of two instincts, the life- and death-instincts can't be ascribed to inanimate objects. The theory of the life- and death-instincts sees a sharp division between the animate and the inanimate. The theory of the life- and death-instincts should be supplemented by a more comprehensive view, a view that embraces both the animate and the inanimate; we discussed such a view in earlier chapters.[1]

15. *Nietzsche On Decadence* Nietzsche's theory of a will to power is not as clear, not as comprehensive, as Freud's theory of life- and death-instincts. But if one looks at Nietzsche's entire philosophy, one realizes that Nietzsche's ideas on human nature are similar to Freud's. Nietzsche thought that every human being represents either ascending life or descending life, either a will to life or a will to death, either renaissance or decadence, either the Dionysian or the Apollinian, either a strong, healthy will to power or a weak, tired will to power. Thus, Nietzsche's view of

---

[1] see Chapter 1, #15 and ch. 3, #19

13. LIFE- AND DEATH-INSTINCTS

human nature was similar to Freud's theory of life- and death-instincts.[1]

Freud didn't attempt to apply his theory of life- and death-instincts to history and culture. Nietzsche, on the other hand, applied his ideas on human nature to history and culture. Nietzsche called certain philosophers renaissance-type and others decadent; he called certain artists renaissance-type and others decadent; he called certain historical epochs renaissance-type and others decadent. For example, Nietzsche called Schopenhauer decadent; he thought that Schopenhauer's pessimistic, negative attitude toward life was decadent.

Some might say that Schopenhauer took a pessimistic, negative attitude toward life because life really is filled with suffering, the world really is hell, and Schopenhauer had the genius to understand the nature of life and the nature of the world. Nietzsche, however, realized that life is what we perceive it to be, life has no nature independent of our perception. Therefore, any general judgment about life teaches us about the judge, not about life. For example, when Schopenhauer passes a negative judgment on life, he teaches us about his own nature, not about life; when Schopenhauer passes a negative judgment on life, he reveals that he himself is decadent.

Nietzsche thought that renaissance-type philosophers and artists, unlike Schopenhauer, had positive, affirmative attitudes toward life. Nietzsche himself wanted to be a renaissance-type philosopher, he wanted to take a positive, affirmative attitude toward life. Nietzsche developed a theory of eternal recurrence, according to which everything that has occurred on earth will eventually occur again. Nietzsche thought that if we accept eternal recurrence, if we accept the repetition of life, then we're renaissance-type people. On the other hand, if we reject eternal recurrence, if we can't bear to have life repeated again and again, then we're decadent. Nietzsche thought that by joyfully accepting eternal recurrence, he affirmed life, as the renaissance people

---

[1] "I was the first," Nietzsche wrote, "to see the real opposition: the degenerating instinct that turns against life... versus a formula for the highest affirmation."(*Ecce Homo*, "The Birth of Tragedy," 2)

of the past had done. In fact, Nietzsche thought that his acceptance of eternal recurrence was the most powerful affirmation of life ever made.[1]

16. *Shaw's View*   The central ideas of a historical period are usually shared by several thinkers, not possessed exclusively by one thinker. In Darwin's time, for example, the idea of evolution was shared by several thinkers. In Nietzsche's time, the idea of life- and death-instincts was shared by several thinkers, including Freud, Nietzsche and George Bernard Shaw.

Shaw was interested in philosophy, and expressed philosophical ideas in his plays. Shaw was especially interested in the biological side of philosophy. Shaw spoke of a "Life Force," and said that the Life Force was obstructed by the forces of "Death and Degeneration." Shaw argued that the Life Force impels man to serve not only his own personal interests, but the interests of his society and his species.[2]

17. *A New Theory*   Schopenhauer perceived the importance of unconscious instincts in human nature. But Schopenhauer didn't perceive a will to death in human nature, he perceived only a will to life. Nietzsche perceived both a will to death and a will to life. Furthermore, Nietzsche pointed out how these two opposing instincts manifested themselves in history and culture.

But Nietzsche never developed a theory of decadence and renaissance based on life- and death-instincts; Nietzsche never developed a philosophy of history. Nietzsche perceived Schopenhauer's decadence, but he didn't explain Schopenhauer's decadence. Nietzsche didn't explain why certain philosophers, certain artists, and certain historical epochs are decadent, and others are renaissance-type. Nietzsche perceived decadence and renaissance, but didn't explain them. Nietzsche never developed a systematic theory of decadence and renaissance.

---

[1] Nietzsche spoke of, "the idea of the eternal recurrence, this highest formula of affirmation that is at all attainable."(*Ecce Homo*, "Thus Spoke Zarathustra," 1)
[2] See Shaw, *Man and Superman*, 3, and *Back To Methuselah*, Preface

13. LIFE- AND DEATH-INSTINCTS

Unlike Schopenhauer and Nietzsche, Hegel developed a philosophy of history. Hegel argued that the individual is the product of his time, the product of his society. But Hegel didn't have a biological perspective on human nature, didn't understand the importance of the unconscious, and didn't understand decadence and renaissance.

Philosophy advances by utilizing the insights of earlier thinkers, and filling in the gaps in earlier thinkers. The theories of our time can surpass earlier theories by utilizing Nietzsche's psychological insights, by filling in the gaps in Hegel's philosophy of history, and by making the life- and death-instincts the basis of a theory of decadence and renaissance.

18. *The Idea of Our Time* Individuals live and die, grow and decay, as the result not only of external forces, but also as the result of internal forces, of unconscious forces, of unconscious instincts. Societies are similar to individuals. Like individuals, societies live and die, grow and decay, as the result not only of external forces, but also internal, unconscious forces. If we can understand the unconscious forces that affect societies, then we can understand the phenomena of decadence and renaissance, and deepen our understanding of history.

This deeper understanding of history will give us a deeper understanding of the individual. Since the individual is part of the historical process, and is moved by the forces that move society, this new theory of history is also a new theory of the individual, a new perspective on many branches of the humanities. It must be left to posterity to explore the full implications of this new theory of history; what one generation discovers, the next explores.

This new theory rests on three pillars: Hegel's theory of society as an organism, Freud's theory of the life- and death-instincts, and Nietzsche's theory of decadence. This theory isn't the final stage in the evolution of philosophy. It's the idea of our time, not the final chapter in the history of ideas. The next philosophy will go beyond this philosophy, and reach new heights.

19. *A Flash of Intuition* Only recently, only since the development of the psychology of the unconscious, has it become possible to apply a psychological perspective to history. Earlier philosophies of history—including Hegel's, Spengler's and Toynbee's—have lacked a psychological perspective. A philosophy of history can't be constructed simply by studying history, it needs the help of philosophy and psychology. It can't be constructed by laborious research, but only by a flash of intuition. Thus, we shouldn't expect a philosophy of history from one who specializes in history. (In science, those who make revolutionary discoveries are often people who don't specialize in the field that they revolutionize. Dalton, for example, who revolutionized chemistry, didn't specialize in chemistry; Dalton revolutionized chemistry by applying to chemistry insights that he had acquired from meteorology and physics.)

Spengler and Toynbee tried to construct philosophies of history simply by studying history. Since they knew Western history best, their theories reflect the general course of Western history. They tried to apply their view of Western history to other civilizations—to Indian civilization, Chinese civilization, etc. Instead of moving from general ideas to particular cases, they started from a particular case (Western civilization), then tried to move to a general idea, a general theory of history. Spengler and Toynbee were preoccupied with historical research, and didn't utilize the latest findings of philosophy and psychology, didn't utilize the findings of Nietzsche, Freud, etc. The works of Spengler and Toynbee fill thousands of pages because they aren't true philosophies, and aren't based on intuition.

Ortega had a profound understanding of history, though he didn't construct his own philosophy of history. In an earlier chapter, we saw that Mill recognized the need for a new religion, but wisely refrained from trying to fill that need himself.[1] Likewise, Ortega saw the opportunity for a new philosophy of history, but wisely refrained from trying to seize that opportunity himself. Ortega said, "We are now approaching a splendid

---

[1] See ch. 3, #15

13. LIFE- AND DEATH-INSTINCTS

flowering of the historic sciences."[1] This splendid flowering would start with bold theory, Ortega said, not with painstaking research.

The philosophy of history set forth in the next chapter combines philosophy, psychology and history, instead of looking only at history. It's set forth concisely—far more concisely than the theories of Spengler and Toynbee. It aims to describe the forces, the unconscious instincts, that underlie history. But it doesn't attempt to explain all events or all civilizations, and it doesn't attempt to predict whether present-day civilization will flourish or perish. Thus, it's less ambitious than the theories of Spengler and Toynbee. (Likewise, new scientific theories are sometimes less ambitious, and explain less, than earlier theories. For example, the theories of Newton and Lavoisier explained less, in some respects, than earlier theories had explained.[2])

The philosophy of history must concentrate on cultural history rather than political history. The human spirit expresses itself more clearly in the cultural sphere than in the political sphere, just as one who sings alone expresses himself more clearly than one who sings in a chorus. In the political sphere, the human spirit interacts with foreign countries, with the physical environment, etc. Since events in the political sphere are shaped by a multitude of factors, it's difficult to describe the role of unconscious instincts in political history. In the cultural sphere, on the other hand, there are fewer factors shaping events, and the role of unconscious instincts is clearer. Though the philosophy of history can deepen our understanding of political history, its primary focus must be on cultural history, on showing how unconscious instincts affect culture, and cause decadence and renaissance.

---

[1] *Man and Crisis*, ch. 1
[2] See T. Kuhn, *The Structure of Scientific Revolutions*, ch. 12; on Dalton, see Kuhn, ch. 10.

14. Decadence and Renaissance

1. *Seven Theses*

I. Organisms have life- and death-instincts.
II. Society is an organism.
III. Society has life- and death-instincts.
IV. When the life-instinct is predominant in a society, the result is a renaissance-type society; when the death-instinct is predominant in a society, the result is a decadent society.
V. When the death-instinct in a society reaches an extreme, it turns into its opposite, the life-instinct.
VI. Decadence, or the death-instinct, has now reached an extreme in most Western societies.
VII. The death-instinct, having reached an extreme in most Western societies, will now turn into its opposite, the life-instinct. Thus, most Western societies are at the start of a renaissance.

I'd like to discuss each of these seven theses, beginning with Thesis Two (Thesis One was the subject of the previous chapter).

2. *Thesis Two: Society is an organism* That the best Italian painters were born within forty years of each other violates the laws of probability and demands explanation. And why were the

14. DECADENCE AND RENAISSANCE

best Greek dramatists and the best Roman poets and the best Russian novelists also born within forty years of each other? Why was the Renaissance so fruitful for various kinds of culture, in various countries? History includes a series of decadent eras, as well as a series of renaissance-type eras. What are the causes of decadence and renaissance?

The organic theory of society provides a clue to the causes of decadence and renaissance. According to the organic theory of society, a society is an organic whole; though it is not actually an organism, it behaves like an organism. A society is not composed of separate individuals, as a pile of rocks is, but rather of inter-connected individuals, individuals whose instincts are determined by the instincts of their society. One might borrow a phrase from physics and say that individuals in a society are like particles whose wave functions are correlated.

No individual can escape his society; every individual is born with his society's instincts, and will die with them. Every branch of culture—philosophy, literature, music, visual art—is under the sway of the same instinct. During the Periclean age in Greece, for example, all branches of culture flourished together. During the late Roman empire, on the other hand, all branches of culture declined together, and creativity dried up. Not only is every branch of culture under the sway of the same instinct, but political behavior, too, is influenced by that same instinct. In short, society is an organic whole, and everything in a society reflects that society's predominant instinct.

3. *Thesis Three: Society has life- and death-instincts* What makes society an organic whole? What knits together the individuals in a society? The individuals in a society are connected by living together, by a common history, by a collective unconscious, and by a shared life- or death-instinct. Although societies resemble organisms, insofar as they have life- and death-instincts, societies don't necessarily die, as real organisms do. Societies may die accidentally, but they don't die necessarily.

4. *Thesis Four: When the life-instinct is predominant in a society, the result is a renaissance-type society; when the death-*

instinct is predominant in a society, the result is a decadent society Just as all organic life contains both a life-instinct and a death-instinct, so too every society contains both a life-instinct and a death instinct. Most epochs are neither completely renaissance-type nor completely decadent; most epochs are moderately renaissance-type or moderately decadent, that is, most epochs are a combination of the life-instinct and the death-instinct, with one of these instincts slightly stronger than the other.

A few epochs, however, are completely renaissance-type or completely decadent. Epochs that are completely renaissance-type are more noticeable, more visible, more memorable, than those that are completely decadent. The Periclean age in Greece, and the Renaissance age in Italy are two examples of completely renaissance-type epochs. In epochs like these, the life-instinct is markedly stronger than the death-instinct.

The average man doesn't express the instinct of an era; although the average man shares this instinct, it remains latent in him. Only the genius expresses the instinct of an era; as Hegel would say, only the great man expresses the Spirit of the Age. Genius sublimates its instincts, and only in sublimated form can instincts become visible to the eye of history.

5. *Thesis Five: When the death-instinct in a society reaches an extreme, it turns into its opposite, the life-instinct* Philosophers have long noted that many aspects of life have a dialectical nature—in other words, many aspects of life move toward an extreme and then turn into their opposites. An extreme of happiness, for example, often turns into sadness, and an extreme of liberty often turns into tyranny. In the West, the theory of the dialectic originated with Heraclitus, who believed that everything moved toward its opposite; Heraclitus spoke of *enantiodromia*, running toward the opposite. The dialectic played an important role in Hegel's philosophy. The dialectic was not unknown to Chinese philosophers, and it can be found in the Chinese

14. DECADENCE AND RENAISSANCE

theory of *yin* and *yang*; "*yang* at its highest point changes into *yin*, and positive into negative."[1]

The instincts of society oscillate back and forth. A decadent society will reach an extreme of decadence before turning into a renaissance-type society; the darkest hour is right before the dawn. The life-instinct, however, declines gradually before turning into the death-instinct, it doesn't reach an extreme before turning into the death-instinct; day declines gradually into night. Thus, a renaissance-type society will decline gradually into a decadent society.

6. *A Survey of the History of the West in the Light of the Theory of Decadence and Renaissance*[2]

A. Greece

The renaissance-type era in Greek history was the era of Aeschylus, Sophocles and Thucydides. An era like this usually lasts about forty years. In this case, about fifty-four years elapsed between the birth of Aeschylus and the birth of Thucydides. Since instincts are innate, and a long life can't change the instincts with which one was born, date of birth determines one's instincts. That people in a given society are alive at the same time doesn't mean that they have the same spirit or instinct. That people in a given society are born at the same time does mean that they have the same spirit or instinct. As Ortega said, "in history it is important to distinguish between that which is contemporary and that which is coeval," in other words, between that which is alive at the same time and that which is born at the same time.[3]

Before we can understand the shift from renaissance to decadence in Greek culture, we need to consider the significance of a

---

[1] Jung, Collected Works, vol. 15, ¶94. The dialectic plays an especially prominent role in the philosophy of Zhuang Zi.
[2] My theory seems to fit the West best; I haven't tried to carry it outside the West. Perhaps people with a deeper knowledge of China, India, Egypt, etc. will apply my theory to those civilizations.
[3] *Man and Crisis*, 3

writer's views on morality. A writer's views on morality often reveal whether he is renaissance-type or decadent. A moral world view is a sign of decadence, while an amoral world view is a sign of a renaissance spirit.

Though the renaissance spirit is generally amoral, an amoral world view doesn't always indicate a renaissance spirit. Decadence is sometimes amoral, especially in the modern era. Decadence is protean, and takes many different forms. Although decadence has often, in the past, taken the form of repressive ethics, it takes different forms in our time. Modern decadence no longer advocates repression of the unconscious. Thus, in our time, a philosopher's views on morality aren't as reliable an indication of his spirit as they were in earlier times.

Why do decadent writers, especially those from earlier times, often preach morality, and advocate the repression of the unconscious? There are two possible explanations for this. The first is that repression means turning against oneself, doing violence to one's unconscious; repression is related to the death-instinct, and the death-instinct is the essence of decadence. The second is that the decadent person is less healthy than the renaissance person; the decadent person's instincts are less harmonious and more in need of repression and control. Hence the decadent person needs morality and the rule of the super-ego, while the renaissance person can express his whole nature without restraint or repression.

Nietzsche was the first philosopher to see the importance of decadence, and to regard morality as decadent. Nietzsche viewed Socrates and Plato as moralists, decadent moralists. Socrates represents the decadent era that succeeded the renaissance-type era. Socrates is an excellent example of a moralist, of one who champions consciousness over the unconscious, reason over inclination. Knowledge is virtue, according to Socrates, and virtue is happiness.

Euripides, like Socrates, was a moralist. Euripides and Socrates had an affinity for each other. Socrates, it was said, helped Euripides to write his plays. Though Socrates refrained from seeing the plays of the older tragedians, he was willing to walk to the Piraeus in order to see Euripides' latest play. Euripides and

14. DECADENCE AND RENAISSANCE 281

Socrates represent the Apollonian, the moral, the decadent and the death-instinct, in contrast to Aeschylus, Sophocles and Thucydides, who represent the Dionysian, the amoral, the renaissance-type and the life-instinct.

The renaissance-type artist, like the renaissance-type philosopher, is amoral, while the decadent artist is often a moralist. Though Euripides sometimes depicted characters who were swept away by passion, his world view was rational and moral; all his verses, said Cicero, were precepts. By contrast, the world view of Aeschylus and Sophocles was amoral. Euripides probably represents the first signs of the decadent era that succeeded the renaissance-type era, though he was born nine years before Thucydides.

After its brief renaissance era, Greek culture entered a decadent era from which it never emerged. But it didn't become completely decadent immediately; decadence replaces the renaissance spirit gradually. Of the four leading Greek philosophers who came after the renaissance era, three—Socrates, Plato and Aristotle—were moralists and one, Epicurus, was a hedonist. Hedonism, like morality, is decadent. Speaking of the major Greek philosophers, Nietzsche said, "These great philosophers represent one after the other the typical forms of decadence."[1]

Although many of the most illustrious Greek writers were decadent, they were nonetheless great writers. Plato, for example, is among the greatest philosophers ever, despite his decadence. Decadence affects a writer's views, but it doesn't diminish his genius or dull his intellect.

The tragic spirit vanished from Greece after the renaissance-type era. The writers of comedy, especially the writers of the so-called New Comedy, represent the decline of Greek drama and the decline of the Greek spirit in general. Hence the New Comedians admired not the older tragedians from the renaissance era, but the later tragedian from the decadent era, Euripides. One of the New Comedians, Philemon, said that he would gladly hang himself immediately if he could converse with Euripides in

---

[1] *The Will to Power*, §435. Cicero's remark on Euripides is cited in Samuel Johnson, "Preface to Shakespeare."

the land of the dead. What one loves and admires is an indication of what one is.

Some have argued that Euripides caused the decline of Greek tragedy. Others have argued that the early tragedians—Aeschylus, Sophocles and Euripides—exhausted all the best subjects for tragedies, and set such a high standard that later dramatists were afraid to write in the same genre. Similar arguments are made about the decline of English drama after Shakespeare. According to these arguments, writers are weighed down by the burden of the past, the burden of great predecessors. Such arguments are superficial, however; they don't explain why Greek and English creativity declined not only in drama but also in other cultural fields. Only a general theory of renaissance and decadence can explain the decline of Greek tragedy, the decline of English drama, and other cultural phenomena.

Turning from Greek cultural history to Greek political history, we're confronted by the conquests of Alexander the Great. Does the militarism of Alexander represent the Greek spirit or the Macedonian spirit? If the militarism of Alexander represents the Greek spirit, it occurs at the same point in the historical cycle as the militarism of Napoleon and the militarism of Hitler, and this suggests that such militarism takes place about one hundred and fifty years after renaissance-type eras.

B. Rome

When considering the history of Rome, we find an era of political and cultural decadence at the end of the Roman Republic. During this era, there was a general political disintegration—the invasion of enemies, the depredations of pirates, the revolt of allies, the rebellion of slaves.

The era of Julius Caesar and Augustus, which followed the decadent era, was a renaissance era. This renaissance era is represented by Lucretius, Virgil and Horace. The renaissance spirit is one cause of Rome's expansionist tendency during this era. This expansionist tendency was expressed in the conquests

14. DECADENCE AND RENAISSANCE

of Caesar and Pompey. Nations tend to expand during renaissance eras, and contract during decadent eras.[1]

In the opinion of many people, war results in nothing but death and destruction, and is the product of the death-instinct. But the ultimate goal of the death-instinct is to bring the organism to which it belongs back to an inanimate condition, not to send other organisms back to an inanimate condition. War isn't the product of the death-instinct.

War can improve mankind, just as evolution by natural selection can improve species. Civilized nations, because of their superior political and economic structure, have often conquered uncivilized nations, and thus spread their civilization. Roman conquests, for example, spread civilization in Europe. Conquest creates larger political units, within which society can enjoy political stability and economic progress. Without conquest, the world would be fragmented into countless miniature nations, which would be in a state of political instability, economic stagnation and cultural barbarism.

Konrad Lorenz, the expert on animal behavior, rejected Freud's view that aggression is the product of the death-instinct. In his book *On Aggression*, Lorenz argued that aggression often benefits both individual and species:

> Aggression, the effects of which are frequently equated with those of the death wish, is an instinct like any other and in natural conditions it helps just as much as any other to ensure the survival of the individual and the species.[2]

If aggression helps both individual and species, shouldn't we associate it with the life-instinct rather than with the death-instinct? Many of the aggressive acts that are committed by individuals and nations are doubtless the product of evil, sadistic, destructive impulses. But Freud's view that aggression and war

---

[1] "The history of a nation," wrote Ortega, "is not solely that of its formative and ascendant period. It is also the history of its decadence. If the former consists in amalgamation, the latter may be described as an inverse process. The history of the decadence of a nation is the history of a vast disintegration."(*Invertebrate Spain*, ch. 1)
[2] *On Aggression*, Introduction

are always the product of the death-instinct is one-sided, and overlooks the fact that aggression and war sometimes have positive effects—among human beings, and among other animals.

After the Augustan era, Rome gradually declined into decadence. Its chief philosophers during its decadent period—Seneca and Marcus Aurelius—were Stoics. Stoicism is a decadent philosophy since it advocates repression of the unconscious in the name of virtue and morality. Renaissance-type philosophy, unlike Stoicism, advocates the expression of one's whole nature, not the repression of a part of one's nature.

During Rome's decadent period, many religious cults flourished. "The need for superstition," wrote Burckhardt, "was grown the more desperate in the degree that the natural energy with which the individual confronts fate had disappeared."[1] Like Ortega, Burckhardt had a deep understanding of history. Burckhardt saw the importance of energy, and he saw that decadence is a shortage of energy. Burckhardt's concept of "natural energy" is close to the concept of life-instinct.

Decadence—the death-instinct in society—was one cause of the decline and fall of the Roman Empire. There were many other causes of Rome's decline. To enumerate all of these causes, and to say how large a share each had in bringing about the final result, is impossible. The causes of historical events can never be completely understood. A theory of the life- and death-instincts of societies can't explain all historical events, it can only contribute to our understanding of history. In this respect, the theory of the life- and death-instincts is similar to the economic interpretation of history. Both theories can contribute to our understanding of history, but neither can explain every historical event.

C. Modern Europe

---

[1] *The Age of Constantine.* Old people may also have a shortage of "natural energy," and this may prompt old people to become superstitious. Examples of old people who had religious conversions are Newton, Liszt, Wagner, Gogol, Tolstoy, Strindberg and Huysmans.

14. DECADENCE AND RENAISSANCE

Before the major Italian Renaissance, there was a minor Italian renaissance in the early 1300's. Its key figures were Giotto, Dante and Petrarch. Giotto shows an interest in personality and psychology that is characteristic of the renaissance-type painter.

Three leading painters of the Italian Renaissance were Michelangelo, Leonardo and Titian. They were born within twenty-five years of each other. They share with Giotto an interest in personality and in psychology. Though known for its painters, the Italian Renaissance also included a renaissance-type writer, Machiavelli. Like Thucydides, who was also a renaissance-type writer, Machiavelli has an amoral view of the world.

Machiavelli accepts reality, and looks reality squarely in the face; this is characteristic of the renaissance-type spirit, just as fleeing from reality is characteristic of a decadent spirit. Nietzsche praised Machiavelli and Thucydides as renaissance-type spirits:

> Thucydides, and perhaps the *Principe* of Machiavelli, are related to me closely by their unconditional will not to deceive themselves and to see reason in *reality*—not in "reason", still less in "morality."[1]

Nietzsche contrasted Thucydides with Plato, whom he regarded as decadent:

> *Courage* in face of reality ultimately distinguishes such natures as Thucydides and Plato: Plato is a coward in face of reality—consequently he flees into the ideal; Thucydides has *himself* under control—consequently he retains control over things.

If Italy had a renaissance in the early 1300's, and another renaissance in the late 1400's, the question arises, Why did the Italians have two renaissances in a relatively short space of time? A renaissance occurs when decadence, or the death-instinct, has reached an extreme. This seems to happen quickly when society is underdeveloped and barely maintains its organic nature, as was the case with Italian society during this era. Societies of this

---

[1] *Twilight of the Idols*, "What I Owe To The Ancients", #2. Perhaps we should speak of a "Spanish Renaissance"—Cervantes, Velazquez, etc.

type need only a short time to complete a full cycle of renaissance–decadence–renaissance. A society that is completely undeveloped and hasn't reached the organic level, such as European society during the Dark Ages, doesn't seem to have either renaissance-type or decadent eras.

The Dutch renaissance occurred in the mid-1600's and is exemplified by Vermeer, Rembrandt and Spinoza. Rembrandt is a perfect example of the psychological renaissance painter, and Spinoza is a perfect example of the amoral renaissance philosopher. Spinoza denied free will and defined right in terms of power. Because Spinoza was an amoral renaissance spirit, he was admired by other amoral renaissance spirits, such as Goethe and Hegel. Just as what one loves and admires is an indication of what one is, so too what sort of people love and admire one is an indication of what one is.

The French renaissance began in the early 1500's, shortly after the Italian renaissance began. Its leading figures were Montaigne and Rabelais. Like other renaissance-type writers, Montaigne believed in natural ethics, in expressing one's whole nature, rather than in repressive ethics.

> I have... adopted for my own use [wrote Montaigne] the ancient rule that we cannot go wrong in following nature.... I have not, like Socrates, corrected my natural disposition by force of reason, nor used any art to interfere with my native inclinations.[1]

This passage illustrates the difference between decadent philosophers, who believe in repressive ethics, and renaissance-type philosophers, who believe in natural ethics.

Shakespeare and Bacon are the leading figures of the English renaissance, which occurred about forty years after the French renaissance. Shakespeare has the amoral world view that is char-

---

[1] "On Physiognomy." Like Montaigne, Rabelais seems to have believed in natural ethics; the motto of the academy in Rabelais' novel is "Do What You Will." Nietzsche admired natural ethics: "All naturalism in morality, that is all *healthy* morality, is dominated by an instinct of life.... *Anti-natural* morality, that is virtually every morality that has hitherto been taught... turns on the contrary precisely *against* the instincts of life."(*Twilight of the Idols*, "Morality as Anti-Nature" #4)

acteristic of the renaissance mind. Samuel Johnson criticized Shakespeare for not being moral:

> [Shakespeare] sacrifices virtue to convenience, and is so much more careful to please than to instruct, that he seems to write without any moral purpose.

Bacon, like Shakespeare, has an amoral world view. One commentator said, "there is a touch of Machiavelli often in Bacon's counsels of life."[1] Nietzsche praised Bacon for focusing on reality, just as he praised Thucydides and Machiavelli.

During the eras of Shakespeare and Montaigne, the life-instinct reached its zenith. During the period from 1600 to 1800, the life-instinct was no longer at its zenith, but was still stronger than the death-instinct, hence the period from 1600 to 1800 may be called a relatively renaissance-type era, though it wasn't an absolutely renaissance-type era.

France and the English-speaking nations should be grouped together since their historical cycles are synchronous; they had renaissance eras at about the same time, and they had decadent eras at about the same time. Germany and Russia, however, shouldn't be grouped with France and the English-speaking nations, since they followed different historical cycles. Germany entered its renaissance era during the early 1800's, when the other Western nations entered their decadent era. Thus, the historical cycle of Germany is the opposite of the historical cycle of the other Western nations. In today's world, there's more contact between societies, so perhaps all societies will eventually follow the same historical cycle.

The three leading figures in the German renaissance were Goethe, Beethoven and Hegel. Goethe is an example of the amoral renaissance artist. Like Montaigne, Goethe believed in natural ethics rather than repressive ethics. Goethe put the doctrine of natural ethics into the mouth of the "fair saint" in *Wilhelm Meister*: "I freely follow my emotions and know as little of constraint as of repentance."

---

[1] See Samuel Johnson, "Preface to Shakespeare," and Henry Morley's Introduction to Bacon's *Essays*, A. L. Burt, NY.

Hegel is an example of the amoral renaissance philosopher. Like Goethe, Hegel admired the amoral philosophy of Spinoza. Hegel didn't view the world in moral terms. When Hegel discusses politics, he doesn't ask, "What is just? What is legitimate?" Hegel accepts reality, and tries to understand reality. Hegel's political thinking reminds one of the political thinking of Thucydides and of Machiavelli. Hegel sees nothing unjust in conquest: "The civilized nation is conscious that the rights of barbarians are unequal to its own and treats their autonomy as only a formality."[1]

Kant was born just before the German renaissance and Schopenhauer just after it. Kant and Schopenhauer were therefore not renaissance-type philosophers, but decadent philosophers. That they had moral world views is an indication of their decadence. Kant is the antithesis of a natural moralist, since he believed that one's natural inclinations could never be considered moral. Kant's "categorical imperative" is a classic example of rational ethics, as opposed to natural ethics.

In Schopenhauer, the death-instinct may be said to have become conscious of itself; Schopenhauer preached denial of the will to live. Instead of advocating the expression of one's whole nature, as a renaissance-type philosopher does, Schopenhauer advocated the repression of one's unconscious, which he called the "will."

The Russian renaissance occurred in the latter part of the 1800's and is exemplified by Dostoyevsky, Tolstoy and Tchaikovsky. This renaissance is probably one cause of Russia's expansionist tendency in this era. As mentioned earlier, nations tend to expand during a renaissance-type era, and contract during a decadent era. Russia is now at the start, or near the start, of a decadent era. Thus, the historical cycle of Russia, like the historical cycle of Germany, is the opposite of the historical cycle of France and of the English-speaking countries.

Nietzsche noticed the discrepancy between Goethe, a renaissance spirit, and Goethe's times, which were decadent. Likewise,

---

[1] See Goethe, *The Apprenticeship of Wilhelm Meister*, VI, and Hegel, *The Philosophy of Right*, §351.

van Gogh noticed the discrepancy between Tolstoy, a renaissance spirit, and Tolstoy's times, which were decadent.[1] Both these discrepancies can be explained by pointing out that the nineteenth century was decadent only in France and in the English-speaking countries, not in Goethe's Germany or in Tolstoy's Russia. Goethe's Germany and Tolstoy's Russia were renaissance-type societies.

7. *Thesis Six: Decadence, or the death-instinct, has now reached an extreme in most western societies* After their renaissance eras, France and England began to gradually decline into decadence. From about 1600 to about 1800, France and England were in relatively renaissance-type eras, even though they were gradually declining into decadence. From about 1800 to about 2000, France and England were in relatively decadent eras. The four-hundred-year cycle, lasting from 1600 to 2000, began with a renaissance-type era, the era of Montaigne and Shakespeare, an era that lasted about one generation. And the cycle ended with an era of absolute decadence, an era that lasted from about 1950 to 2000.

8. *Thesis Seven: Most Western societies are at the start of a renaissance* Since the death-instinct has reached an extreme in France and in the English-speaking countries, the life-instinct will now emerge in these countries for the first time in about four hundred years. This life-instinct will result in a renaissance, the representatives of which will be born between about 1960 and 2000. The renaissance itself will last from the time these representatives mature until they die. After they die, the era of pure renaissance will end, and won't return for about four hundred years. But the era of pure renaissance won't immediately give way to an era of pure decadence; the renaissance spirit will decline gradually.

Carlyle foresaw the renaissance of our time. In 1831, Carlyle intimated that the West would come back to life in about two

---

[1] See Nietzsche, *Twilight of the Idols,* "Expeditions," §50, and van Gogh, *Dear Theo,* p. 390.

hundred years, like the phoenix rising from its ashes. The renaissance that Carlyle foresaw is now at hand.[1]

Since the renaissance epochs of the past were culturally productive, despite the small populations of the countries in which they occurred, will the renaissance of our epoch be even more culturally productive, since our population is much larger than theirs? No, there seems to be little correlation between cultural productivity and population. In fact, the most creative renaissance epoch was the Periclean epoch in Greece, and the population responsible for that creativity was small.

If population size isn't the cause of differences between renaissance epochs, then what is the cause of those differences? External conditions, as well as innate factors, determine the difference between renaissance epochs. In what sort of environment are writers and artists working? Within what cultural traditions are they working? The renaissance of our time may be held back by an unfavorable environment and by a lack of cultural traditions. It's difficult nowadays to withdraw from the world, to think, to imagine, to dream. Modern man can scarcely appreciate the creations of earlier epochs, let alone create great works himself. Culture demands minimal external stimulation, quiet solitude, leisure. Modern life is over-stimulating, crowded and hurried. Modern man is absorbed by politics and business, and distracted by the mass media. Machinery and technology take him outside himself.

To find quiet solitude, it isn't necessary to go to the wilds of Alaska. If one has high goals, high ideals and inspiring examples, and if one rejects society's goals, society's ideals and society's examples, one will quickly find oneself cast out from society, and one will have to build a world for oneself. Isn't this what the great artists and writers of the past have done? Haven't they built worlds for themselves? Isn't a literary work a little world?

Cultural achievement in our time will be inhibited not only by an environment that isn't conducive to culture, but also by the absence of cultural traditions. Today's young renaissance-type

---

[1] See Carlyle, *Sartor Resartus*, "The Phoenix"

14. DECADENCE AND RENAISSANCE

writers and artists will have difficulty finding suitable models to emulate in the society around them. To find such models, they will have to go back to the late nineteenth and early twentieth centuries, then develop their own styles with the help of those models. The new styles that they create will not be understood or appreciated by their contemporaries. Today's young renaissance-type writers and artists face a difficult task, a task that few will be able to accomplish. The renaissance of our time will probably be represented by a small number of outstanding figures

Index

Note: numbers refer to pages, not sections

Abraham, Karl
  on the origin of genius, 101
  on the unconscious desire for death, 265
Adler, Alfred
  on youngest children, 75
Aeschylus, 279
Akbar, M. J., 245
Alexander The Great
  and Napoleon and Hitler, 282
Ali, Muhammad, 79
Allen, James, 165
Aristotle, 18, 281
  metaphysics of, 24
  on genius, 130
  on the origin of philosophy, 22
Aspect, Alain, 252
Auden, W. H., 109
Austen, Jane
  and Forster, 189
Bacon, Delia, 209
Bacon, Francis, 21
  and Shakespeare, 100
  and the English Renaissance, 286
  and the Shakespeare Controversy, 213
  Twain on, 211
Bacon, Roger
  prescience of, 102
Banfield, Edward C., 240
Basho, 35, 38
Baudelaire, Charles, 109
  and the Hermetic tradition, 171
Beethoven, Ludwig van, 51
  and the German renaissance, 287
  and the nature of genius, 108
Bell, John Stuart, 252
Bentham, Jeremy, 238
Berenson, Bernard
  and Goethe, 203
  and Kenneth Clark, 206
Bergson, Henri, 70
Berkeley, George, 39, 256
Bin Laden, Osama, 117, 245
Blake, William, 162, 171
Blavatsky, Madame, 172
Blyth, R. H., 37
Boehme, Jakob
  and patronage, 46

INDEX

Bohr, Niels, 251
Booth, John Wilkes
   Shakespeare's influence on, 127
Boswell, James, 149
   compared to Dostoyevsky, 155
Botticelli, Sandro, 120
Bradley, A. C.
   on Macbeth, 29
Broch, Hermann, 174
Bruno, Giordano, 6, 11, 115, 119
   and the Hermetic tradition, 170
Buddha, 14, 37, 78, 205
   and Hume, 40
Burckhardt, Jakob, 284
   prescience of, 103
Burke, Edmund, 238
Bury, J. B., 80
Byron, Lord
   and the psychology of genius, 111
   and the psychology of handicapped children, 76
   his prediction of the time of his death, 264
Caesar, Julius, 102, 282
   his love of grammar, 221
Campanella, Tommaso
   his Hermetic utopia, 120
Campbell, Joseph, 6, 42, 60, 234, 247
Carlyle, Thomas, 178
   and Emerson, 146
   and the psychology of genius, 112
   on the rebirth of the West, 289
Carter, Jimmy
   and birth order, 76
Casaubon, Isaac
   and the decline of the Hermetic worldview, 122

Cervantes, Miguel de
   and Proust, 159
Cézanne, Paul
   paranoia of, 105
Chapman, George, 150, 214
Charcot, Jean M., 21
Chateaubriand, Vicomte de
   Hugo's feelings about, 146
   Ortega on, 108
Chaudhuri, Nirad, 243
Chekhov, Anton, 151
   and Joyce's short stories, 157
   feminine character of, 107
Churchill, Winston, 78
Cicero
   on Euripides, 281
   on suicide, 61
Clark, Kenneth, 206
   on Berenson, 205
Clausewitz, Carl von, 118
Clinton, Bill
   early childhood of, 96
Coleridge, Samuel Taylor
   and the Hermetic tradition, 171
Comte, Auguste, 105
Confucius
   and the moral significance of art, 50
Conrad, Joseph
   and Jung, 173
Dalton, John, 274
Dante, 167
Darwin, Charles, 21, 69, 106
De Gaulle, Charles, 78
Defoe, Daniel, 150
Democritus, 256
Demosthenes
   and the psychology of handicapped children, 76
Descartes, René, 21, 68, 122
   and metaphysics, 24

his solitary youth, 87
Dickens, Charles
  on the death-instinct, 263
Dickinson, Emily
  and the psychology of traveling, 48
Donne, John, 170
Dostoyevsky, Fyodor, 94, 106, 110, 150, 154, 159
  and adolescence, 87
  and atheism, 62
  and ego inflation, 36
  and Nietzsche, 63
  and telepathy, 158
  his tendency to go to extremes, 105
  on national character, 90
  The Idiot, 193
Dumas, Alexandre, 150
Eckart, Dietrich
  Hitler's admiration for, 126
Eckermann, Johann P., 149
Eckhart, Meister, 177
Edmundson, Mark, 196
Einstein, Albert, 20, 55, 108, 249, 257
  and the psychology of genius, 111
Eissler, K. R., 217
  and the psychology of genius, 112
Eliot, T. S.
  on Shakespeare's philosophy, 167
Emerson, Ralph Waldo, 13, 17, 27, 149, 194
  and Carlyle, 146
  and Montaigne, 16
  and style, 146
  and the Hermetic tradition, 171
  on consistency, 54
  on travelling, 48
Epicurus, 106, 281
Erasmus
  letters of, 149
Euripides
  Socrates' attitude toward, 280
Existentialism
  and Kierkegaard, 184
Fabius Maximus, 79
Fackenheim, Emil
  and Hitler, 127
Faulkner, William, 47, 77, 102
Ficino, Marsilio, 120
  and the Hermetic tradition, 170
Fielding, Henry, 174
Flaubert, Gustave, 106, 110, 153
  and Montaigne, 16
  his adolescent asceticism, 85
  his belief that literature should be impersonal, 154
  his possible influence on Chekhov, 151
Ford, Gerald
  early childhood of, 96
Foreman, George, 79
Forster, E. M., 109, 141, 194
  and Eastern thought, 186
  and Queer Theory, 193
  as a humanist, 195
France, Anatole, 77
  his attitude toward nature, 110
  on style, 143
Franz, Marie-Louise von, 82, 163
Frazer, James, 253
Freud, 21, 25, 68, 70, 96, 109, 140, 261, 283
  and Nietzsche, 270
  and the occult, 74
  and the Psychology Revolution, 2, 97
  and transference, 93

INDEX

Eissler on, 217
  his relation to Schopenhauer and Nietzsche, 74
  his theory of life- and death-instincts, 262
  his views compared to Tolstoy's views, 156
  on American culture, 231
  on eldest children, 75
  on homosexuality, 110
  on humor, 153
  on precocity, 111
  on Shakespeare's identity, 208
  on the fear of heights, 267
Frost, Robert
  on translating poetry, 149
Fry, Roger
  on Forster, 190
Gandhi, Mohandas K., 243
Gibbon, Edward
  his contempt for religion, 10
Gide, André, 109, 140
  and Proust, 201
  his adolescent asceticism, 85
  on Goethe, 148
Giotto, 285
Goebbels, Paul Joseph
  and the psychology of handicapped children, 76
Goethe, Johann Wolfgang von, 21, 108, 148
  and Berenson, 204
  and *Bildung*, 32, 203
  and natural ethics, 287
  and Shakespeare, 146, 215
  and the Hermetic tradition, 171
  and the occult, 72
  Nietzsche on, 288
Gogol, Nikolai, 105
  and Kafka, 153
Goldschmidt, Meyer, 130

Gombrowicz, Witold, 174
Gorky, Maxim, 64
Handlin, Oscar, 31
Hasek, Jaroslav, 174
Hegel, G. W. F., 24, 25, 59, 273, 278
  and the German renaissance, 287
  and the theory of the dialectic, 278
  Kierkegaard's opposition to, 183
Hegesias, 13
Heidegger, Martin, 239
Heine, Heinrich, 64
  prescience of, 103
Heisenberg, Werner, 55, 253
Hemingway, Ernest, 108
Heraclitus
  and the theory of the dialectic, 278
Herbert, George
  and the Hermetic tradition, 170
Hermetic Worldview, The
  and Shakespeare, 167
  and the art of memory, 119
  in Western literature, 169
Herrigel, Eugen, 37
Hillman, James, 95
Hitler, Adolf, 77, 102, 139, 282
  and child abuse, 95
  and the role of fate in history, 103
  Ibsen's influence on, 125
Hitschmann, Edward
  on the children of genius, 108
Hoffer, Eric, 31, 199
  and Montaigne, 16
Hölderlin, Friedrich, 105
Homer, 150, 154
Horace, 45

Hugo, Victor
  youthful ambition of, 146
Hume, David, 40, 52, 240
  his voracious reading as an adolescent, 86
Huntington, Samuel, 245
Ibsen, Henrik, 108, 153
  and Chekhov, 152
  and patriotism, 136
  and the occult, 157
  and the subjective nature of literature, 154
  and *Wild Duck*, 164
  his influence on Hitler, 126
Ikhnaton, 101
Jackson, Michael, 114
James, Henry, 102
  and Shakespeare, 208
  style of, 143
  Wilde on, 160
James, William, 102
  on suicide, 181
Janet, Pierre, 21
Jefferson, Thomas
  prescience of, 102
Jesus, 57, 205, 245
  and extending morality beyond the family, 91
  and Jung, 67
Johnson, Samuel, 198
  his criticism of the Metaphysical Poets, 171
  on genius, 100
  on Shakespeare, 287
  on suicide, 181
Johnson, Lyndon, 77
Johst, Hanns
  and Hitler, 126
Joyce, James, 108, 150, 152, 157, 158
  and patriotism, 136
  and the Hermetic tradition, 172
Julian the Apostate
  and Ibsen, 126
Jung, Carl, 7, 10, 18, 19, 28, 42, 44, 66, 67, 69, 86, 89, 96, 106, 135, 161, 164, 166, 172, 173, 251, 253, 258
  and ethics, 29
  and Nostradamus, 73
  and patronage, 47
  and the Hermetic tradition, 170
  and the occult, 74
  and the Psychology Revolution, 2, 97
  and transference, 93
  and Zen, 53
  on contradictions, 55
  on Goethe, 215
  on the death-instinct, 263
  on the *I Ching*, 118
Kaczynski, Ted ("the Unabomber")
  and child abuse, 95
  Joseph Conrad's influence on, 127
Kafka, Franz, 102, 145, 147, 152, 157, 158, 174, 199
  and Chekhov, 152
  and marriage, 132
  cheerfulness of, 107
  melancholy personality of, 106
  on modern art, 228
  prescience of, 103
Kant, Immanuel, 52, 68, 70, 139, 166, 255, 260, 288
  and the occult, 19, 73
  and the psychology of genius, 112
  and the psychology of traveling, 48
  Herder on, 107

metaphysics of, 24
Nietzsche's views on, 26
Keats, John, 140, 150, 167, 264, 265
Kedourie, Elie, 241
Kennedy, Ted, 77
Khayyam, Omar, 177
Kierkegaard, Soren, 13, 15, 46, 53, 102, 108, 115, 183, 194, 233, 240
  and style, 145
  and the psychology of genius, 112
  and the psychology of handicapped children, 76
  his anticipation of his early death, 264
  his dramatic life, 128
  moodiness of, 105
  on suicide, 61
  the meaning of his surname, 223
Kircher, Athanasius, 119
Knight, G. Wilson, 29, 78, 166
  on Hamlet, 164
Kristol, William ("Bill"), 238, 239
Kübler-Ross, Elisabeth, 84
Kundera, Milan, 174
La Bruyère, Jean de, 185
  on style, 142
Lao Zi, 34, 70
Lawrence, D. H., 64
Leibniz, Gottfried Wilhelm
  on the history of language, 219
Lenin, Vladimir, 102
Leonardo da Vinci, 21, 101
  Freud on, 107
  prescience of, 102
Leopardi, Giacomo, 106
Lévi, Éliphas

  and the Hermetic tradition, 171
Lichtenberg, G. C., 106
  and the occult, 167
  and the psychology of handicapped children, 76
  on excessive learning, 225
Lincoln, Abraham, 117
  his anticipation of his early death, 264
Locke, John, 39
  and natural rights, 52
  his worldview contrasted with the Hermetic worldview, 171
Looney, J. T.
  and Shakespeare, 208, 209, 212
Lorenz, Konrad
  on aggression, 283
Luther, Martin, 55, 223
Macaulay, Thomas B.
  and the psychology of genius, 111
Machiavelli, Niccolo, 285
  and Francis Bacon, 287
Maecenas
  as patron of Virgil and Horace, 45
Mallarmé, Stéphane, 172
Mann, Heinrich
  and telepathy, 73
Mann, Thomas
  and longevity, 266
  and the nature of genius, 101
Mansfield, Harvey, 238
Marcus Aurelius, 284
Marvell, Andrew, 170
Marx, Karl, 21, 238
Medici, Cosimo de
  his interest in Hermetic texts, 121

Melville, Herman, 108, 145
Mendel, Gregor J.
　and the psychology of genius, 112
Mercurius, 67
Merlin, 67
Michelangelo, 36, 50
　loneliness of, 108
Mill, John Stuart, 50, 65, 71, 182, 231, 274
　and the psychology of genius, 112
Mill, James, 238
Miller, Henry, 255
Milosz, Czeslaw, 177
Milton, John, 169
　compared to Shakespeare, 16
　feminine character of, 106
Monboddo, Lord
　on the history of language, 222
Montaigne, Michel E., 15, 17, 21, 115, 202
　and Renaissance philosophy, 13
　and the French Renaissance, 286
　on suicide, 61
Mozart, Wolfgang Amadeus
　childlike character of, 107
Muhammad, 106
Mulisch, Harry
　and Hitler, 127
Musil, Robert, 174
Mussolini, Benito, 102
　and telepathy, 73
Napoleon, 50, 102, 118, 266, 282
　and the role of fate in history, 104
　his voracious reading as an adolescent, 86
　on Goethe, 216

Negroponte, Nicholas
　on peer review, 216
Newton, Isaac, 20, 105, 250, 254, 269
　and the psychology of genius, 112
　his worldview contrasted with the Hermetic worldview, 171
Nietzsche, Friedrich, 8, 11, 12, 13, 17, 18, 21, 22, 25, 27, 28, 49, 52, 63, 64, 65, 81, 105, 106, 114, 149, 177, 200, 204, 226, 236, 261, 266, 270, 272, 280
　against skepticism, 194
　and *amor fati*, 84
　and atheism, 62
　and E. M. Forster, 190
　and ego inflation, 36
　and eugenics, 62
　and Freud, 74
　and meditation, 32
　and Montaigne, 16
　and patriotism, 136
　and Ruskin, 89
　and Schopenhauer, 146
　and style, 145
　and the psychology of genius, 111, 112
　and the will to power, 261
　and Zen, 36
　attitude toward Schopenhauer, 26
　contrasted with Jung, 18
　his dislike of democracy, 232
　Kundera on, 175
　on connecting culture with life, 202
　on excessive learning, 225
　on Francis Bacon, 287

INDEX

on Goethe, 288
on Machiavelli and Thucydides, 285
on psychology, 97
on suicide, 61
on the death-instinct, 263
prescience of, 103
Nostradamus, 73
O'Neill, Eugene, 108
Obama, Barack
  early childhood of, 96
Ortega y Gasset, José, 21, 108
  and the philosophy of history, 274, 279
  and *The Revolt of the Masses*, 230
Ovid, 214
Parmenides
  and the origin of metaphysics, 23
Pascal, Blaise, 101, 106
  and Montaigne, 16
  and the psychology of genius, 112
  on Biblical prophecies, 58
Pater, Walter, 7
  and Zen, 176
  his new religion, 9
Perceval
  and adolescence, 86
Perennial Philosophy, 8, 119
Petronius, 157
Philemon
  and Euripides, 281
Pico della Mirandola, 6, 119
  and the Hermetic tradition, 170
Plato, 18, 51, 205, 209
  and style, 145
  and the Hermetic tradition, 169
  and the moral significance of art, 50
  and the psychology of genius, 112
  metaphysics of, 24
  Nietzsche on, 280, 285
  on eugenics, 62
  on simplicity, 142
Pollaiuolo, Antonio del
  Berenson on, 203
Pope Benedict, 238
Pope, Alexander
  and the psychology of handicapped children, 76
Potter, Beatrix, 81
Presley, Elvis, 114
Proust, Marcel, 46, 82, 109, 130, 149, 150, 152, 158, 160, 161, 185, 248
  and the occult, 163
  and the psychology of traveling, 48
  and the publication of *Swann's Way*, 201
  his asthma, 106
  on meeting people for the first time, 83
Rabelais, François, 157
Rank, Otto
  on the connection between sex and death, 182
Raphael
  Berenson on, 204
Rasputin, Grigori Y.
  and telepathy, 73
Reagan, Ronald, 117
Rembrandt, 286
Renan, Ernest, 154
Riesman, David, 235
Rimbaud, Arthur, 109, 172
  and the psychology of genius, 111
Robertson, Morgan

foresees *Titanic* disaster, 119
Rousseau, Jean-Jacques, 115, 149
   as a parent, 108
   prescience of, 102
Rumi, 245
Ruskin, John, 8, 105, 149
   and Nietzsche, 89, 232
   and Proust, 160
   on economics, 202
   Tolstoy on, 159
Sachs, Hanns, 110
Saddam Hussein, 246
Sage, Steven
   his Hitler-Ibsen theory, 127
Schiller, Friedrich von, 106, 216
Schlegel, Frederick
   on the history of language, 222
Schopenhauer, Arthur, 18, 21, 22, 27, 46, 52, 70, 105, 199, 260, 261, 269, 270, 272, 288
   and E. M. Forster, 191
   and Eastern philosophy, 32
   and eugenics, 62
   and Freud, 74
   and metaphysics, 25
   and Nietzsche, 146
   contrasted with Jung, 18
   importance of, 25
   Kierkegaard's interest in, 130
   Nietzsche on, 271
   Nietzsche's early attitude toward, 26
   on the origin of genius, 101
   on traveling, 48
Schumann, Robert, 105
Scott, Sir Walter, 148
Seneca, 102, 284
   on the death-instinct, 263
Shakespeare, William, 29, 78, 92, 100, 135, 145, 146, 152, 161, 162, 164, 165, 173, 217, 258
   and Goethe, 215
   and *Macbeth*, 29
   and *Othello*, 175
   and the English Renaissance, 286
   compared to Milton, 16
   his influence on Twain, 179
   his last years, 84
   Oxford Theory, 207, 214
   Tolstoy's dislike of, 269
   Twain on the identity of, 209
   Whitman on, 212
Shaw, George Bernard, 64
   and eugenics, 62
   and longevity, 267
   and the idea of life- and death-instincts, 272
   Joyce's dislike of, 157
Shih-t'ao, 124
Socrates, 51, 80, 115, 205
   his comment about marriage, 151
   Kierkegaard's admiration for, 183
   Montaigne on, 286
   Nietzsche on, 280
Solzhenitsyn, Aleksandr, 82
   on modern art, 227
Sophocles, 81, 279
Sorokin, Pitirim A., 21
Spengler, Oswald, 21, 274
Spinoza, Baruch, 286
   and metaphysics, 24
   Hegel's admiration for, 288
Stalin, Joseph, 139
   and child abuse, 95
Stapp, Henry, 250, 258
Stendhal
   and suicide, 182
   on national character, 90
   Ortega on, 108

Sterne, Laurence, 157, 174
Strauss, Leo, 54, 185, 238, 239, 240
Strindberg, August, 105, 106
  moodiness of, 105
Suzuki, D. T., 37, 78, 255
Swedenborg, Emanuel
  and telepathy, 73
Swift, Jonathan, 105
Swinburne, Algernon Charles, 109
Synesius
  his dream book, 121
Tagore, Rabindranath
  his attitude toward death, 267
Tai Chen, 262
Talleyrand, Charles Maurice de
  and the psychology of handicapped children, 76
Tarot, 118
Tasso, Torquato, 105
Thoreau, Henry David, 7, 13, 15, 17, 27, 28, 38, 127, 145, 178, 199
  and the psychology of genius, 112
  and Whitman, 176
  and Zen, 42
  on national character, 90
Thucydides, 279, 285
Tindall, W. Y.
  on the Hermetic Tradition, 172
Titanic, 119
Tocqueville, Alexis de, 49, 232
  on style, 144
  prescience of, 102
Tolstoy, Leo, 77, 83, 150, 152, 159, 192, 289
  as a literary critic, 185
  compared to Dostoyevsky, 155
  his attitude toward death, 268
  his criticism of Shakespeare, 165
  his suicidal feelings, 181
  his views compared to Freud's views, 156
  on Ruskin, 159
  on the death-instinct, 263
  on the hunting personality, 83
Toulouse-Lautrec, Henri de
  and the psychology of handicapped children, 76
Toynbee, 21, 244, 274
Turner, J. M. W., 254
  and landscape painting, 123
Twain, Mark, 178
  and Shakespeare, 208, 209
  on style, 143
Van Gogh, Vincent, 105, 115, 289
  and the psychology of genius, 102
  his prediction of the time of his death, 264
Verlaine, Paul, 109
Virgil, 45, 145
  feminine character of, 106
Voltaire
  letters of, 149
Wallace, Alfred R., 21
Watts, Alan, 10, 34, 37, 267
Weber, Max, 50, 168
  on extending morality beyond the family, 92
Wells, H. G., 64
  and eugenics, 62
  his adolescent asceticism, 85
Whitman, Walt, 7, 10, 109, 178
  and Shakespeare, 208, 212
  and Zen, 176
  his influence on E. M. Forster, 186

Wikipedia, 217
Wilde, Oscar, 10, 31, 109, 110, 149, 163, 205
and telepathy, 73
his self-destructive impulses, 266
on Henry James, 160
Wittgenstein, Ludwig, 102
and the origin of genius, 102
Wolfe, Thomas, 147
Woolf, Virginia
and Forster, 189
Wordsworth, William, 38

Xerxes, 23
Yates, Frances
and the Hermetic worldview, 120
Yeats, William Butler
and the Hermetic tradition, 172
Young, Arthur
on bodily functions and national character, 90
Zhuang Zi, 34
Zola, Émile
and Chekhov, 152
Zukav, Gary, 252, 253, 254

Feedback

Note: the following e-mail messages react to my book and to my website, LJHammond.com

Hello, I live in Nova Scotia, Canada. I'm 35 years old and just lost my younger brother to complications after Brain Tumor Surgery. He was a self-taught man who knew much about the Humanities.... I cannot begin to describe the loss and the pain I endure on a daily basis. I am completely stuck on the age-old question, What is the meaning of life? The only comfort I get at the present time is to educate myself in more of the great works. I stumbled across your site and it has brought me much comfort. I have made it my home page. I just wanted to say Thank you very much. Tim

If you lack a general liberal education and would like to fill that gap, you may have noticed that it's very easy to get lost. Pick any topic and you are faced with an overwhelming number of classical texts, authors and theories, each requiring a large investment of time and energy to understand and appreciate. What would be really helpful is a high-level overview of entire areas of study, and, incredibly, this very slim book attempts to provide just that.... The book is incredibly easy to read and presents often impenetrably abstract ideas in a comprehensive and entertaining manner. Highly recommended! Mycha, Princeton, NJ (posted on Amazon)

I am a college student at Fudan University, Shanghai, China. I read your book, published by China Film Press. I just want to say thank you. Your book was very easy to understand, but I was amazed by the power in those plain words! I bought your book when I was in high school, and I've been reading it again and again through the years, and it was among the very few books I took to Shanghai with me. Your book made me re-find my interest in philosophy and literature, and also re-find myself. Loretta

FEEDBACK

Just a short note to say how enormously I have been appreciating the pages on your website. What a find, what a treat! And a big thank-you for bringing my attention to Montaigne. How I have gotten to my mid-fifties with three decades of avid interest in mind-full things, and not having 'discovered' this man's writing is a great mystery to me. Perhaps that aphorism of the teacher arriving when the pupil is ready is relevant in my case! Vincent, Cape Town

Thank you for the delightful narrative on your visit to England. My wife and I have been on several tours to England, and your account brought back wonderful memories. We will be looking forward to hear the "rest of the story".... As a college biology instructor at a junior college, you expand my horizons in philosophy and literature. Clyde, Texas

Thank you Hammond. You introduced me to the world of culture, wherein I now live and grow. I should say that were the first great influence in my life. I am 19, from Toronto Canada.... I am very interested in Nietzsche, Emerson, Thoreau, your CWGT book, Phlit, meditation, the good life, ancient Egypt and the occult, and so on. Adam

Great great essay from 2005 on the sonnets, Goethe and much more. Really enjoyed your ideas and will come back.... After reading the article on the sonnets, I stayed at your site and read several more articles. Nothing disappointed me. I like your wide breadth of knowledge. I like your balanced and calm presentation of arguments. I like your choice of subjects. I want to read every back issue of the newsletter. Chris, Pennsylvania

Just a short note to say how valuable I found your pages. Without reservation I can say that they are the most illuminating, not to mention, concise and clear, pages I have yet found on the web. I chanced upon them in a general search, but have returned again, and again. I would like to wholeheartedly congratulate you not just for their style and content, but also for the generosity that prompted you to put them online. Nick, London

CPSIA information can be obtained at www.ICGtesting.com
Printed in the USA
245255LV00001B/77/P